eBay® Listings That Sell

FOR

DUMMIES®

eBay® Listings That Sell For Dummies®

Cheat Sheet

Following the XHTML Trend

The World Wide Web Consortium (W3C at http://www.w3.org/) is the governing body that develops protocols and guidelines to ensure the progression of the Web. This group offers standards that everyone can follow to code Web pages that play well with the ever-changing tools and technologies making up the Web environment. W3C is responsible for formulating the current HTML and XHTML standards, and has made sure that the advances in XHTML stay *backward-compatible* with HTML (meaning that all your commands still work).

TIP

If you want to be current with the trends in XHTML (and you do!), begin **now** to write the HTML code for your eBay listings so that it is XHTML-compatible. Doing so allows your listings to display properly in virtually any browser and on all of the newest Web-enabled devices. Remember these four important points if you a want to bring your HTML code up to XHTML standards:

- **All XHTML elements must be properly nested:** For example, HTML accepted coding such as `<strong><em>text</strong></em>` (notice how the `</em>` closing tag appears after `</strong>`).

  But for XHTML, the code must close tags in the proper sequence and would look like `<strong><em>text</em></strong>` (with the `</em>` closing tag coming before `</strong>`).

- **Tag and attribute names must be in lowercase:** Use `<font>` instead of `<FONT>`.

- **All XHTML elements must be closed:** For example, HTML allowed a `<p>` tag without a closing `</p>` tag, but all closing tags must be present in XHTML.

- **Attribute values must be enclosed in quotes,** as in `<font color="silver">this text is silver</font>`.

Replacement commands for converting to XHTML

If You Used This in HTML	Use This for XHTML
`<b>` and `</b>`	`<strong>` and `</strong>`
`<i>` and `</i>`	`<em>` and `</em>`
`<font size="+1">`	`<big>` and `</big>`
`<font size="-1">`	`<small>` and `</small>`
` `	` `
`<hr>`	`<hr />`
`<img src="http://www.yourdomain.com/yourpicture.jpg">`	`<img src="http://www.yourdomain.com/yourpicture.jpg" />`
`<p>`	`<p>` and `</p>`

REMEMBER

If you want your code to show up on newfangled telephones and handheld devices (and whatever else comes down the pike), be sure to use the XHTML commands!

eBay® Listings That Sell For Dummies®

Cheat Sheet

Marsha & Patti's Absolute Essentials for eBay Listing Success

Must-Dos for Photography

What to Do	Here's Why
Use a tripod!	What more can we say? Taking pictures in Macro (highly magnified) mode requires a very steady hand. Why go crazy dealing with out-of-focus images? Anchor your camera to a tripod (or a Cloud Dome) so that the shakies are no longer part of your photography problems.
Use a neutral background.	As you look at bad examples in this book (and while visiting eBay), you're bound to see lots of items pictured with distracting backgrounds. Don't handicap your own listings by confusing the buyers. Keep it simple!
Put your clothing on a mannequin.	If you can't afford a mannequin at first, use a dressmaker's form or even a half-body display model. Clothing just won't sell well when photographed flat on the floor (or the bed). And that's even truer when it's folded up.
Avoid modeling clothing on a person.	One benefit of a mannequin is that it's a neutral object. The buyers know that the mannequin has a better figure than they do, and can picture mentally what the outfit might look like on them. Also, very few of us have the perfect mannequin body, and we can't show off the clothing to its best advantage.

Must-Haves for a Successful Listing

What to Have	Here's Why
Crystal-clear item descriptions.	Talk about the item! Mention all the necessary facts about the item, so the buyer can picture exactly what it is or (when appropriate) does. Think infomercial! Tell buyers all the reasons why they must have this item to make their lonely lives complete. Most of all, as Marsha's sixth-grade English teacher said, "Keep the description like a woman's skirt: long enough to cover the subject but short enough to keep it interesting!"
Quality photographs!	That's what this book is trying to tell you. You can't sell an item without a good photograph. A picture is worth a thousand words, so if your description is somewhat lacking, your picture will pick up the slack.
Clearly outlined selling terms.	Give your buyers all the necessary information regarding payments, shipping, and return policy. Don't leave any questions in the buyers' minds, or they may misconstrue, causing you problems down the line. Be sure to phrase your description in a polite, inviting manner so as to attract (rather than repel) prospective bidders.
Flawless customer service!	Preserve your feedback rating; the better your reputation online, the higher the bids and the higher the selling price for your items. Remember that there are already enough jerks online, and you don't need to be one of them. Your customer service, courtesy, and warmth should shine through at every turn!

For Dummies: Bestselling Book Series for Beginners

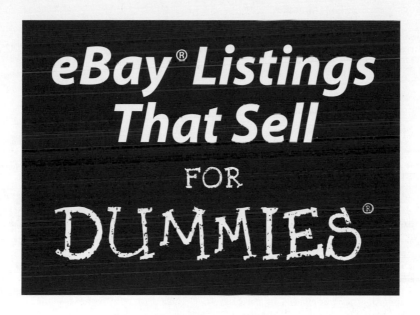

eBay® Listings That Sell

FOR DUMMIES®

by Marsha Collier
and
Patti Louise Ruby

WILEY

Wiley Publishing, Inc.

eBay® Listings That Sell For Dummies®

Published by
Wiley Publishing, Inc.
111 River Street
Hoboken, NJ 07030-5774

www.wiley.com

For general information on our other products and services, please contact our Customer Care Department within the U.S. at 800-762-2974, outside the U.S. at 317-572-3993, or fax 317-572-4002.

For technical support, please visit www.wiley.com/techsupport.

Wiley also publishes its books in a variety of electronic formats. Some content that appears in print may not be available in electronic books.

Library of Congress Control Number: 2005939204

ISBN-13: 978-0-471-78912-3

ISBN-10: 0-471-78912-7

Manufactured in the United States of America

10 9 8 7 6 5 4 3 2 1

1B/RT/QU/QW/IN

WILEY

About the Authors

Marsha Collier spends most of her time on things related to eBay. She's a charter member eBay PowerSeller, as well as one of the original instructors for eBay University. As a columnist, an author of four best-selling books on eBay, a television and radio expert, and a lecturer, she shares her knowledge of eBay with millions of online shoppers. Thousands of eBay fans also visit her Web site, www.coolebaytools.com, to get Marsha's latest insights on e-commerce.

Out of college, Marsha worked in fashion advertising for the *Miami Herald* and then as special-projects manager for the *Los Angeles Daily News*. She also founded a home-based advertising and marketing business. Her successful business, the Collier Company, Inc., was featured by *Entrepreneur* magazine in 1986, and in 1990, Marsha's company received the Small Business of the Year award from her California State Assemblyman and the Northridge Chamber of Commerce.

Bargains drew Marsha to eBay in 1996, but profitable sales keep her busy on the site now. Marsha applies her business acumen and photography skills to her eBay business — and in this book, she shares her knowledge about what makes good, profit-promoting listings on eBay.

Patti "Louise" Ruby, an Indianapolis native, was born to work on a computer. In junior high, she took a class in the programming language Fortran. She excelled and enjoyed the class: The die was cast. Patti went through several jobs as a programmer and then became a consultant.

In the late '90s, Patti was part-owner of an antique mall, and coincidentally found a Web site called AuctionWeb (the original eBay). She was fascinated by the concept, and began selling on the site. She also became an integral part of the chat rooms, which initially served as loose customer support where users helped other users. Patti's ease with computers helped many a new user feel comfortable on the boards — and with using the AuctionWeb system.

In February 1997, Patti was hired as AuctionWeb's second Customer Support Representative. In this position, she became the main interface between the engineering staff and the user community, where she communicated members' "bug" reports and suggestions for site enhancements. When AuctionWeb became the new eBay site in the fall of 1997, she headed up a "live" question-and-answer board that was set up to help members make the transition between platforms.

In 1999, eBay started a traveling show called eBay University (where Patti first met Marsha), and she has been a lead instructor since its inception. Patti "retired" from eBay in February 2002, after five challenging, exciting years. Being a part of the early eBay years gave her the opportunity to watch the company grow from a small neighborhood market to the worldwide marketplace it is today. She has continued to buy and sell on eBay. She laughs, ". . .once you've discovered eBay, there is no escape!"

Dedication

Marsha and Patti dedicate this book to the thousands of members of the eBay community who strive for better listings and higher revenues. We know just how difficult the striving can be and want to help in every way we can. We hope to meet as many of you as possible at eBay University classes and eBay Live.

We take our lead from the legions of sellers who continue to inspire us to do what we can to carry them through the fun, challenging, and profitable journey we call eBay.

Authors' Acknowledgments

Without the amazing talents of Leah Cameron and Barry Childs-Helton, this book would not be one iota as good as it is (and it really is darn good). They are one top-drawer editorial team, and only by working with them can you possibly know how very talented (and patient) they are. We'd also like to thank our tech editor, Cindy Lichfield, for going over the book — and checking it twice!

Steven Hayes, thank you. You're always thinking and working a new angle. Its part of what makes working with you fun.

Andy Cummings, it's wonderful that someone as high up on the corporate food chain as you really cares about the writers. You're a rarity in the publishing field.

Patti would like to thank Marsha for sharing this book with her. Patti says, "I always admired Marsha for what she was able to accomplish; now I know firsthand what a tremendous job it is she does! I'd also like to acknowledge my family, who has continued to display their unfailing belief in me, and David, as always, most of all."

Publisher's Acknowledgments

We're proud of this book; please send us your comments through our online registration form located at www.dummies.com/register/.

Some of the people who helped bring this book to market include the following:

Acquisitions, Editorial, and Media Development

Editors: Leah Cameron, Barry Childs-Helton

Acquisitions Editor: Steven Hayes

Technical Editor: Cindy Lichfield

Media Development Manager: Laura VanWinkle

Editorial Assistant: Amanda Foxworth

Cartoons: Rich Tennant (www.the5thwave.com)

Composition Services

Project Coordinator: Erin Smith

Layout and Graphics: Andrea Dahl, Stephanie D. Jumper, Barbara Moore, Lynsey Osborn, Jill Proll, Heather Ryan

Proofreaders: Jessica Kramer, Techbooks

Indexer: Techbooks

Publishing and Editorial for Technology Dummies

    Richard Swadley, Vice President and Executive Group Publisher

    Andy Cummings, Vice President and Publisher

    Mary Bednarek, Executive Acquisitions Director

    Mary C. Corder, Editorial Director

Publishing for Consumer Dummies

    Diane Graves Steele, Vice President and Publisher

    Joyce Pepple, Acquisitions Director

Composition Services

    Gerry Fahey, Vice President of Production Services

    Debbie Stailey, Director of Composition Services

Contents at a Glance

Table of Contents

. . . .

Introduction

If we were to catalog all the misinformation we've seen about selling on eBay, it might take days! We wrote this book to get you started in the right direction, and even provide some shortcuts.

Marsha has been writing eBay reference books since 1998, selling on eBay since 1996, tracking the buying trends as they change from year to year, and keeping her readers clued in about the differences as they crop up. In her ongoing quest for eBay accuracy in the midst of complexity, she's joined forces with Patti Ruby, her ace technical editor on previous books. Result: a fearless venture into the intricacies of selling, of taming the dreaded HTML, of attracting more eBay profits!

(By the way: Thank you if you've bought *eBay For Dummies* books before — and if this is your first one, welcome. We're sure this book will add some high-caliber know-how to your eBay selling arsenal.)

There are good ways to display your eBay listings, and there are bad ways. How many times have you opened an item on eBay and found barely enough of a description to identify the item — especially if the listing had no picture! (Let's see . . . you didn't buy that item, right? Call it a hunch.) That one example is just the tip of the eBay-mistake iceberg. In this book, we set you on the path to efficient listing content and attractive online appearance for your item — and we show you how to produce your listings in record time. The aim, of course, is to beat out your competition and rake in those elusive bidder-dollars.

The pictures that display your item online are an entirely separate ball of wax (so to speak). Lots of books supposedly tell you how to take good photos for eBay auctions, but it seems to me that those books try to teach you how to take high-quality family pictures instead. They don't seem to take into account that photography for eBay has to be rapid-fire and accurate. Your goal is to produce an image of decent quality that will last for the next 7 to 10 days, maximum. Because your time is valuable, this book doesn't bog you down with pages of unnecessary technical garbage. It gives you the information you absolutely need to know to produce the right kind of product image, and nothing more.

We can help you!

Patti Ruby — or "Louise" as she was known on the eBay chat boards — was one of the very first pinks on eBay. (A *pink* is a customer-support person whose job includes posting on the chat and message boards. These posts are highlighted in pink so eBay members will know that they come from "official" eBay employees.) In February 1997, Patti joined eBay as a contractor, handling customer support from her home in Indianapolis. She was the second person that Pierre (eBay's founder) contracted with to handle the ever-growing chat on the eBay community boards. The first person in those trenches was eBay's indomitable Jim "Griff" Griffith, who made eBay posts from his computer in his Vermont studio. Patti "retired" from her eBay employment in 2002, and Griff still carries the flag for the rest of us at eBay.

Both Patti and Marsha have spent many hours buying and selling on eBay. In her mysterious past, Patti was a *coder* — one of those wizards smart enough to write the code that makes computer programs do their magic. Meanwhile, Marsha was working in the hustle and bustle of retail advertising — and as a photo stylist for retail catalogs, she gleaned arcane tips from professional photographers (including gurus of product photography). So you can see why we wanted to write this book: We wanted to share some really useful stuff from our earlier careers.

Well, okay, we also had an ulterior motive: To elevate (in our own little way) the quality of the item listings on eBay — and to add to the bottom line of the sellers who heed our advice. We promise to make things as simple as possible — hey, we know you can handle the complexities, but why bother if you don't have to? We'd rather see you spending your time packing and shipping profitable items!

In our spare time (what's that?), we teach in various venues around the country for eBay University with Griff. We are both "lead" instructors — which means we don't ever get to teach at the same time. But we've both watched eBay change from a homey community of friendly collectors to a behemoth Web site, now teeming with tens of thousands of categories of items and over 150 million registered users. Funny, the rules for listing a successful auction now aren't much different from what they were back in the day. People still make money by following them.

The bulk of the information you find in this book is not covered in depth in any of the other *For Dummies* books on eBay. Due to the nature of the other books, there just wasn't the space to devote to such specifics about HTML and photography. So this book gives you all the handy, practical information on these topics that you've asked for over the years — and having put it down here, moves on. Enjoy!

About This Book

This book isn't written in a linear style, and you don't have to read it right through like a novel, either. You can check out the titles of the chapters in the Table of Contents, and when you find something that interests you, just flip to that page and start reading. When you have a question on something particular, we suggest you slide to the back of the book and visit our very-nicely-put-together Index. (Our publisher, Wiley Publishing, Inc., does a thorough index, and you should be able to connect to just about anything in this book from there.)

There's no need to even take notes when you read this book. Just dog-ear the corner and use a highlighter. That's the sign of a well-read, well-studied book. While you're folding and marking, you can find answers to lots of important questions as we take you through the following tracks:

- ✔ Seeing what makes eBay photography different from traditional digital camera work
- ✔ Discovering "just-enough" HTML to make an attractive listing and yet not waste your time
- ✔ Designing your own reusable listing templates (or use ours!)
- ✔ Setting up for specific, unique photographic situations
- ✔ Deciding what additional software you might need for your eBay listings
- ✔ Finding and using the right camera and equipment
- ✔ Getting what you need to produce quality images for eBay

Our Foolish Assumptions

Anyone who buys this book is either currently selling on eBay or is seriously planning on making some money online. In our tenure at eBay University, we have seen documentation stating that the average eBay user takes about 80 minutes to put together an eBay listing. We can hear the chorus now: *An hour and 20 minutes . . . are you kidding? How could anyone possibly list enough items to run a business if listing one item takes this long?*

Our goal is to shave those 80 minutes into a maximum of 5. Five minutes from start to finish. Time is money, and the more items you can list, the more money you can make. We assume that making money is a serious goal for you as well.

Are we right? If it's time to buckle down and make some serious cash, this is the book for you. Below are some other foolish assumptions we've made about you:

- ✔ You have a computer and an Internet connection.
- ✔ You've bought and sold at eBay and are fairly familiar with how it works.
- ✔ You would like to have nicer-looking listings than you currently have.
- ✔ You've had an issue or two with taking a good picture.

✔ You'd like to doll up your listings and give them some extra, added punch.

✔ You feel that working from home in jeans and a sweatshirt is a great idea.

If you can say yes to our foolish assumptions, we're off and running! Both Patti and I are about to flood your head with lots of stuff that can (upon thorough digesting) speed up your day and boost you toward reaching your sales goals! Take a few moments to read the following section to get a feel for how we've put together this book.

Conventions Used in This Book

Our publisher loves that word *conventions,* and we like it because it reminds us of going to parties and collecting free stuff that we can resell on eBay. But that's not the type of convention they want us to talk about here. The publisher's conventions are consistent ways of presenting the stuff in this book. So here's how they work . . .

Tiptoeing through the steps

When faced with a somewhat daunting task, we often take you through it in a numbered, step-by-step fashion. We separate and number the steps, like this:

1. **Acquire a bag of cookies.**

2. **Carefully tear open the bag.**

   Make sure that you leave the bag opening in good enough shape that resealing is possible — assuming, of course, that you don't plan to eat all the cookies at once.

3. **Insert three fingers and pull out selected cookie.**

   We like to use three fingers because using more just gets messy and too much chocolate on your fingers can really be a bother, but you may find that two will do in some instances.

4. **Stuff cookie in mouth and chew.**

We like this method! (Of course, we're talking about the instruction method, but we like how it works for cookies, too.) And we try to keep the instructions simple — pretty much because we also prefer easy-to-follow instructions.

Watching the icons, yes, I con . . .

You're going to see some icons and sidebars in this book; our editors seem to think that some of this is optional reading material. Harrumph. We want you to know that we feel every single word is indispensable. (Okay, sure, you may be more drawn to some topics than to others.) Although the sidebars will be separate from the text, we put them in to add a little spice — to give you an extra bit of information to emphasize the current lesson. We write 'em because we want you to read 'em. Enough said?

You'll also notice some clever little icons in the margins that point out some very important facts that you need to know. They're often the online equivalent of the laws of nature: truths that it would be foolhardy to ignore.

And about that HTML code . . .

If you've ever suspected that telling a computer to do something means using language weirdly, you're right. So we use a strange font to highlight the HTML commands that are plentiful in the book. If, for example, you want to tell your computer to set off type in bold text (with italics for emphasis), the HTML that does that job looks like this:

```
<b>My auctions look gud</b>, now all I <i>need</i> is a spell-checker!
```

How This Book Is Organized

As with all the books in the *For Dummies* line, the information in this book is neatly tucked into several different parts. The goal is to make it easier for you to progress through from the beginning to the advanced information we're offering — or, if you jump around in it like a Jack Russell Terrier, to make sure you always know where to find what you're jumping to.

We've laid out this book in five parts.

Part I: Getting Chummy with the Basics

We start you off gently with the basics of online presentation, HTML, and photography — exclusively as they apply to eBay sellers. Remember that selling is the goal of this book. It's no accident that we focus these important topics in that direction.

Here in this part you find out why our philosophy of "eBay, HTML, and Photography" is different from everything you may have encountered in other books. The way we see it, all you want to do is post clean listings that sell your items for high prices. Okay, that's our bias as eBay sellers with backgrounds in marketing and selling. We figured you wouldn't mind.

Part II: Lining Your Pockets with HTML

Following our theory that "less is more," here's where you go to discover how to set up some good-looking auctions yourself — and move the stuff with minimum fluff. That means (be brave) venturing into HTML, but the good news is that some of the best tools for working with it already exist on your computer. For example, did you know that the Verdana font was developed exclusively to make video-monitor text easier to read? It was designed by a world-renowned type designer, Matthew Carter, and Monotype's Tom Rickner. In the family of Verdana sans-serif fonts, you can see unique examples of type design that's just right for the computer screen.

We show you, step by step, how to gussy up your listings *efficiently*. As we get into more and more advanced HTML coding, Patti's no-baloney approach speeds up your learning curve to Warp Factor 9. She'll have you designing listings with all the cool options you need in no time at all. You'll be glad to have her expertise at your side as you design your auctions.

Part III: Turning Pictures into Dollars

In Part III, we get the benefit of Marsha's years in professional photography. We've based this part on a pretty safe hunch: that 98 percent of all digital camera users haven't a clue about how to use half the options available on their cameras. This part is where you see how to use your camera to its fullest — and get the skinny on setting up your own eBay photo studio.

Since lighting is so crucial to tweaking out the details of an item, this part also gives you the scoop on how lighting affects your final images. It's almost scary to know that changing a mere light bulb can mean a big change in the way your camera (and later, your buyer) sees your merchandise. But it's true.

We also get into the best ways to photograph metals and gems. Part III shows you how to get the correct coloring the first time without having to drag your digital photo into Photoshop for major alterations. The "secrets" are all here. When you have pondered these matters deeply, grasshopper, you'll be able to move from camera to listing in three minutes flat.

Part IV: Advanced Applications for Your Newfound Skills

In Part IV, you find out which software programs can help you with your listings with a minimal amount of pomp and circumstance. (Remember that making money and saving time are our goals — not entering our images in an art contest.) We point you in the direction of easily available software that you can use to generate and edit digital images that grab the viewer (figuratively) and sell the item (literally). Hey, it's an art.

We also expand your selling horizons beyond eBay. This part introduces you to some extended skills that can help you design and open a super eBay Store (without paying extra for pre-built graphic on-screen nonsense). We also show you how to get your listings seen on other selling Web sites such as Amazon.

Part V: The Part of Tens

Tradition dictates that nobody can write a *Dummies* book without including the very traditional Part of Tens. (We also get to have some fun in this section, but don't tell our editors we said so.) We debunk some online photography myths and show you ten tips for your auction designs.

Icons Used in This Book

If there's something we really want you to know, we interrupt our (and your) train of thought with a tip. We're a very excitable pair when it comes to getting folks up to speed on these subjects — and sometimes things we've learned just bubble up until we can't hold them in. So here they are, with the *For Dummies* Tip icon in the margin next to them. Follow the tip, and you'll be right on target!

We think that "senior moment" is an unfair term. We've been forgetting things since the early '70s (hmmmm, I wonder why?). At any rate, we point out these important-to-remember ideas with the "finger" (the one with the string around it), so you won't forget them.

Yep, we've all become victims of our own foolishness at one time or another. We put this little bomb icon next to things that can figuratively "blow up in your face." (We've left out the traditional photos of the guy taking photos of large polished silver vessels in his underwear — but if we did publish them, they'd definitely have the Warning icon next to them.)

Occasionally, as memory serves, we'll throw in an interesting little story that applies to the current topic. Each story is either something that we've done ourselves, or something we've learned from other eBay sellers. Whatever these stories' origins are, we promise they'll be fun (and don't be surprised if they're useful, too).

Where Do You Go from Here?

Take the information we give you in this book and, well, *play* with it. HTML coding can be fun (really, we promise) — and so is taking pictures. Play with our instructions and use the knowledge to post better listings.

Better Listings + Better Photographs = More Money

Isn't that the goal we're working toward?

Our goal is to give you a boost toward building your eBay business. Marsha's Web site has been garnering good stuff for that purpose for years:

```
www.coolebaytools.com
```

CooleBayTools is the Web site for the *For Dummies* books regarding eBay. Here you'll find interesting articles by Marsha and a special area where you can reach Patti. We also have a monthly newsletter you can sign up for that (with any luck) arrives every month. (Auction Anecdotes are also gratefully accepted! Please, send only true ones that we can publish, okay?) Also, please realize that we read every e-mail — in our (ahem) copious free time. But because we have our own eBay businesses, teach for eBay U, and try to have lives, we can't respond to everyone individually. But we do send out a newsletter that answers many of questions we get. Like eBay, it's as much a life as it is a living.

Part I
Getting Chummy with the Basics

The 5th Wave   By Rich Tennant

"Look—you can't just list an extraterrestrial embryo on eBay without using some catchy phrases or power words to make it seem interesting and unique."

In this part . . .

In this part, you run through a crash course in eBay-listing essentials that you may already know — or, at least, kind-of know. The purpose of this part is to get you grounded with the important how-tos and what-fors. Once you have this subject matter under your belt, you'll be ready to build on that knowledge and become an expert at creating listings that sell.

Chapter 1

Attracting Buyers with Your eBay Listing

- -

In This Chapter

▶ Matching listings to your goods and your style

▶ Attracting attention to your listings

▶ Using the tools and techniques that make catchy listings

▶ Copywriting, eBay style

- -

Why is it that some eBay sellers are successful while others can't seem to move their similar items? We get e-mails every day from sellers who just can't figure out why their listings aren't generating sales. For some reason, they're not moving items as quickly as they feel they should. And they sense that other sellers are highly successful despite those sellers' confusing and overly graphic ads.

This quandary sets the stage for the advice in this chapter and the how-to information in this book. Your item listings (and more specifically, the text and images you include there) become your face to the buyers, and your auctions reflect your image. When you walk into a retail store; the décor projects an image. A visit to K-Mart (with the *Blue Light Special* blaring from above) gives you an entirely different feeling than does your stroll into Nordstrom (and subsequent lull into shopping heaven via the music of a pianist). This is the goal for your eBay listings: ***to make prospective customers feel comfortable spending their money with you.***

Creating Listings That Are Uniquely You

As a seller, you may be tempted to adopt the selling style of other people whom you perceive as successful (imitation is the sincerest form of flattery?). But have you done the research to see whether the "professional" you're tempted to emulate is truly a "success?" Heck, even the pros have been known to do it; rumor has it that Marsha (early on in her eBay days) tried copying the style of a seller who sold hundreds of items a day. (Hey, learn by doing.) But no matter how she tried, no dice — until she did a little homework and figured out that there was more to this seller than met the eye.

Sometimes the only way to know the real story is to do some online research. Marsha looked at the completed listings from the "big-time" seller — and found that only about 1 in 20 of the listings resulted in the item being sold. So how on earth could this person be such a huge success on eBay? Here's the scoop:

- **Quantity does matter:** The seller listed hundreds of items per day, and whatever sold, sold. If it didn't sell on eBay, the item then came up for sale in the seller's retail location.

- **Service fees make money, too:** This seller was an *eBay Trading Assistant* (a seller who sells items on eBay for those who choose not to sell their own) — and charged clients a minimum fee to cover the time and expenses for every item listed.

Research — whether it's for an item you plan on selling or buying, or for just about any situation you face on eBay — is your number-one tool for success. If you think that a certain seller is a whiz-bang success, confirm your suspicions by taking a look at that seller's completed listings.

As sellers, you need to concentrate on what works best for your own style of listings and the type of items you sell. Learning from other sellers can be helpful, but copying the look of someone else's listings is really a waste of time (not to mention unfair to the person who worked hard to develop his or her own branded templates).

Oddly enough, whether you sell auto parts or designer dresses, the basic rules for successful listings (which we outline in this book) are the same. You may choose different colors for your descriptive text (as an automotive seller versus a fashion peddler), but all the information this book provides about the structure and content of your listing still applies.

A successful listing gives prospective buyers the right information — in a pleasing manner that entices them to either place a bid or click the Buy It Now button. It's as simple as that!

Making Your Listing Stand Out from the Others

Aside from all the sage advice we give you in this book, eBay — not so surprisingly — offers you a good many options to up the value of your listings. Prudent use of these options (*translation:* not spending too much of your profits on them) can bring greater attention to your listings; Figure 1-1 shows a typical listing that uses them successfully. Here are a few of the more popular options:

- **Buy It Now (BIN):** Gives your buyers the benefit of their two favorite options: auctions and fixed-price sales. For a fee from 5 to 25 cents (depending on the BIN price), you can sell your item directly to the first buyer who meets the fixed price (optional), or if someone places a bid, the Buy It Now option disappears.

Figure 1-1: This listing gives prospective buyers an option on how to buy your item.

- **Subtitle:** Wow. When eBay first came out with this option, we thought that it was a pretty darned expensive tool. Fifty cents is an awful lot of coin to pay for additional text to appear next to your title — especially since that text is findable only when a potential buyer searches for title *and description*. But (being the open-minded sellers we are) we thought we'd give it a try. Double wow, son-of-a-gun, it works.

REMEMBER

All but a miniscule number of searches for items are run for "title only," so the cost of including a descriptive subtitle can be worth it! For example, a subtitle works really well when you have a lot of competition (meaning lots of other sellers are selling the same item). By putting together a well-phrased, 55-character subtitle, you can pull the buyers' eyes right off the competition's listings and onto yours. Figure 1-2 shows you a listing that takes full advantage of the subtitle option.

Figure 1-2:
Use the subtitle option to show buyers that your item has more value than does the competition's similar listings.

124 items found for **desk reference**					Add to Favorite Searches	
List View | Picture Gallery		Sort by: Time: ending soonest ▾			Customize Display	
Compare	**Item Title**	**PayPal**	**Price**	**Bids**	**Time Left** ▲	**Shipping**
☐ 📷	The New York Public Library Desk Reference New	📷⊙	$1.99	-	17m	$2.95
☐	Ebay Business All-in-one Desk Reference For Dummies ... Over 850 pages of eBay Selling Savvy direct from Author	📷⊙	$24.68	3	41m	$4.99
☐	Windows Xp All-In-One Desk Reference for Dummies by ...	📷	$9.90	2	15h 15m	$4.22
☐	PDR, PHYSICIANS DESK REFERENCE, LOT, MUST SEE!	📷⊙	$29.99 =Buy It Now		16h 18m	$15.00
☐ 📷	CCNP All-in-one Desk Reference for Dummies - CISCO	📷⊙	GBP 7.99	-	17h 17m	See description
☐	Networking All-in-one Desk Reference for Dummies	📷⊙	GBP 7.99	-	18h 47m	See description

✔ **Bold Title:** When you select the Bold option, your listing appears in boldface type in searches, as well as in category browsing. It's a good option to use if you're in competition with other sellers hawking the same items. But we suggest you use this option only if your item can sell for a good price; otherwise the $1 bold fee can take a large chunk out of your profits!

✔ **Highlight:** Let's hear it for the big yellow highlighter! Nothing like it for getting to the gist of a book. Strangely, however (beats us as to why), the eBay highlight feature is lilac. Be sure to look at the category in which you choose to list before selecting this feature. Some categories (such as Home Page Featured) are overwhelmed with sellers using the highlight option — the pages look completely shaded in lilac. In these categories, *not* using highlight (and using perhaps a bold title instead) might make your listing stand out even more.

Five dollars is a pretty large investment to make in an option, so be sure that it will really work for you before laying down that kind of scratch.

- **Box border:** Here's one of my personal favorites. You can put a box around your listing to draw the page viewers' eyes right to your item. Using a box border is attention-getting — and a real bargain to boot — at only $3! For some reason, sellers occasionally choose to use this option in combination with the Highlight option, which hikes their additional fees to $8. Why use both when the box alone will do the trick for your item?

- **Home Page Featured:** *Location, location, location* is the byword for prime real estate; the Home Page Featured option gives you the highest level of visibility at eBay: a spot on the home page. Your listing may show up in that captivating little box that appears smack dab in the center of the eBay Home page — although there's no *guarantee* that it will. But since a huge percentage of visitors to the eBay site enter through — and scour — the home page, they tend to be attracted to this boxed area, and usually click the <u>See All Featured Items</u> link. This link leads them to the special Featured Items auction section. When you list with this option, your item is also featured (at the top of the page) on the individual category pages of the featured items (kinda hard to miss).

   Bidders browse the Featured Items tabs (Auctions, Buy It Now, or All Items) to see what's listed in there, just as you might make a beeline to the New Releases section of your video store. The charges that put your listing in this special area are $39.95 to list a single Home Page Featured item and $79.95 for multiple items.

   Figure 1-3 shows a typical example from The eBay Home Page Featured section, featuring some popular options: Bold, Highlight, Box and Gallery. (And yes, sometimes the Home Page Featured sellers go a bit overboard on the options!)

- **Featured Plus!:** To get top billing on an eBay page, you can list your item with the Featured Plus! option for $19.95. This option puts your listing on the first page of your item category, as well as at the top of most search-results pages that find it. This option works well for moving special merchandise and setting yourself apart from the competition. Remember your budget: Will your item bring in enough profit to make it worth the 20 bucks to list it at the top of the page? If you feel this is the case, go for it. Figure 1-4 shows how items appear when listed at the top of the page after they're "Featured" in Category listings or searches.

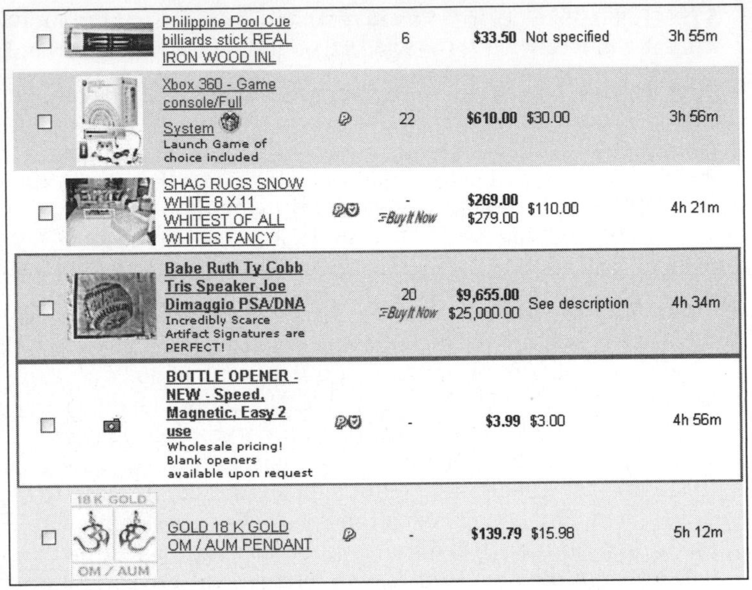

Figure 1-3: An example from The eBay Home Page Featured section.

Figure 1-4: Featured items appear at the top of a search page or at the top of the category listings, as illustrated by these interesting A4 items.

✔ **Gallery Picture:** This is one of the few "musts" in our eBay repertoire. For only 35 cents, you can display a mini-postage-stamp-size version of your item's picture next to its title. This Gallery picture shows up when a prospective buyer is browsing in a category or performing a search and perusing the results.

If you don't use a Gallery picture and just include a picture in your description, eBay displays a silly green camera icon next to your listing. There's no way that the little camera icon can compete with the other sellers' appropriately placed Gallery images. Bottom line: If you're going to sell, you'd better spend that 35 cents for the extra exposure.

If you're selling a media product such as a book, CD, or DVD, eBay supplies the picture for you; it doesn't get any easier than that. For the same 35 cents, eBay will show a stock picture (and some pre-filled text) fed in from an online media library. All you have to do is type in the number below the barcode (the ISBN or UPC code number) as found on the back of your item in the Pre-filled information, find your item area, and eBay does the rest. You can also input the author's or artist's name, or the work's title. If you choose this input method, eBay presents you with a page of images to select from. eBay also adds stock information (a prewritten description of the item) about your media item in the description.

Figure 1-5 shows you the area from the Sell Your Item (SYI) form where you input your data, and Figure 1-6 shows you how the picture appears in the listing.

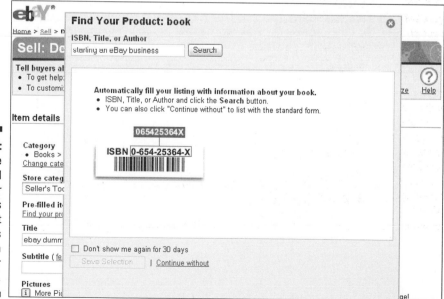

Figure 1-5: Type in the book's ISBN number (or author's name or just the title) as prompted in the Sell Your Item form.

Figure 1-6:
Here's the
book detail
as it
appears in
the
description
of the media
item.

Constructing Catchy Listings

You have several things to keep in mind when creating listings that will draw the eyes (and the wallets) of the buying market. For example, you need a catchy title and a winning description. Read on to see the ultimate tips to luring bidders to your sales.

Writing a title that sells

Your title is (next to your Gallery image) the most important way to draw people to your listing. eBay buyers are search-engine-driven — they find most of their items by typing selected keywords into the search box and clicking the Search button. Those keywords should be all your title consists of. No fancy prose. No silly words that people won't search for. Here are a few examples of eBay's worst title words:

- L@@K
- Nice
- WOW
- RARE

Do yourself a favor — *never* include these words in your title. No one ever searches for these words — ever! (For that matter, nobody's looking for "!!!!!!" in the title, either. Can't think why . . .)

Okay, we're gonna say it up front: If you've finished writing your item title and you have spaces left over, **please** fight the urge to dress it up with lots of exclamation points and asterisks. No matter how gung-ho you are about your item, the eBay search engine may overlook your item if the title is encrusted with meaningless ****, $$$$, and !!!! symbols. If bidders do see your title, they may become annoyed by their virtual shrillness and ignore them!!!!!!!! (See what I mean?)

Another distracting habit is overdoing capital letters. To buyers, seeing everything in caps is LIKE SEEING A CRAZED SALESMAN SCREAMING AT THEM TO BUY NOW! Using all caps online is considered *shouting* — it's annoying and tough on the eyes. Use capitalization SPARINGLY, and only to finesse a particular point or name.

Look for keywords that pay off

Hands down, the most valuable real estate on eBay is the 55-character title of your item. The majority of buyers do title searches, and that's where your item must come up if it's going to be sold!

Here are some ideas to help you fill in the keywords in your item title:

- Use the most common name for the item, and only if there's room, list the alternate name. For example, say *salt shaker,* and if there's room, add *saltcellar.*

- If the item *is* actually rare or hard to find, okay, mention that. But instead of the word *RARE* (so overused it's practically invisible), include the acronyms (OOAK, OOP, or HTF) that eBay users have come to rely on. (No, they aren't cartoon noises; the table in the next section lists what they mean.)

- Mention the item's condition and whether it's new or old. When applicable (as with gently used items), include the item's age or date of manufacture.

- Mention the item's special qualities, such as its style (for a handbag), model (for a camera), or edition (for a book).

- Include brand names, if those names are significant. If you're selling a for-real Tiffany lamp, you want people to know it!

- State the size of the item or other descriptive information, such as color or material content.

eBay lingo at a glance

Here's a crash course in eBay lingo that can help bring you up to speed on attracting buyers to your auction. Table 1-1 summarizes some abbreviations used frequently in eBay auctions; they can do wonders to jump-start your title.

Also, a whole smattering of acronyms that abbreviate item characteristics are part of the eBay business experience. As eBay has grown, so has this specialized lingo. Members use these acronyms as shortcuts to describe their merchandise.

So here, as promised, is Table 1-1: a handy list of common acronyms and related phrases used to describe items on eBay. (**Hint:** *Mint* means "may as well be brand new," not "cool chocolate treat attached.")

Table 1-1	A Quick List of eBay Acronyms	
eBay Code	*What It Abbreviates*	*What It Means*
MIB	Mint in Box	The item is in the original box, in great shape, and just the way you'd expect to find it in a store.
MIMB	Mint in Mint Box	The box has never been opened and looks like it just left the factory.
MOC	Mint on Card	The item is mounted on its original display card, attached with the original fastenings, in store-new condition.
NRFB	Never Removed from Box	Just what it says, as in "bought but never opened."
COA	Certificate of Authenticity	Documentation that vouches for the genuineness of an item, such as an autograph or painting.
OEM	Original Equipment Manufacture	You're selling the item and all the equipment that originally came with it, but you don't have the original box, owner's manual, or instructions.
OOAK	One of a kind	You are selling the only one in existence!
NR	No Reserve Price	You can set a *reserve price* when you begin your auction. If bids don't meet the reserve, you don't have to sell. Many buyers are leery of reserve prices because they're after a more obvious bargain. If you're not listing a reserve price for your item, let bidders know.

eBay Code	What It Abbreviates	What It Means
NWT	New with Tags	An item, possibly apparel, is in new condition with the tags from the manufacturer still affixed.
HTF, OOP	Hard to Find, Out of Print	Out of print, only a few ever made, or people grabbed up all there were. (HTF doesn't mean you spent a week looking for it in the attic.)

Normally, you can rely on eBay slang to get your point across, but make sure that you mean it *and that you're using it accurately.* Don't label something MIB (Mint in Box) when it looks like it's been Mashed in Box by a meat-grinder. You'll find more abbreviations on Marsha's Web site at www.cool ebaytools.com.

Use the spell checker to verify your titling! It bears repeating: Check and recheck your spelling. Savvy buyers use the eBay search engine to find merchandise; if the name of your item is spelled wrong, the search engine can't find it. In addition, poor spelling and incomprehensible grammar reflect badly on you. If you're in competition with another seller, the buyer is likelier to trust the seller *hoo nose gud speling.*

Adding information with a subtitle

eBay allows you to buy an additional 55-character subtitle, which will appear under your item title in a search or in a category browse. The fee for this extra promotion is 50 cents; in a few circumstances, it may be worth your while. Any text you input will *really* make your item stand out in the crowd — but (You knew there would be a *but,* didn't you?) these additional characters don't come up in a title search. So if you have the same words as your subtitle in your description, the words will be found either way with a title and description search. The benefit of the subtitle is that it makes your listing stand out when users browse or look up searches.

Gathering the tools you'll need

Throughout this book, we talk about adding selling power to your listings by applying your skills with photography and HTML. A little knowledge and a few tools are all you need to compete with the big guys. As a matter of fact, you may not need every bit of information in this book. But we want to give you plenty of options and insight into what you need to know to compete.

The big guys — Bose, Hewlett Packard (HP), Sony, Disney, all those big-time merchants that sell on eBay — attract buyers with exactly the same methods you find in this book. Pick out your chapters and use the information that applies to your needs, as follows:

- ✔ If you're interested in spicing up the appearance of your listing text, get yourself a text editor and get ready to brush up on your HTML skills. For example, you can use Windows Notepad and the free "try before you buy" version of a major program: CuteHTML 2.3.

- ✔ If you want your product photos to do the work, check out the photography tricks that you can accomplish with a simple digital camera and inexpensive accessory equipment. Try a snappy little software called Fast Photos (there's a free trial on the `coolebaytools.com` Web site).

We promise that this book's advice on improving the text and pictures you use in your listings will serve you well. Your mission (should you decide to accept it) is to ease into using them. At first, take baby steps toward enhancing your item listings. As your online business grows, you can expand your methods and offerings — but only if you want to.

Copywriting, eBay-style

A fabulous description goes a long way to upping your bottom line. Those aforementioned big guys don't leave any details out of their descriptions, so why should you? Don't think Hemingway here; think *infomercial*. Figure 1-7 shows a listing with a great description — and yours can be magnificent. All you have to do is click in the Description text box of the Sell Your Item form and start typing — glancing at this book now and then for sage guidance, of course.

Figure 1-7: Writing a good description can mean the difference between auction success and failure.

Pyrex 14-Piece Bake and Serve Set

Pyrex is the first name in bakeware. From the kitchen, to the oven, to the table, to the refrigerator--all in one bowl. This set is just the thing for the on-the-go family that doesn't have time to wash lots of dishes (and who does)!

This 14 pc. set from the Pyrex Bake and Serve line features

- 9" x 13" x 2" dish with dark blue plastic storage cover
- 8" x 8" x 2" dish with dark blue plastic storage cover
- 2 natural wood and wrought iron baskets
- (4) 2-cup round storage dishes with dark blue plastic storage covers

If you like this item and are looking for other kitchen applications, please visit Kitchen Kountry, our fully-stocked eBay Store.

Here's a list of suggestions for writing an effective item description:

- **List the item's benefits.** Give the buyer a reason to buy your item and be enthusiastic when you list all the reasons everyone should bid on it. Unlike the listing's title, you can use as much space as you want. Be precise in your description: tell how big it is, what color, what kind of fabric, what design, and so on. Also, mention any alternative uses for the item — perhaps those pantyhose can also be used for straining yogurt?

- **Include the negative.** Don't hide the truth of your item's condition. Trying to conceal flaws costs you in the long run — in terms of (for openers) returned items, bad feedback, or (at very worst) a fraud investigation. If the item has a scratch, a nick, a dent, a crack, a ding, a tear, a rip, missing pieces, replacement parts, faded color, dirty smudges, or a bad smell (especially if cleaning might damage the item), mention it in the description. If your item has been overhauled, rebuilt, repainted, or hot-rodded, say so. You don't want the buyer to flip out because you weren't truthful about imperfections or modifications.

- **Promote your other listings.** The pros always do a little cross-promotion, and it works. When the hosts on the morning news tell you to tune in for something special, they're trying to prevent you from turning to the competition. So, a word to the wise: If you're selling photography equipment and cat toys, be sure to point to *both* store categories.

- **While you're at it, promote yourself, too.** As you build your feedback rating, point out your terrific track record to potential bidders. Add statements like "I'm great to deal with. Check out my feedback." You can even take it a step farther by inviting prospective bidders to your About Me page (where you may also include a link to your personal Web site if you have one).

- **Spell out pre-sale details.** Occasionally, sellers offer an item as a *pre-sell*, or an item that the seller doesn't yet have in stock but expects to. If you're offering this kind of item, make sure that you spell out all the details in the description.

eBay policy (and Federal Trade Commission law) states that you must ship a pre-sell item within 30 days of receiving payment, so be sure you will have the item within that time span. Also don't forget to include the actual shipping date. And don't forget that putting up an item for sale *without actually having it in hand* is a practice fraught with risk. The item you are expecting may not arrive in time, or it may arrive damaged. We've heard too many sad tales of sellers who got caught in this situation — and had to go out and purchase an item at retail for a buyer in order to preserve their feedback.

- **Invite questions.** Make the buyer comfortable with the idea of e-mailing you with a question. Some sellers seem way too busy (or full of themselves) in their text to make you want to ask a question. Remember, customer service is the key to high bids.

✔ **Wish your potential bidders well.** Communication is the key to a good transaction, and you can set the tone for your auction and post-auction exchanges by including some simple phrases that show your friendly side. Always end your description by wishing bidders good luck, inviting potential bidders to e-mail you with questions, and offering the option of providing additional photos of the item if you have them.

Like stores that hang signs saying "No shirt, no shoes, no service," eBay members can refuse to do business with other members. You have the right to be selective (within reason and the law, of course) about whom you want as a prospective buyer for your item. The listing is yours, and you can protect your investment any way you want. However, you can't discriminate or break any state or federal laws in your description. If you've had bad experiences with certain members of the eBay community, you may block them as bidders from your business. Just don't be rude and negative. There's no faster way to turn off a bidder than by having more warnings and rules than you have description. Take a look at Figure 1-8 for a listing that doesn't exactly exude customer service.

Figure 1-8:
Is this any
way to
start your
description?
Is it any way
to attract
new
customers?

Description
DO NOT BID IF YOU DO NOT AGREE TO THESE TERMS!!!!!!!! IF YOU HAVE LESS THAN 10 POSITIVE FEEDBACKS, EMAIL ME FIRST!
PLEASE READ LISTING VERY CLOSELY BEFORE YOU BID! PAYMENT WITHIN THREE DAYS OF AUCTION. PAYPAL ONLY. DO NOT BID IF YOU DO NOT INTEND TO PAY. PLEASE KEEP EBAY SAFE FOR THE HONEST EBAYERS!!! US ONLY. DO NOT BID ON THIS AUCTION IF YOU HAVE LESS THAN 10 POSITIVE FEEDBACKS!! CHECK OUT MY OTHER AUCTIONS!

Following our tips will go a long way to helping you raise your bottom line. Since there are two of us, we offer two unique perspectives for enhancing an item description. Here they are:

✔ **Remember what your English teacher taught you.** Make your description like a woman's skirt: Long enough to cover the subject but short enough to keep it interesting.

✔ **Write your description as if you didn't have a picture.** Use words to draw a mental image of your item. That way, your prospective buyer will know what the item looks like if the photo server fails and the image doesn't show up. ("Electric guitar" just doesn't say much if what you're selling is a "near-mint Fender Stratocaster, American Deluxe Series, maple neck, abalone inlays, Transparent Crimson finish, gold hardware, in original plush-lined hardshell case.")

Remember these pearls of wisdom next time you write up a listing.

Chapter 2

Getting a Quick Start with the Sell Your Item Page

In This Chapter

▶ Understanding the Sell Your Item form

▶ Carefully filling in the blanks

▶ Knowing what all the options mean

*E*very item listed on eBay has been set up on the eBay Sell Your Item (SYI) form (or something very similar sent through a third party provider). However you approach selling an item on eBay, you always have to make the same decisions, fill in the same blanks, and check the same boxes — kind of. There are variations. So, in this chapter, we take you step-by-step through the Sell Your Item page — the page you fill out to get your sales going on eBay. We explain all the facets of this page, offer some advice that can increase your odds of making money, and provide pointers on the best way to position your item so buyers see it and bid on it.

Remember that eBay's technocoders are constantly changing things (we all have to justify our paychecks, you know), so perhaps the next time you go to sell an item on eBay, the form may look a tad bit different. But never mind this minor inconvenience. The basic questions and decisions will stay the same.

Understanding the Sell Your Item Area

After you've decided you're ready to list your item, the first order of business is to sit down and settle on your title and description copy. With this well-thought-out text in hand, it's time to face the eBay Sell Your Item form. To find eBay's SYI page from the eBay Home page, click the Sell link on the navigation bar at the top of the page, and you're whisked there immediately.

Every eBay page has a navigation bar at the top, so click the word Sell, as shown in Figure 2-1.

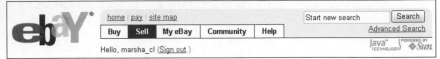

Figure 2-1:
Clicking Sell
gets you on
the way!

Now comes decision time. You're going to have to nail down a slew of details about *how* to list your item. Believe it or not, each of these small choices can have a strong effect on whether your sale is a success. So, pay attention.

Decision #1: Choosing a category (or two)

Your first decision is what category you want your item to appear in. Figure 2-2 shows you the category-selection page where you find several useful tools:

Figure 2-2:
Type
keywords to
help select
your
category.

Enter words about your item to find a category for it.

`[                    ]` `Search`

Browse category directory | Recently used categories

✔ **Recently Used Categories link.** Clicking this link takes you to another page, as shown in Figure 2-3, to select a category from among those you've already used for listing items on eBay.

✔ **Browse Category Directory selector.** Click this link to get to a Java-based selection page, as shown in Figure 2-4. When you click Continue at the bottom of the page, you're transferred to yet another page where you can drill down into the sub, sub-sub and sub-sub-sub categories to list your item (even if it's a submarine).

✔ **Keyword Finder box.** Type the specific name of your item in this box (see Figure 2-2), and you're presented with a list of the categories that have items to match your keywords.

We prefer to run a complete item search with our keywords so we can see which categories are likely to gross the highest dollar amounts for our items.

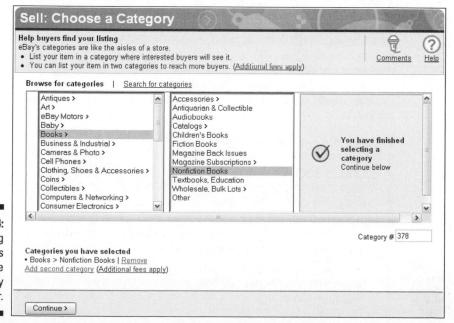

Sell: Choose a Category

Help buyers find your listing
eBay's categories are like the aisles of a store.
- List your item in a category where interested buyers will see it.
- You can list your item in two categories to reach more buyers. (Additional fees apply)

Comments   Help

Search for categories | Browse for categories

[Search]

Categories: select up to two for your listing

☐ Cameras & Photo > Lighting & Studio Equipment > Other Lighting & Studio Items
☐ Books > Nonfiction Books
☐ Cameras & Photo > Lighting & Studio Equipment > Continuous Lighting
☐ Cameras & Photo > Digital Camera Accessories > Accessories > Other Accessories
☐ Home & Garden > Pet Supplies > Dogs > Dog Leashes
☐ Home & Garden > Lamps, Lighting, Ceiling Fans > Table Lamps > Other
☐ Home & Garden > Pet Supplies > Cats > Cat Toys > Other Cat Toys
☐ Art > Prints > Contemporary (1950-Now) > Limited Editions > Other

[Continue >]

Figure 2-3:
Looking at
your
recently
used
categories.

After you select your category, you have the option to list your item in a second category. The caveat here: You're charged double your listing fee if you list in two categories.

Sell: Choose a Category

Help buyers find your listing
eBay's categories are like the aisles of a store.
- List your item in a category where interested buyers will see it.
- You can list your item in two categories to reach more buyers. (Additional fees apply)

Comments   Help

Browse for categories | Search for categories

Antiques >	Accessories >	
Art >	Antiquarian & Collectible	
eBay Motors >	Audiobooks	
Baby >	Catalogs >	
Books >	Children's Books	**You have finished**
Business & Industrial >	Fiction Books	**selecting a**
Cameras & Photo >	Magazine Back Issues	**category**
Cell Phones >	Magazine Subscriptions >	Continue below
Clothing, Shoes & Accessories >	Nonfiction Books	
Coins >	Textbooks, Education	
Collectibles >	Wholesale, Bulk Lots >	
Computers & Networking >	Other	
Consumer Electronics >		

Category # 378

Categories you have selected
• Books > Nonfiction Books | Remove
Add second category (Additional fees apply)

Figure 2-4:
Using
eBay's
browse
category
selector.

[Continue >]

Here's how to use eBay's Enhanced (filmstrip-style) category selector:

1. **Select a main category by clicking it.**

   The appropriate subcategories appear in the next square.

2. **Select the most appropriate subcategory.**

   More subcategories appear in the next square.

3. **Continue selecting subcategories until you have narrowed down your item listing as much as possible.**

   You know you've come to the last available subcategory when you don't see any more arrows on the category list.

Most bidders scan for specific items in subcategories. For example, if you're selling a Swaroski crystal pin, don't just list it under Jewelry; keep narrowing down your choices (fortunately, eBay makes that easy: Just keep clicking until you hit the end of the line).

Selecting your category can make or break your listing. For more about savvy category selection and other eBay techniques, check out any of Marsha Collier's eBay books in the *For Dummies* series. And if you're looking to start an online business, there's also a book for that: *Starting an eBay Business For Dummies,* 2nd Edition.

Decision #2: Choosing a listing type

Another important decision is what type of listing you want to post on eBay. As with the dizzying menu at your favorite restaurant, there are three ways to sell an item on eBay (flip over to the first figure in Chapter 1 for a quick visual refresher). There is a fourth way — selling real estate — but we're dealing with consumer items here. Four ways to list may not seem too dizzying (unless you're trying to psychically decide just which format will be the best for you).

Here are the pros and cons of each type:

✔ **Online Auction.** This is the original, traditional sale format on eBay. This is what those eager new shoppers look for when they come to the eBay site in search of bargains. Remember that this option is flexible; you can combine an auction listing with a Buy-It-Now option for those who want to purchase the item immediately. The Buy-It-Now option will give the prospective buyer the opportunity to buy the item at the price you post.

Experience has taught us that when we're selling a collectible item, letting it go to auction often nets a much higher final selling price.

- ✔ **Fixed Price.** Fixed-price sales make shopping on eBay as easy as going to the local mall. It's an easy transaction for the buyer to complete. The only problem is that many prospective buyers get confused when they see this option. ("This is eBay — where's the auction?") Also, they may prefer an auction because of the innocent perception that they *may* get a better deal automatically.

- ✔ **Store Inventory.** After you've opened your eBay Store, here's where you click to list an item in the store. It's a convenient place to sell items related to your auctions or your fixed-price sales.

For this stroll through the Sell Your Item form, we want to list an old-fashioned eBay auction. We might be willing to sell the item for a fixed price, but we're also willing to let the item go to auction. After you've put a check mark next to that option, you're off to the races.

Filling in the Blanks — Carefully

Now is the time to get exacting with your listing. In Chapter 1, we discuss the pros and cons and the pluses and minuses of your listing's title, optional subtitle, and description. Figure 2-5 shows you where to begin in the main part of the Sell Your Item form.

eBay is constantly working on perfecting the layout of these forms, and when you look at the SYI page, it may be set up a bit differently than the page depicted in this book. But regardless of the look, please recognize that you still have to make all these decisions and fill in the blanks about your item listing.

If you have an eBay Store, the first thing you do is customize in which store categories you want your new item to appear. You may select 2 of your possible 20 custom listing categories from two drop-down menus. Here's a chance to get creative — why not list your items in more than one category? And remember to check out Chapter 5 for instructions on setting up links to your store on your listings.

Now, if you haven't set up photo hosting elsewhere, you can list one picture with eBay's Picture Service for free; additional pictures will cost you 15 cents each. Alternatively, you can put all the pictures you want in your auction's description — for free. (Chapter 15 gives you the lowdown on how to use eBay's Picture Services, list images in your description, and make the most of third-party photo-hosting services.)

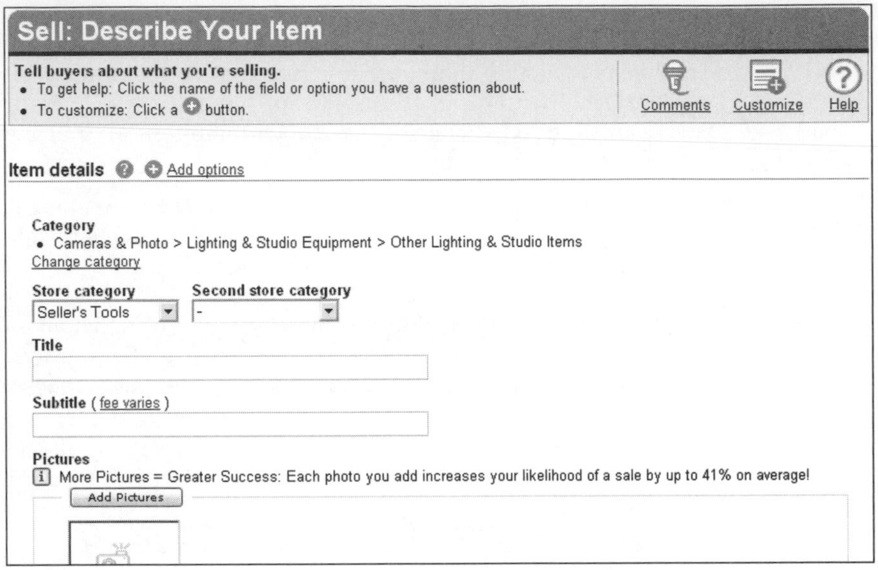

Figure 2-5:
Here's
where you
put the
beginnings
of your
listing
description.

Deciding on your Item Specifics

Every eBay category gives you the opportunity to list *Item Specifics* (shown in Figure 2-6), even if those specifics are as simple as the Item Condition selection — that is, choosing whether the item is New or Used. Most categories have a more elaborate setup — and the more complex the item, the more it needs those extra details (for example, Item Specifics for the Apple Laptop category tend to be more complicated than those for, say, Jeans).

These specifics are used during an eBay search. Many eBay search pages show a product *finder* (at the left of the screen) that helps the shopper narrow down their choices.

Different categories offer specifics for their unique products. For example:

- **Women's Jeans Finder**: Style, Size Type (as in Misses, Juniors, Maternity, and so on), Size, and Condition. Take a look at how these filled-in specifics appear in the description shown in Figure 2-6.

- **Men's Shoe Finder**: U.S. Size, Type, and Condition.

- **Golf Club Finder:** Club Type, Brand, Model, Condition, Shaft Material, Dexterity, and Gender.

- **Wristwatches Finder:** Gender, Brand, Condition, and Age.

Get the picture? Be prepared to know the answers about your item and fill in these specifics. You don't want to loose a sale because you forgot to indicate that your item was new.

Figure 2-6:
Checking
out the
Jeans
specifics in
a nutshell.

Description		
Item Specifics - Women's Jeans		
Style: **Boot Cut**	Size Type: **By Waist Size**	
Condition: **New: With Tags**	Size: **30**	

Writing up the description

Chapter 1 lays out the basics of item description; here's where we get down to the basics of putting the description into the eBay system. If you don't want to monkey around with HTML (not just yet, anyway), you can use the Standard way of inputting your text — which is (blessedly) much like using a word processor. Figure 2-7 shows you the standard input area for creating your description.

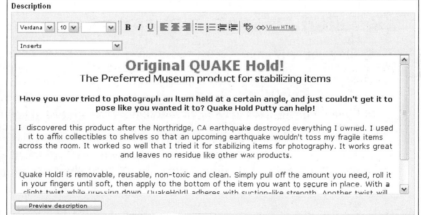

Figure 2-7:
Dolling up a
listing here
is as simple
as using a
word
processor.

For those not familiar with the boxes, bars and menus, we list them here (from left to right):

> ✔ **Font Name:** This is a drop-down menu that will change the type face of the text on your screen. Merely highly your text to select the text you want to change, and then use your cursor to select the typeface of your choice from the drop-down menu. You have choices of Arial, Courier, Times, and Verdana.
>
> The Verdana font was designed exclusively for legibility on computer screens.

✔ **Size:** Here's another drop-down menu that allows you to select the size of your type. The numbers in the drop-down menu indicate the types point size. The higher the number, the larger the text.

✔ **Color:** Want some fiery red text? Here's your chance! You can change your highlighted text to Black, Blue, Brown, Red, or Green.

✔ **B:** Stands for **Boldface.** Clicking the B changes your type from regular text to bold.

✔ **I:** I is for *italic.* You want to slant the text in part of a sentence for effect? Just highlight your text and click here.

✔ **Flush Left:** When you want your text to align to the left, just highlight it and click the simulated left-aligned text.

✔ **Centered Text:** Sometimes text looks best centered (especially when your picture is a horizontally-based rectangle). Highlighting the text and clicking here centers your text perfectly.

✔ **Flush Right:** Sometimes the most effective look aligns your text to the right side of the page. Just click here and voilà!

✔ **Numbered List:** Highlight a group of paragraphs and click here for a nicely ordered, numbered list.

✔ **Bulleted List:** We use this one a great deal for listing an item's features. Highlight (just as in the numbered list) and eBay's magic will produce a cleanly ordered, bulleted list like this one.

✔ **Move Right:** This pushbutton command moves the entire selected paragraph of text to the right.

✔ **Move Left:** Surprise! Clicking here will move your block of text to the left.

✔ **Inserts:** Here's a drop-down menu that helps you insert certain pre-assigned links into your text — or, for that matter, create a link. Figure 2-8 shows the range of choices on this drop-down menu.

After you create a link using eBay's system, you can choose to save it to use again.

✔ **Spell Checker:** Hallelujah! Finally we'll be able to check the spelling in our listing before going live. What we can't understand is why we still see plenty of misspellings in eBay listings. Be sure to use this feature — *and* check your work carefully! (A word to the wise: Try reading it out loud to catch some of the embarrassing typos that spell checkers can miss.)

✔ **Help:** The question-mark button permits you to access eBay's help menu for this form.

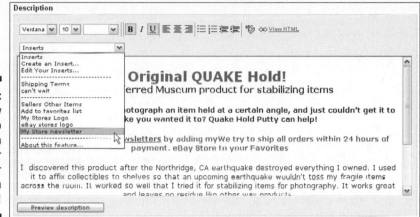

Figure 2-8:
Look how
easy it is to
create an
insert for
your
description
page!

After you've input all of your description, you still have to go step-by-step
through the form, indicating some very important essentials:

1. **Pricing and duration:** Here's where the hard part starts again: Think like
   a marketer! Can you give the prospective buyer the option of making a
   low, low opening bid? (No guts, no glory.) Or do you want to play it safe
   with a middle-of-the-road opening bid? (Okay, that's my usual approach.)
   Whatever your strategy, list your opening price here. If you want to
   place a reserve or a Buy-It-Now price — well, now's your chance.

   To list an item with Buy It Now, you must have a feedback of ten or be ID
   Verified.

   There's also a drop-down menu where you select the number of days
   you want your listing to run. You can choose anywhere from one to ten
   days.

2. **Start Time:** If you'd rather not schedule your listing just now, put it off
   till the future. You can schedule a future time for the listing to start;
   here's where you kick in the extra 10¢ fee to do it.

   If insomnia has you up in front of the computer listing your auctions at
   0-dark-thirty, don't let your auctions *close* in the middle of the night —
   say, at 2:30 a.m.? Unless you're prominent in the community of vampires
   and werewolves, there aren't enough bidders around to cause any last-
   minute bidding wars that would bump up the price. Of course, if you're
   hoping to get bids from the other side of the globe (which also means
   the other side of the clock), that's a different story.

3. **Charity Auction:** If you want to donate a portion (or all) of the money from your listing to a charity, select one from your pre-registered list here. To register to sell for a charity, visit the eBay GivingWorks hub page at www.ebay.com/givingworks.

4. **Quantity:** Unless you're planning to sell multiple items, the number of items is always 1 — which means you're holding a traditional auction. If you need to change the quantity number from 1 to something bigger, just type the number in the box. In this case, the number of items you're offering is always 1. (Of course, you could run a Dutch auction or a multiple-item fixed-price listing — in which case, the quantity would be more than 1.) You may also indicate a single "lot" of multiple items; say a "lot" of 5 dolls.

5. **Item Location:** The region, city, and country from which the item will be shipped (this is a required field). The usual eBay default is to put your registered ZIP code and hometown in this field automatically. If you want to list a larger metropolitan area along with your ZIP code, you can. Just click the *Change* link and you can change from the suburb of Encino to the metropolitan area of Los Angeles.

6. **Listing Designer:** If you'd like to contribute ten cents to eBay's coffers to use one of their pre-designed graphic listing frames, here's where you can make your donation. (On the other hand, we show you how to make your own listing templates in Chapter 8.) Also, you can always drop by our Web site (at www.coolebaytools.com) for a few free ones that you can download.

7. **eBay's Options Gallery:** Here's where you get to use all those fancy options that we talked about in Chapter 1. Make your selections carefully and be sure the money you spend has a good chance of coming back to you in higher bids.

8. **Page Counters:** If you want to avail yourself of Andale.com's free page-view counters, indicate that here.

   Using Andale's counters requires registration on the Andale service.

9. **Payment Methods:** Here's the place you the information on what payment methods you will accept. If you want your buyer to pay with a PayPal, mention that here. This information appears at the top of your sale page when the sale is completed, at the bottom of the auction while it's active, and in the End of Auction e-mail.

10. **Ship-to-Locations:** Here's where you can indicate exactly where you're willing and able to ship an item. If you don't want the hassle of shipping out of the United States, just check the box that denies this option. You can individually select different countries, as well. (Sorry, no different planets. At least not yet.)

11. **Shipping and Sales Tax:** Indicate whether you're charging flat rate for your shipping (as in Figure 2-9), calculated or calculated freight (for items over 150 pounds).

    There's also a place for you to input the sales-tax percentage that you may (or may not, depending on your state) have to charge for purchases within your own state. eBay keeps this figure in the SYI form as a default until you decide to change it.

Figure 2-9:
eBay
shipping at
its simplest:
using the
flat rate that
more buyers
adore!

Shipping ❓ ❶ Add options

Cost ▦ Research rates and services
[Flat: same cost to all buyers ▾] [Apply]

Domestic shipping services
[US Postal Service Media Mail (2 to 9 working days) ▾] $ [3.50]
[US Postal Service Priority Mail ▾] $ [4.99]
[- ▾] $ [ ]

International shipping services
[USPS Global Priority Mail ▾] $ [17.50]
[- ▾] $ [ ]
[- ▾] $ [ ]

Shipping insurance
[Optional ▾] $ [1.30]

12. **Returns Policy:** If you accept returns, you can outline your policy here. Unfortunately, eBay has no way for you to indicate that you do *not* take returns, but if that's the case, just type that message in the refund policy box and hope people read it.

13. **Payment Instructions:** If you want to put in a little speil about how fast you ship — or (ahem) that you don't take returns — you can do that here. If you want buyers to pay with a different payment service, mention that as well. This information will appear at the top of your sale when the sale is completed, at the bottom of the auction while it's active, and in the End of Auction e-mail.

14. **Buyer Requirements:** This is a little-known-but-hugely-important option for sellers. eBay lets you take the "no shoes, no shirt, no service" philosophy all the way from the '60s into the new century. If there are some folks you don't want to sell to, here's where you may (within eBay standards) say so.

    When you indicate the folks you'd rather not do business with, it's good practice to be businesslike and specific about it. Figure 2-10 (for example) shows my choices for bidder blocking.

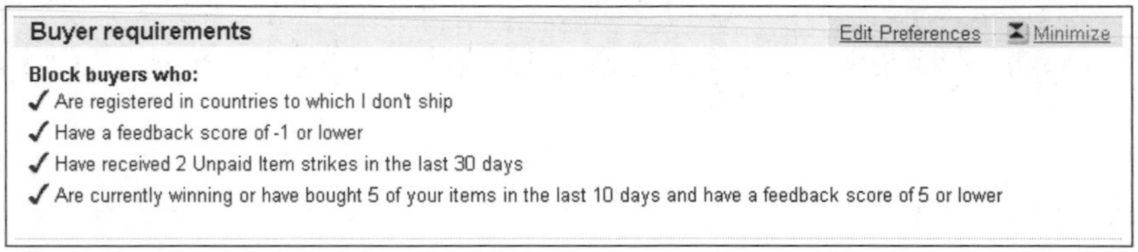

Figure 2-10:
I've set
my eBay
account
to block
bidders who
fulfill these
"sorry,
but . . ."
require-
ments.

Buyer requirements   Edit Preferences   ⅹ Minimize

Block buyers who:

✓ Are registered in countries to which I don't ship

✓ Have a feedback score of -1 or lower

✓ Have received 2 Unpaid Item strikes in the last 30 days

✓ Are currently winning or have bought 5 of your items in the last 10 days and have a feedback score of 5 or lower

Figure 2-10: I've set my eBay account to block bidders who fulfill these "sorry, but . . ." requirements.

Checking Your Work and Starting the Listing

When you've filled out all the blanks on the Sell Your Item page, you are ready to — you guessed it — check your work. After clicking Continue, you can review your work before listing. This is the place where you can catch embarrassing mistakes and take them out before your item is listed. The Review page shows you a condensed version of all your information, and tallies up how much eBay is charging you (in fees and options) to run this auction. You also get to see how your action description and pictures will look once they're up there on the site.

Chapter 3

Knowing How HTML Works

Although the title of this chapter might make you think it has more technical information than you will ever need to know, its purpose is to demystify the "geek-ness" of HTML (HyperText Markup Language). Starting with HTML (and all of its confusing permutations), through CSS (Cascading Style Sheets), and even the term WWW (World Wide Web) itself, the language of the Internet is a myriad of acronyms and abbreviations.

But behind all those seemingly unpronounceable words are relatively simple meanings. By the time you finish reading this chapter, you'll not only know what each of these terms mean, but you'll also know which ones are important for you to understand and learn to use. Understanding how HTML works is like learning to play a musical instrument, programming the time on your VCR, or becoming a marathon runner: Take it one step at a time, and break it down into manageable portions.

Getting to Know HTML and the Web

The terms *Internet* and *World Wide Web* (*Net* and *Web* for short) are often used interchangeably, but technically, the Internet is composed of the World Wide Web *and* many other functions. Here's a short list of the more commonly used Internet features:

- ✔ **E-mail:** Electronic mail is by far the most popular Internet application.

- ✔ **Real-time "chat" programs:** Advanced far beyond the early days where only text was used for conversations on the Internet, a plethora of programs allows conversations between two (or many more) users.

- ✔ **Telephony:** Using the Internet to make phone calls has been around for a while, but recent advances in hardware and software that use VoIP (Voice over Internet Protocol) make this one of the fastest-growing Internet applications.

- ✔ **File transfers:** Huge amounts of data are transferred on a continual basic through the Internet, independent of information transferred via Web site links.

The term "World Wide Web" brings to mind, of course, a spider web. Now is the time to envision a spider web, with all of its intricate intersecting threads. No matter where you start on the web, you can reach another point by following a path made up of individual strands. The World Wide Web works the same way; no matter which page you start on, you can reach virtually any other page by following links, which are the intersections of the individual strands. These intersections can all be on the same computer, or they can be on many different computers, anywhere in the world, as long as they are connected to the Internet.

Hypertext

Before the Web became popular, the primary source of information for most of us was a shelf full of reference books such as dictionaries and encyclopedias. Most entries in these references were full of cross-references to other entries for more information. Researching a subject could become an exercise in futility, flipping back and forth in volume after volume, chasing these cross-references. The Web has allowed users worldwide to create the ultimate encyclopedia, with more information and more cross-references, but a much easier way of accessing them.

There's an amazing amount of information available in the wink of an eye on the Web. But remember to take any information you find with a grain of salt — because bad information can be retrieved just as quickly as good information. Quantity and speed isn't always a guarantee of quality, and "what you see" on the WWW isn't always "what you want to get." *Anyone* can say *anything* they want — and they do! — and as my momma always told me, just because someone says it, doesn't mean it's true.

Even more important in the "what you see isn't what you want to get" line of thinking is this: The incidence of spoof sites is growing exponentially. *Spoof* sites are Web sites whose main goal is tricking you to freely give up your personal financial information and set yourself up as a target for identity theft. Always make sure that you know where you are in the cyber universe when entering sensitive information. And never, ever click on a link in an e-mail that *looks* like it came from eBay, PayPal, or any other organization. Go directly to the Web site in question and sign in to check on the status of your account.

HTML — the language of the World Wide Web — is what makes all those cross-references work as easily as the click of a mouse. The "HT" in HTML stands for *hypertext*, a set of computer instructions that acts like glue to stick together the individual strands of the Web, creating intersections so you can navigate from one point on the Web to another. A *hypertext link* is a portion of information, usually one or more words, that serves as both a snippet of text and an active control; it's linked to another portion of information — on the same page, the same computer, or another computer somewhere on the Internet — and when you click the link, you go there.

Markup

The "ML" in HTML stands for *markup language* — essentially codes or instructions included in a file of text that indicate how that text should be displayed by an Internet browser. These codes are invisible when the file is ultimately displayed, but they are essential to making the screen show more than just a steady stream of characters. Imagine what trying to read this page would be like if there were no paragraph breaks, no headings, or no cute little icons to draw your attention to something important!

Markup languages are used not only for pages on the Web, but also in virtually any program that handles text (whether it's e-mail or a word processor) to make the text readable when displayed, as well as easy to print. Often — as with the interface between your e-mail program and your printer — your computer provides the markup language automatically. Understandably, the commands to display a document on your computer screen are completely different than those required to print those same words on a piece of paper.

Chapter 19 introduces some programs you can use to automate the markup language for you — but you might as well know what it is you're automating, so for the moment, hang in there. After you get a handle on how these languages work behind the scenes, you can boss them around more easily.

Browsers

Most of us have a preference for one browser over another; it's similar to our preference for a particular model of car. A car will get us to and from the grocery store, no matter who made it. There are differences in options, of course — automatic or a manual transmission, MP3 or CD player (or, for retro fans, a cassette tape player). Obviously you can't work the clutch if your car has an automatic transmission, or play your CDs on that cassette player. Same deal with Web browsers: They all work similarly, but some commands work in one browser, but not in the other. We'll point out some of those commands as we go along.

For example, the `marquee` command, which provides a scrolling message when viewed using the Microsoft Internet Explorer browser, displays only nonmoving text when viewed with early versions of the Netscape browser. Conversely, the `blink` command works only in the Netscape browser (although, in our quest to reduce irritating distractions, we don't recommend using that command in either case).

Okay, back to the automotive analogy. Carmakers bring out a new version of each model at least once a year; browser manufacturers do the same. Sometimes these new car models are introduced with great fanfare to tout major new changes. Other years, only minor changes occur. Similarly, Web browsers are updated at varying levels on a regular basis.

At this point, it's worth noting that a Web browser is simply another computer program used to navigate the Web — and computer programs keep coming out in new versions, normally designated by a number, a decimal point, and another number. If you see *version 7.1* (for example), the first digit denotes a major version; the second digit indicates only a minor change. Some browser-savvy Web sites tell you, right up front, which browser (in which version) will display them best. A typical notice might read, "Best viewed with Internet Explorer version 6.0 and later."

As of this writing, the most popular browser is Internet Explorer; throughout 2005, Firefox emerged to take a firm hold on second place.

It's a good idea to have the top two or three browsers available on your computer — after all, you don't know which one an average visitor to your site may be using. When you're testing out new HTML commands you should be sure to view your listing description using each browser, to make sure the effect of your careful HTML coding is displayed as planned for the majority of your customers.

Some of your customers might not always upgrade their Web browsers to the latest version when it becomes available, especially if the new version includes major changes. If you decide to try out a fancy new HTML feature, keep in mind that some of your customers might be using an antiquated version of a browser that can't translate a command it doesn't know about. For this reason, avoid using those newer features in order to keep your listing from displaying improperly. For instance, both the `frame` attribute of the `table` command and the `legend` command (which you can use to draw borders around text) don't work in older browsers.

Web servers

A *Web server* is a program that runs on a computer connected to the Internet. Think of the Web server as a restaurant which provides delivery service, and users on the Web are patrons, or "clients" of the restaurant. The Web server is a very specialized program that answers an order submitted by a client computer for a page to be displayed, or "served." This order can be a direct request for a portion of text, HTML, an image, or a sound file (to name a few) or it can be triggered by the user clicking on a hyperlink. See Chapter 5 for a detailed explanation of the construction of hyperlink HTML commands.

Deconstructing an HTML Tag

The anatomy of an HTML command isn't nearly as complex as it may appear at first glance. Here's the general parts-is-parts breakdown for an HTML command:

- ✔ **An opening character:** This is the trigger to the Web browser (which will be interpreting the command), telling it not to display the characters that follow, but to act on them.

- ✔ **The actual command:** This text string defines what to do when the browser displays the page — and how to make it look the way you intend.

- ✔ **Optional attributes:** These non-displayed text strings define, in more detail, how the command is to be executed. (Fuss, fuss, fuss.)

- ✔ **A closing character:** This is the signal to the Web browser that the command is complete.

Most HTML commands are used as paired tags; one command signals the start of a change in the way that text is to be displayed, and another command signals the end of that change. If the ending command is omitted, the change in display is never turned off, which may provide an interesting, unwanted effect.

You can use a pair of simple HTML tags to center text on a Web page: The starting command `<center>` signals the place where the centering is to begin, followed by the word (or words) to be centered. This formatting ends with the ending command `</center>`, which signals where the centering is to end.

- ✔ Opening character: `<`
- ✔ Command: `center` or `/center`
- ✔ Closing character: `>`

A more complex pair of commands changes the font size and color of the text: The starting command `<font size="4" color="green">` signals the place where the font change is to begin, followed by the word (or words) to be displayed in the different size and color. Those are followed by the ending command `</font>` — which signals the place where the change is to end — here's the rundown:

✔ Opening character: <

✔ Command: font or /font

✔ Optional attributes: size="4" and color="green"

✔ Closing character: >

Most ending commands are identical to the associated starting command but are immediately preceded by the / character.

Cascading Styles Sheets (CSS)

The latest innovation in markup language for the Web is *Cascading Style Sheets* (CSS). No, this isn't the latest fashion in intricately flowing bedcoverings; CSS provides you the ability to more precisely define how you want a page to be displayed. This extra control may be necessary because specific Web browsers can easily override (or ignore) basic HTML commands.

A major benefit of using CSS is that you can define *once* (at the top of the page) the elements that are normally optional attributes for individual commands (such as body, hr, or ul). If you decide later to make a global change to the look of your page, you will need to change only one portion of the page (the top).

With Basic HTML, you would need to edit each occurrence of the command and its attributes. Even better, CSS enables you to create a separate file with the definition of the entire "style" of a page. You then refer to that same style from multiple pages. If you decide to make a major change to the look of your pages, you need to edit only the file that contains the overall style definitions, rather than every page that refers to the file.

You need to upload (to the Internet) the file containing your CSS style format information — just as you would upload an image you want to embed in your listing description. (See Chapter 15 for the scoop on how to get this uploading done.) As with any other critical data, make sure that you have a backup copy of the file containing your CSS style information. Anytime you make a change, make a copy of the file and edit the *copy* for testing your new formatting. We recommend you keep the last several versions of your style-file — just in case!

Okay, it's true — a simple change to a CSS external style-definition file can distribute the change to multiple pages that refer to the file. But that convenience comes with an associated danger: If the external file is damaged, or a change is made incorrectly, the error also gets distributed to all pages that refer to it. So what if the CSS style-file gets corrupted or you make a change incorrectly? After you scream in despair and before you start pulling out your hair, remember that you've followed the best practices from the preceding tip. That is, you edited only the copy of your CSS style-file, and you also kept the last several versions of this file. So the solution to your corrupted file or incorrect change is a simple file substitution!

Cascading Style Sheets are a relatively new method for defining how content displays on the Web. Up to now, each browser implements CSS a bit differently to suit its own features. For this reason, be sure to test your pages in the most popular browsers to make sure they display your pages correctly.

Interested in learning more about CSS? We've put a tutorial on Marsha's Web site www.coolebaytools.com that will help you get started!

Sure and Simple Formatting Tricks

One of the simplest tricks that can make things easy when you're adding HTML commands to your text is to put each command on a separate line. When a Web browser interprets a page that includes HTML commands, it ignores which lines they're on, and doesn't bother to display any extra blank lines or spaces. That means you can write your HTML so it makes the best possible sense to you (what a concept!) and still have it *work*. The following code, for example, will be interpreted and displayed as shown in Figure 3-1:

```
<font size="+1">
It doesn't matter whether your text is
all
on
one
line, or if you have  some    extra     spaces or


blank lines

in your text, it will all be formatted
properly when the HTML commands are interpreted
and displayed by a web browser.
</font>
<p>
To make it easier on yourself, put each opening and
closing HTML tag on a
<strong>
separate
</strong>
line.
</p>
```

Figure 3-1:
Formatted
description
from
unformatted
text and
HTML
commands.

File   Edit   View   Favorites   Tools   Help

It doesn't matter whether your text is all on one line, or if you have some extra spaces or blank lines in your text, it will all be formatted properly when the HTML commands are interpreted and displayed by a web browser.

To make it easier on yourself, put each opening and closing HTML tag on a **separate** line.

Want to save your sanity — and maybe keep from pulling your hair out later when you discover that the formatting doesn't end where you thought it did? Always enter the closing tag when you enter the opening tag, and just put your text between 'em. That way you avoid forgetting to close the tag later.

Uh-oh. We just said that extra blank spaces won't be displayed. What if you *want* more than one space at a time — that is, how do you create an area of "white space" in your description? Don't panic; there is a special HTML command that accomplishes this feat: the *non-breaking space*. To get one, just insert   in your text for each space you want to include: & nbsp;& nbsp;& nbsp;& nbsp; will force the display of five blank spaces in a row.

The non-breaking space comes in handy in several other ways. For instance, if you have two or more words that should stay together, no matter what, the   can make it happen. Here are some examples of how to use this command to keep words from being separated:

Los Angeles, CA - Los Angeles, CA

September 4, 1995 - September 4, 1995

4:00 PM - 4:00 PM

Though some browsers recognize and interpret the non-breaking space command without the semicolon (;) character at the end, not all browsers do. Be sure to include that semicolon; otherwise the actual characters   will be displayed instead of any space at all, making your text messy.

The non-breaking space command stands alone; no need for angle brackets or a corresponding closing tag.

Part II
Lining Your Pockets with HTML

The 5th Wave   By Rich Tennant

"Oh, Anthony loves working with HTML. He customized our eBay listings to greet customers with a 'Badda Bing!'"

In this part . . .

This is it. Part II is just what you need — especially if you want to work a little on-screen magic from behind the scenes. We're constantly hearing from people who want to do just that — by learning the ways of HTML coding. Figuring out the best way to format your listings can be a challenge at first, but this part helps you bypass any confusion. We make the most essential HTML easy — spelling out its syntax in simple terms, offering advice on the structures that give you attractive, repeatable results — and impart just enough HTML know-how to make your listings stand out from the crowd.

Chapter 4

HTML Text — Formatting Basics

*T*hough some eBay pundits would argue that the text description in your listing isn't the most important part, we beg to differ. The words you use to describe the item you have for sale (along with essential information such as terms and conditions of purchase) are what could make or break the success of your sale.

Think of your listing description as a barren plot with nothing showing but tilled soil. With just a little work and the magic of HTML code, you can transform your listing into an inviting, beautiful garden — or an eye-jarring, overwhelming jungle (if you're not careful)!

Just as a garden benefits from a planned layout and choice flora, your listing's verbal description benefits from the structure of HTML coding that's selectively applied. In this chapter, we show you how to change the color, size, shape, and look of the words in your description. Also, because one long, unbroken block of text is difficult to read, we show you how to break up your description into smaller, attention-getting pieces by using paragraph breaks, bullets, and centering. We finish up with how to create a template that can give all your listings a uniform look and feel — a real marketing plus.

Making Text Clear but Catchy with HTML

When you get your first look at a page of text that includes HTML tags, you might be a tad overwhelmed — you're not alone — but we'll be taking it one tag at a time. Each of them is a building block that you can add to your listing description as you become comfortable with it. You probably won't use all the commands we describe in this book, but careful use of the ones that give you the look you want is a piece of cake — if you take it one layer at a time.

Formatting builds strong listings

HTML functions mainly to modify the appearance and the placement of text in your listing. The appearance of the text can be modified by changing its size, color, or typeface. The placement of the text can be changed by centering sections of text, creating neatly ordered lists, or breaking up large blocks of text — either with white space or with an actual drawn line.

Only what you need to know about coding HTML

As we explain in the previous chapter, an HTML tag is simply a signal to the browser to display text in a particular way from a specific starting point to a specific ending point. In almost all cases, HTML tags come in pairs — one to mark the beginning and the other to mark the end of the change made to the displayed text.

HTML tags always start with the < character and always end with the > character. In between these two characters are an HTML command and, optionally, some attributes that focus the formatting change.

In the remainder of this chapter, we go over the HTML commands that give you the biggest bang for the buck. For each one, we provide an explanation of how it works, and how it can be (or not be) used effectively. The example commands we provide help make clear how the commands are written.

Getting Bolder (Or Larger, or More Colorful) as You Go

Text by itself can be rather blah and not very expressive. You can spruce up your listing by indicating (via HTML) that you'd like to see your text displayed more creatively. For example, consider using HTML to specify a *font* (a particular typeface and size) to boost the fun factor of your listing text. You don't want your listing to look run-of-the-mill, and a good way to make your words stand out from other listings is to change the font in which they appear on the Web page.

Using different fonts can be fun — but as with all other text enhancements, too much can be, well, *too* much. Be careful to not blast your reader with a page full of unrelated fonts that are difficult to read! In general, you rarely need more than two fonts to get the job done.

Picking fun (but readable) type

You can choose from two categories of typefaces to use for the text in your listing description: those with serifs and those without. Typefaces without serif are called *sans-serif* or *gothic*. (*Serif*, by the way, means that the typeface has those small, fine lines that finish the ends of each letter and carry your eye to the next letter.) The serif typeface was developed with its smooth-flowing upper- and lowercase letters to make printed text easy to follow. A standard serif font often used in books is Times New Roman.

A commonly used sans-serif typeface is Arial. In sans-serif type, the letters don't have the fine lines that finish the letters, so the letters end abruptly at the bottom or top. In general, sans-serif letters are easier to read from far away than serif letters, so it's pretty commonplace to see road signs done in sans-serif fonts and book text done in serif fonts. See Figure 4-1 for examples of these two categories of typefaces.

Figure 4-1:
Serif and
sans-serif
typefaces.

> File   Edit   View   Favorites   Tools   Help
> ← Back ▾ → ▾ ⊗ ⊠ ⌂ | ⊗Search ⊡Favorites ⊗Media ⊗ | ⊟▾ ⊒ ⊠ ▾ ⊟ ⊡ ⊼ ⊜ | Address ⊜Y »
>
> **Times New Roman** has the fine, finishing lines on letters.
>
> Arial doesn't have the fine, finishing lines on letters.
>
> ⊕ Done   ⊒ My Computer

Fancy fonts are fun for printing out, but it's a different ballgame online. Be sure to select standard typefaces that are available on all computers. Otherwise your potential customers' computers may display completely different (and perhaps highly unreadable) type when they view your listing. (Check out the sidebar "Your computer can become a font of fonts" to find out more about what happens with nonstandard typefaces.) Refer to Table 4-1 for ideas on choosing a standard typeface and deciding how you might want to use it.

Table 4-1	Readily Available Fonts and How to Use Them		
Typeface Name	*Category*	*Suggested Use*	*At This* SIZE *Attribute*
Arial	Sans serif	Listing headings	4
Verdana	Sans serif	Listing headings	4
Courier New	Serif	Tables, lists	2
Times New Roman	Serif	List body text	2
Comic Sans MS	Sans serif	List body text	2
MS Sans Serif	Sans serif	List body text	2

After you select a typeface you'd like to use, place the following command at the location where you want the chosen type to start:

```
<font face="Typeface name">
```

Your computer can become a font of fonts

Each operating system contains a set of standard fonts (typefaces and sizes) that are installed on the computer when it's brand new. Then, as people install different programs on their computers — especially word-processing or desktop-publishing programs — additional fancy fonts are added.

What can happen then looks like this: You browse through all the fancy fonts you have available on your computer, and pick out one that's easy to read and has just the right oomph for your listing! After all, the point is to enhance your description,

not make it difficult to read. Use HTML code to insert the font to be used in your description, and then happily submit your listing. So far, so good! But you then discover, when looking at your listing on someone else's computer, that what you see is not the font you picked at all. It's a completely different one! What gives?

Actually the problem has to do with the other computer. Either the precise font you selected isn't available on that computer, or its browser settings don't allow a change of font. So all your fancy fontwork has gone for naught!

As with most HTML commands, `font` is one that must be turned off (or closed) when you're done with it. Simply place the following command where you want the special typeface to end (and take special note of the / character):

```
</font>
```

`font` is one of the HTML commands that can have options (called *attributes*), and `face="typeface name"` is one of those options. You can define all the attributes together in one command, as we show you in the following sections. But you can also use separate commands — one `font` command to define the `face`, one to define the `size`, and yet another to set the `color`. Just don't forget that if you define these attributes independently, you have to turn off each one independently!

For the main body of your listing, select a font (typeface and size) that's easy to read and readily available on all computers. Use only one or two additional fonts for emphasis. Enlarged titles and separate text blocks with instructions for international customers are good examples of areas where changing fonts can be effective.

By and large, resist the urge to use a different font for each paragraph (it screams "newbie!") — and don't use fancy, obscure fonts that are difficult to read or unavailable on all computers (they may be better for flyers than for Web pages). Check out Figure 4-2 for a look at some commonly used fonts that show up well on-screen.

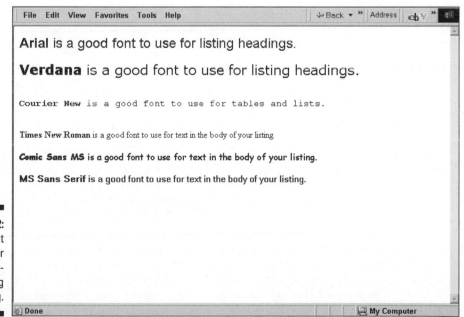

Figure 4-2:
Fonts that make for a good-looking listing.

Trying out different sizes

HTML sets up a type-size standard for all Web pages. On the HTML scale (ranging 1–7), the standard size for text displayed in eBay listings is 2. But as you notice in this book, or in the newspaper you read with your coffee this morning, different font sizes make pages more interesting to read and help set apart different groups of text. You can (and should!) do the same thing with your listing. At the very least, headings that appear in a different size help distinguish the different types of information you want your customers to see. For example, you may need headings to point out your item description, terms of purchase, shipping information, and so on.

You can use several different commands to tell HTML to change your text size:

✔ `<big>` **tag:** Use this tag when you want the enclosed text to appear one increment larger than the standard text.

```
<big>The BIG command makes your text larger by one
        size.</big>
```

✔ `<small>` **tag:** Use this tag when you want the enclosed text to appear one increment smaller than the standard text.

```
<small>The SMALL command makes your text smaller by
        one size.</small>
```

✔ `size` **attribute:** Use this attribute with the `<font>` tag when you want to increase the size of the enclosed text or specify a particular size on the HTML scale.

```
<font size="+1">Makes your text larger by one size (if
        the number is a 3, the text will be 3 sizes
        larger).</font>
<font size="-1">Makes your text smaller by one size
        (if the number is a 2, the text will be 2
        sizes smaller).</font>
<font size="4">Makes the text a specific size of
        4.</font>
```

To combine the `font` tag's `size` attribute with another optional attribute (such as the `face` attribute used in the previous section), try the following command:

```
<font face="Arial" size="4">
```

This command changes the typeface to `Arial` and makes it size 4 at the same time. And if you combined these two attributes into one command, you now need only one command to turn off the text formatting:

```
</font>
```

Figure 4-3 shows how the combined command can affect the type in a listing.

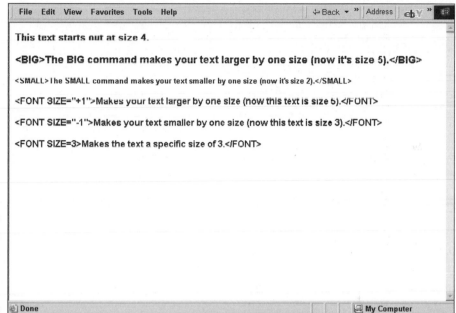

| File | Edit | View | Favorites | Tools | Help | ← Back ▾ » | Address | 🔍Y » |

This text starts out at size 4.

<BIG>The BIG command makes your text larger by one size (now it's size 5).</BIG>

<SMALL>The SMALL command makes your text smaller by one size (now it's size 2).</SMALL>

<FONT SIZE="+1">Makes your text larger by one size (now this text is size 5).</FONT>

<FONT SIZE="-1">Makes your text smaller by one size (now this text is size 3).</FONT>

<FONT SIZE=3>Makes the text a specific size of 3.</FONT>

🖉 Done   🖳 My Computer

Figure 4-3:
Changing
and sizing
the type in
your listing.

Use a larger font to emphasize titles and section headings within your description, but keep the following guidelines in mind:

✓ Don't use a font so huge that the text is wider than your potential customers' screens can handle. You don't want to make them scroll left and right just to read your text.

✓ Don't use a font so small that the viewers have to put their noses right on the screen to read it. Some folks would rather go away than squint.

Showing your text in different colors

First, decide what colors you're going to include on your page. Just as with a garden, you don't want to go wild and use *all* the colors available to you! A multitude of contrasting colors won't be easy to read, just as a garden with many different colors would be difficult to look at for very long. A few subtle colors that work together well, used with care, can make your point without being overbearing.

Say you've picked out an easy-to-read typeface and decided on the proper size. Now you get to decide what color(s) you want your text to be! Remember your excitement when you got a brand-new box of 64 crayons? (Whoa — look at all the colors to pick from!) Hang on to your hat, because now you have 216 standard colors in your box! There are actually 256 standard on-screen colors, but only 216 are designated as *Web-safe* (available on all computers) because Microsoft and Apple reserved the other 40 colors for use in their own operating systems. Even though your computer is probably capable of displaying *millions* of colors, 216 should be more than enough for eBay purposes.

In Chapter 8, we talk about using color in the background and for other design purposes, but right now we're talking about changing the colors of your text. Following are some guidelines for using color in your listing text:

✔ **Decide on a limited set of colors to include in your listing.** And then, stick to your decision! Just as you don't infuse your garden with plants in every color of the rainbow, you don't want to go wild by using all 216 colors available to you! Using a multitude of different colors won't make your listing easy to read (quite the opposite), but carefully pulling in a few colors that work together well can help make your point without making your readers' eyes burn.

✔ **While choosing colors for your text, keep in mind whether you plan to change the background color.** You don't want the background and text colors to clash with each other! Text will fade into a background color that's too similar, but too strong a contrast can bring a viewer to tears.

✔ **Recognize that some potential customers may be colorblind or have other difficulties with viewing specific colors.** Yellow is one color that many people can't read easily. Readability is the watchword here!

Once again, HTML comes to your rescue and makes changing your text color an easy task. Although all 216 colors have designations in HTML, 16 colors have standard names — which you can specify to select a particular color: aqua, black, blue, fuchsia, gray, green, lime, maroon, navy, olive, purple, red, silver, teal, white, and yellow. The rest of the 216 available colors are designated by unique *hexadecimal numbers* (each using the numeric digits 0 through 9 and including letters A through F).

You can find a handy chart of colors on Marsha's Web site at `coolebaytools. com/html_hex_colors.html`. This chart shows each color around the number used to select it. To change your font color to bright lime green (okay, maybe not the most appropriate for readable text, but allow us a funky example), you can use either of the following commands:

```
<font color="lime">
```

or

```
<font color="#00FF00">
```

As with all other `font` commands, don't forget to turn off your color change by using the `</font>` command.

Use color changes carefully and only for emphasis. Make sure that the colors don't clash, are easy to read, and are limited to no more than two. Don't use a white or light-colored text because you're planning to have a dark background color or image. If your reader's browser can't display the background you've chosen, your white text will appear on a default white background — impossible to read (think polar-bear-in-a-snowstorm).

There are three different ways of looking at the colors on a color wheel. *Analogous* colors sit next to each other, like blue, blue-green, and green. *Complementary* colors are opposite each other on the wheel — think red and green, or blue and orange. *Color triads* can be made by superimposing an equal sided triangle on the wheel, and taking the three colors at the points of the triangle (red/yellow/blue or purple/green/orange). Analogous colors should be used for the major color scheme of your listings. Complementary colors and color triads can be used for accents, but should be used very sparingly.

Drawing attention with bold and italics

You may notice, as you read this book that we use **bold** or *italics* to make certain words or phrases stand out when we have something important to bring to your attention. Consider doing the same thing in your listings. As with the enhancements we talk about in prior sections, remember that such treatments lose their effectiveness when used too often. Think of your HTML commands as the spices that you add when cooking — you don't want to be heavy-handed with the salt (or the italics)!

HTML gives you two ways to define text to be bolded, and both are commands made up of paired tags. The following snippet shows both ways:

```
To make a word or phrase bold, you can use either the
        <b>bold</b> or <strong>strong</strong>
        commands.
```

You also have two ways to define text as italicized, and both also must use paired tags. Check out the following:

```
To make a word or phrase italicized, you can use either
        the <i>italics</i> or <em>emphasis</em>
        commands.
```

For several reasons, the strong and em tags should be used in lieu of the bold and italics tags. After all, bold and italics are only formatting commands; the strong and em tags actually define the content. When analyzing pages, search-engine programs give more weight to content designated with these two commands. Browsers that "speak" (screen readers) will interpret strong and em tags more appropriately, giving the listener speech closer to someone talking.

Use bold and italics to make single words, phrases, or short sentences stand out from the remainder of the text. But don't make an entire paragraph or item description bold; this treatment simply has the same visual effect as putting the paragraph in a different font, and the emphasis gets lost.

. . . etc.

After you change typeface and text size, enhance your text with color, and format with bold and italics, what's left? HTML offers tags for many other text enhancements — but most are either not available in all browsers (such as flashing text and scrolling marquees) or they're not appropriate for use in text descriptions.

We want a word with you about <u>underlining</u>. As with **bold** and *italics,* underlining is a way of emphasizing text to make it stand out from surrounding text. We don't recommend using the HTML underline tag when creating listing descriptions for a good reason. That is, most links (which we discuss in Chapter 5) are automatically underlined. If you underline some of your text, many customers will think that text is a link, and you'll have them click-click-clicking without any result. Then when you include a link later on — maybe one that takes them to your eBay Store — they may not click it because the last "link" they tried didn't work. It's like the boy who cried "Wolf!" — if your customers don't believe you, you can't expect them to buy what you're offering.

Grouping and Positioning Your Listing Text

A second major group of HTML tags can help you spice up your listing text. These tags help you group and position your text to direct the reader's eye, distinguish related information, and draw attention to important points. Let's face it: One large block of text is just a bunch of words — and if there are no breaks in the page, your customer will give up trying to pick out the description from the shipping terms. By simply grouping each relevant portion of your description into paragraphs and lists, with headings in appropriate places, you put the right information in the right place.

Centering sometimes fits the bill

You may want to center a small part of your text. The `<center>` tag, like most others, requires a paired closing tag to complete it. If you neglect to include the closing tag, all the remaining text on-screen will be centered. The following command centers the enclosed text on-screen:

```
<center>This command will center the text between the left
          and right sides of the screen.</center>
```

Don't succumb to the temptation to center all your text! Although this treatment might look all right on your screen, remember that not all your customers' displays will be set to the same resolution as yours — and they may find your text hard to read. You can often achieve a nice appearance for your listing by centering headings, images, or individual items that you specifically want to stand out. We say again, lest anybody forget — a little goes a long way when enhancing your text.

Center titles, images, or special instructions. But don't center large blocks of text. Doing so makes the left and right edges of the text vary widely, and the listing becomes much more difficult for your customer to read.

Breaking up large text blocks

Okay, suppose you've written a standout item description that answers every possible question your potential buyers could have about the item you're selling — and what they should expect for completing the transaction. Congratulations — you're halfway there. *Presenting* all this information will require putting a lot of text on-screen — and one large, dense paragraph can be difficult to read. Fortunately, HTML gives you several commands that can break up your text into bite-size groups. Breaking up the text not only makes your listing easier to read, but it also helps your potential customers go back after reading it and find specific details to review if they have questions.

To ensure that your HTML can be read by the newest versions of all browsers, review the format of the commands given in the next section. They might be a little different from the way you learned them; as given here, they're based on the most recent definition of HTML.

All three HTML commands that we recommend for breaking up large groups of text are *single tags* — they don't require closing tags. (But we also note that you should close the one that can be closed — and why you should do so!) The following bullet list gives you the breaking news (so to speak) on these tags used for structuring your description:

✔ **
:** This is the Break command that inserts a line break and puts any following text on the next line without an intervening blank line. This command is useful when you're making a list that you don't want emphasized with bullet points or numbers. It looks like this:

```
<br />This text will begin on a new line.
```

✔ **<p> and </p>:** This is the Paragraph command that inserts a line break and makes any following text appear on the next line, after inserting a blank line first. This command is useful for separating *paragraphs* of text (d'oh!) to make them easier to read. When used without attributes, this tag doesn't require a paired closing tag to go with it. Even so, it's still a very good idea to get in the habit of closing all your tag pairs. The </p> tag is only four keystrokes; go ahead and close it! Here's what that looks like:

```
<p>This text will start on a new line, with a blank
        line just above it.</p>
```

✔ **<hr />:** This is the Horizontal Rule command — useful for separating vastly different sections of text by drawing a line horizontally across the screen. For example, you can use <hr /> to separate the description of your item from your payment and shipping policies — both sections are important to the reader, but are vastly different in content. A horizontal rule, used in conjunction with other text enhancements (such as a centered header in bold or italic type), can help you effectively distinguish these sections of your description.

Like the Break and Paragraph commands, the Horizontal Rule command doesn't require a paired closing tag. But it does have several optional attributes you can specify when using it. One such attribute (which you may use often) is the width option, which defines the span of the line across the display. If you omit the width option, the horizontal line is drawn all the way from left to right side across the viewer's screen. You may also want to use the align attribute in conjunction with width. Using align, you can specify whether the less-than-full-length line displays centered, or to the left or right side of the screen. Here it is:

```
<hr width="50%" align="center" />
```

Break up large groups of text with the Paragraph command to make your text easier to read. Use the Horizontal Rule command to separate different sections of your description. We don't, however, recommend using the color attribute as an option with the Horizontal Rule command; not all browsers can display this option. Also, don't use the `width` attribute without specifying the percentage (%) to show that you're defining the line width as a percentage of the screen width, rather than a specific length of *pixels* (those little dots that make up lines and text on the reader's screen).

Both the `br` and the `hr` commands are single tags and must be used inside two other paired tags such as `<p>` and `</p>`. They also have the closing / inside the brackets, placed at the end (not the beginning) and preceded by a space.

Emphasizing with bullets

No, we're not talking about ammunition! (You can't sell that on eBay anyway.) Bullets, or *bullet points*, are those little dots (or sometimes numbers) that often appear to the left of text that's arranged in a list. The bullets help the reader's eye separate the list items.

Making bulleted lists is a little more difficult than using other HTML commands, if only because it requires two different sets of paired tags. The first set of tags marks the beginning and ending of the entire list. The second set separates items in the list by marking the beginning and ending of each one. (And after you get all these commands in order, you can make sublists inside your lists — but always remember to keep the tags paired!) Here's a bulleted list of things to remember about lists:

- ✔ Numbered lists — another way to itemize details in your listing — are called *ordered lists* in HTML. And the tags that start and end these lists are `<ol>` and `</ol>`, respectively.

- ✔ Lists that aren't numbered (just bulleted) are called *unordered lists*. You got it: The starting and ending tags are `<ul>` and `</ul>`.

- ✔ The command that designates each List Item (for either Ordered Lists or Unordered Lists) starts with `<li>` and ends with `</li>`. The following HTML commands create a numbered list to show the tracks on a CD:

```
<ol>CD Title
<li>Track 1</li>
<li>Track 2</li>
<li>Track 3</li>
<li>Track 4</li>
<li>Track 5</li>
</li>
```

Use bullets if you have a list of items that you want to emphasize. Use a numbered list if the order of the items is important (such as book chapters or CD tracks). But please, don't use bullets just because you can.

Setting Up Your Own Auction Template

When you enter a store that is part of a chain, did you ever notice that the store is laid out similarly to other stores in the chain? Retailers do that to make the surroundings familiar so customers feel comfortable the minute they enter the store. They know right where to find what they're looking for: in the back-left corner (for instance), they'll find dairy products, and in the right-front corner will be the fresh produce.

Any chain store worth its salt doesn't want its customers overwhelmed and confused when they walk in the door. Consistency encourages a feeling of familiarity, so customers can easily locate the sections of the store. Time wasted looking up and down every aisle to locate a specific department is time that isn't spent determining which items to purchase.

With all the text enhancements available to you through HTML, you can design a listing layout that's easy to read, provides all the information your customers need, and feels consistent with your other listings. You can carefully group and delineate information so your shoppers can easily locate the information they need to make a decision to purchase your item. As you're designing the look of your listings, keep in mind all the different types of items you sell; format the layout so you can use it for most — if not all — of your products.

Experiment with HTML formatting and put together the best layout you can; then save this layout as a *template,* or a pattern, to use when you create your listings. Creating an HTML template benefits you in two ways:

- You don't have to rewrite standard sections of text (such as payment terms and shipping schedules) that are common to each of your listings.

- The visual consistency creates a "brand" for each of your listings. Returning customers — or customers who look at several of your items to take advantage of combined shipping for multiple purchases — will feel right at home looking at your listings. They'll know where on the page to find the information they need, won't have to scan the entire page to find a specific detail — and just might end up in more of a mood to buy what they're looking at.

When saving your template, use the most elementary text-editing program you have available. Complex word-processing programs insert additional commands (similar to HTML commands, but specific to that program) — which can cause problems when you try to reuse the template to create other listing descriptions. The Microsoft Notepad program (a classic text editor included with Windows) works well for eBay purposes; it doesn't insert additional commands and it preserves the HTML commands you used to format the easy-to-read layout you designed.

Follow these steps (on a computer running Windows XP) to create and save a handy, reusable listing template:

1. **Choose Start⇨All Programs⇨Accessories⇨Notepad, or open your simple text editing program of choice.**

2. **Start with a blank page, at the top of which you type your listing header.**

3. **Include the HTML for at least one picture.**

4. **Finish with your standard payment and shipping sections.**

   You might want to review this chapter while you're at it.

5. **Choose File⇨Save As to save your completed template.**

   The Save As dialog box appears.

6. **In the Save In drop-down list, choose a location where your template is readily available for use when creating your listing descriptions; type a logical name for your template in the File Name text box.**

7. **Click Save to save your template.**

Figure 4-4 shows a template we created with a blank area to be filled in with the differentiating information for each item.

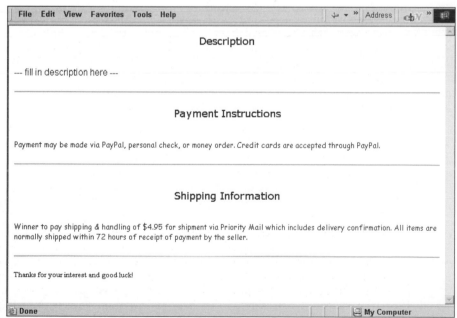

Figure 4-4:
An easy-
to-read
template,
ready to be
completed.

Work up a description layout that you're comfortable with, and make a template of it to use for all your listings. But don't be so rigid about it that you feel pressured to use your standard template in every single listing. If the design doesn't fit a specific item, then it just doesn't fit! You wouldn't try to squeeze into a pair of pants that don't fit any more (would you?), and you shouldn't try to force every listing you create into a one-size-fits-all template. Remember, however, that you can still use that lovely (and consistent!) color scheme you came up with, as well as those fonts you so tastefully selected, to preserve the familiar look and feel that makes your customer feel welcome.

Chapter 5

Playing the (Hyper) Links

* *

* *

*A*lthough you might never step foot (with or without cleats) on a putting green, learning how to play the links is essential when designing your listing description. Links are the *HT* (the *hypertext*) in HTML, and you click links to make something happen. Usually this action displays a different Web page. Or clicking a link can move you to a different location on the same Web page. You can also use a link to open an e-mail message and automatically fill in the send-to e-mail address (and other information, if you'd like).

A link can appear on-screen as text or as an image; you can tell you've found one when your cursor changes to a hand with a pointing finger. Recognizing text links on a Web page is easy! These links are most often automatically underlined and displayed in bright blue text.

The code to generate a link may look more complicated than other HTML commands, but it works essentially the same way. The command starts off with an opening tag; then you find the hyperlink text (or the HTML coding for an image), followed by the closing tag. Chapter 3 shows you the basic HTML command syntax, and this chapter shows how the basics work for adding links to your listing.

You also find out about the attributes, or options, available to enhance your linking commands. Although most commands have attributes, not all attributes are useful when writing listing descriptions. So in this chapter, we discuss only those attributes that we find especially handy.

As with most other HTML commands, a linking command must end with a closing tag. If you don't set the end where you want it, your link will extend to the end of the page!

Teeing Off with Simple Links

The most common link is one that displays a new Web page when a customer clicks it — and for good reason: Why would you want to take your customer away from your listing description? The point of linking is not to take customers off to online limbo-land, but rather to direct them toward shopping aids or opportunities — including other valuable information, goods in your eBay Store, or a list showing some (or all) of the items you have for sale.

You can even link to your own Web site, as long as that link is on your About Me page. Don't make the mistake of putting a link to your off-eBay Web site in your listing description; this is against the eBay Links policy (read it at `http://pages.ebay.com/help/policies/listing-links.html`), and if the link is reported to eBay, your listing will be ended prematurely.

Here's how to use HTML to construct the most common links:

✔ **To link to another Web page,** find out the address, or URL (Uniform Resource Locator) of the page. After you've got the address, create an *href* (Hyperlink REFerence) command by including the anchor `href` tag (with URL), the hyperlink text (which identifies the link), and the closing tag. Here's an example.

```
<a href="http://www.yourisp.com">Hyperlink text</a>
```

✔ **To jump directly to a specific location on the current page,** place a required matching `name` tag at the location on the page you're jumping to. The `name` tag is formatted as follows:

```
<a name="location_name"></a>
```

The actual name you give the location is unimportant, but it must exactly match its reference in the anchor `href` tag. Although you may wonder why this command needs a closing tag, don't leave it out; logical or not, you have to include it!

After you define the place to jump to, creating the link that jumps you there is as simple as referring to that same *location_name* in a standard anchor `href` tag. If the `name` tag is at the top of the listing description (for example), the following HTML will jump directly there so your customer doesn't need to scroll all the way back to read it again:

```
<a href="#location_name">Return to top of
        description</a>
```

The *location_name* you use must exactly match the associated `name` tag, and you must include the # character, but only in the `href` tag.

We don't recommend putting links near the top of your listing description if clicking that link could allow your customer to skip past important information without reading it! An appropriate position for these location links is at the bottom of your description, allowing your customers to return easily to areas they would like to review.

Linking to your eBay Store

You might want to include a direct link to your eBay Store at several places within your listing. After customers discover an item you have for sale (due to your outstanding marketing techniques, of course), directing them to your eBay Store gives your customers a look at your entire array of merchandise for their shopping pleasure! eBay automatically provides several direct links to your eBay Store, but you should also provide your own; this is one place where more is better!

Savvy sellers offer shipping discounts to customers who purchase more than one item at a time; in these days of rising energy costs, who isn't looking for a way to reduce expenses? Be sure to emphasize multiple-purchase shipping discounts in each of your listing descriptions — and give each one a link to your eBay Store to make it easier for your potential buyer to find more items to purchase; that convenience might clinch the deal! Marsha creates a link to her eBay Store ("Marsha Collier's Fabulous Finds") as shown here:

```
<a href="http://stores.ebay.com/Marsha-Collier's-Fabulous-
        Finds">Visit my eBay Store for low prices on
          handy seller tools and Cloud Dome Products</a>
```

You can also provide a link to your eBay Store from your own Web site; it's easy, and it might save you money on your eBay fees! As of this writing, if a customer arrives at your eBay Store from an external site by clicking a specially coded link — and then makes a purchase — eBay will reduce the Final Value Fee (commission) that the seller pays for that sale by 75 percent! That should be enough of an incentive to learn the simple HTML command to direct your Web site visitors to your eBay Store.

You can create this money-saving link just like the preceding direct link, but be sure to add the referral code ?refid=store to the URL. That way eBay knows the link that sent the customers to your eBay Store came from you. Here's what that looks like in practice:

```
<a ref="http://stores.ebay.com/yourstorename?refid=store">
          Visit my eBay Store for more fabulous buys</a>
```

For the latest information about saving money on your fees, search eBay's help system for *Store Referral Credit*.

Linking to specific items or categories in your eBay Store

If your eBay Store is chock-full of wonderful stuff, you might want to link to only one specific item or category of items. The more merchandise you have in your store, the more important these directional links are. After all, in the brick-and-mortar world, the larger the department store, the more store directories there are to keep shoppers from feeling overwhelmed and leaving in frustration.

Creating directional links — to either a single item or a category — is easy and works much the same in either case. Just do the following:

✔ **To link a listing to a single store item,** simply view the item in your eBay Store where you can see its unique item number. This number is part of the URL that points to the single item. Copy the URL from the location bar in your Web browser and paste it into the `href` tag. Your linking command should look something like this one:

```
<a href="http://cgi.ebay.com/ws/eBayISAPI.dll?
      ViewItem&item=7551201712">eBay For Dummies</a>
```

URLs can have parameters, and most aren't necessary for linking directly to a single eBay item. Parameters in URLs begin with either a `?` (question mark) or `&` (ampersand) character, and the only parameter required for linking to a single item is `&item=999999999`. You can delete anything in the URL that follows this parameter.

✔ **To link a listing to a specific store category,** go to your eBay Store and select the appropriate category. The URL displayed is the one that you use in the anchor command's `href` attribute, which should look something like this:

```
<a href="http://stores.ebay.com/yourstorename_
      W0QQdptZ0QQsclZallQQtZkm">Need seller's tools?
      Find them in my eBay Store.</a>
```

Linking to other listed items

If you don't have an eBay Store, you can link to a single item (or only a subset of items) you have for sale. Doing this provides the same benefit as linking directly to a store category: You avoid overwhelming your customer with too much information at one time. Less confusion makes for easier sales!

To display some (or all) of your listed items, first you need to determine the URL which will show only those items you want displayed. Follow these steps:

1. **Go to eBay and access any of your item listings.**

2. **Click the link labeled *View seller's other items (List view)* to view all items you currently have available for sale on eBay.**

   - If you want to display all of your items, this is the URL to include in the linking `href` attribute.

   - If you don't want to display all your items, you need to perform a search to narrow down the results from the full list.

3. **To display a subset of your items, type the appropriate search word(s) in the Search box at the top of the list (just under the All Items tab) and then click Search.**

   Under Search Options at the left, make sure that the check box next to *Items from seller* remains checked, and that your eBay user ID is the one displayed, as shown in Figure 5-1.

4. **When you winnow down the search results to exactly the items you want displayed, copy the URL from the location bar of your browser, and paste it into the `href` command.**

   The resulting HTML linking command looks something like this:

```
<a href="http://search.ebay.com/search/search.dll?
      sofocus=bs&sbrftog=1&from=R10&catref=C6&
      satitle=%22eBay+For+Dummies%22&sacat=-1%26
      catref%3DC6&bs=Search&fsop=1%26fsoo%3D1&
      coaction=compare&copagenum=1&coentrypage=
      search&sadis=200&fpos=91325&ftrt=1&ftrv=1&
      saprclo=&saprchi=&seller=1&sass=marsha_c">
      Looking for a good starting place to learn
      about eBay?</a>
```

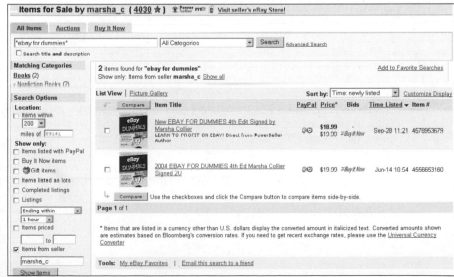

Figure 5-1:
Search your
results for
a subset
of items
to link to.

Linking to related Web sites

You may sometimes have more information about an item you're selling than you want to include in your description. For example, if including the extra info slows down the loading of the page, better trim down that description.

The longer a page takes to load, the greater the chance that your customer will get tired of waiting and leave to find something else to purchase.

If you run into the too-long-listing situation, you can put the additional information on another Web page and link to this page from your listing description. Extra listing information can include expanded item specifications, additional detailed images, or a broader description of your payment-and-shipping terms and conditions.

After you create the page containing the additional information, simply refer to its URL address in a simple `href` link like this:

```
<a href="http://www.yourisp.com/photos.html">View
          additional pictures!</a>
```

Providing an e-mail link

You might want to let your potential buyer know how to contact you directly via e-mail in case they have any questions. You can do this by simply including your e-mail address as part of your listing description. Or you can give buyers a better, easier way to send you an e-mail by using an HTML command that opens their e-mail client programs and fills in *your* e-mail address automatically. You can even get a little fancier and have the program fill in the subject line so they don't have to!

Don't rely solely on the `mailto:` command described in this section because it won't always work — this is one of those commands that depends on a setting in your customers' browsers. If they haven't told their browsers which e-mail program they're using (or the browser doesn't recognize their e-mail program), this command won't work! So make sure your e-mail address is visible in your listing — or that you give your customers another way to contact you, just in case!

To open an e-mail message automatically, you start with the anchor tag and the `href` attribute — but instead of linking to a Web page, filename, or location marker, you include a special command and your e-mail address, as follows:

1. **Type** `<a href=` **to begin the link for opening an e-mail message.**

2. **Type** `mailto:` **and then your e-mail address, all in quotation marks.**

   The HTML line you start looks something like this:

   ```
   <a href="mailto:seller@yourisp.com"
   ```

   This command has several attributes available, but the only one we find convenient is the one that designates the subject line of the e-mail.

3. **To define the subject line, type** `?subject=Your Desired Subject Line` **immediately following your e-mail address, and inside the quotation marks.**

4. **Type the closing tag** `>` **to finish the link.**

   Usually the text in between the anchor tag and the closing tag (that is, the text that becomes the hyperlink) is your email address, but you can also display a message such as *Got Questions?* as the hyperlink.

5. **Type the** `</a>` **tag to close the** **anchor** **command.**

   Here's how a command looks when it includes both a subject line and hyperlink text:

   ```
   <a href="mailto:seller@yourisp.com?subject=I've got a
        question!">
   Got questions?</a>
   ```

 If you decide to specify a subject line for the e-mail link, remember that the sender can change this line. So don't count on using the words you provide to filter these e-mails when they arrive in your mailbox!

If you want to get even fancier with your linking, you can use a picture of a mailbox, a stylish question mark, or some other image in place of the hyperlink text. Want to know how? Read the next section!

Making a Hole-in-One: Linking to an Image

Sometimes it makes more sense to use an image instead of text for your hyperlink. For example, if you have a logo for your eBay Store (silly comment — of course you do!), use it as the link to your store. The bigger the target, the easier it is to click!

You display an image in your links with the help of the `img` (Image) tag and several attributes, which we describe in Table 5-1.

Table 5-1		Attributes of the Image Tag
Attribute	**Sample Value**	**What It Does**
src=	"http://www.yourisp.com/yourimage.jpg"	Defines the location of the image you want to display.
width=	"400"	Defines the width (in pixels) of the image to display. Using both this and the height attribute efficiently makes your description load faster.
height=	"300"	Defines the height (in pixels) of the image you want to display.
border=	"0"	Turns off the blue border that identifies the image as a hyperlink. Turn off this distraction, but tell your customers that they can click the image, and what happens when they do.
alt=	"alternate text"	Defines the text that appears when the cursor passes over the image. This attribute doesn't work in all browsers, so don't put any important information here! If the image won't load, this text is what is displayed in its place.

The img command is then surrounded by the href (Hypertext REFerence) command, and voilà! You have an image that's also a link!

When you make an image that's a link, your customers' cursors change when passing over the image, indicating that they can click there — but don't assume they'll see that! Be sure to include in your text that the image is clickable — say it more than once if necessary.

The following code displays a set of images, each of which takes your customer to a different category of your eBay Store. Figure 5-2 shows you how effective this linking technique can be.

```
<center>
<font face="Verdana" size="+2">
There are many more exciting items in my eBay Store -
        Check them out by clicking on one of the
        departments below</font>
```

```
<br /><br />
<a href="http://stores.ebay.com/yourstorename_category1">
        <img src="http://www.yourisp.com/category1.jpg"
        width="230" height=50" border="0"></a>
<a href="http://stores.ebay.com/yourstorename_category2">
        <img src="http://www.yourisp.com/category2.jpg"
        width="230" height=50" border="0"></a>
<br />
<a href="http://stores.ebay.com/yourstorename_category3">
        <img src="http://www.yourisp.com/category3.jpg"
        width="230" height=50" border="0"></a>
<a href="http://stores.ebay.com/yourstorename_category4">
        <img src="http://www.yourisp.com/category4.jpg"
        width="230" height=50" border="0"></a>
</center>
```

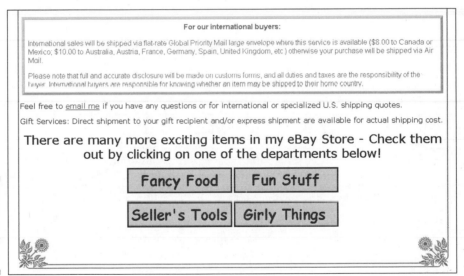

Figure 5-2:
Show all the
departments
in your
eBay Store.

You've got lots of other wonderful items available for sale, and you want to let your customers know what they are! Putting a list of those items in your description would make you guilty of *keyword spamming* — a definite no-no on eBay! There is a way — just make images of the words describe the other goodies you have. Display those images, making each one a hyperlink to the appropriate category in your eBay Store, or have each one launch a specific search of a subset of your listings, as shown in Figure 5-2. Using this approach, you can provide this essential information to your customers without breaking any rules!

The Nineteenth Hole: Using Silly Linking Tricks

Actually, the linking tricks we tell you about aren't *all* silly, but be careful when using them. If a link you're using doesn't do what a link normally does, it only makes sense to warn your potential buyer of the different behavior *before* it happens. If clicking a link will open a new window (and there are times when this is a good thing), provide a note that this will happen, and include a cordial reminder that your customer will need to *close* the new window to return to your listing. Clarity is always a good idea online.

Opening a new browser window

Sometimes you want to provide your customers with additional information that's hanging around on another Web page, but you don't want to take them away from your listing description. The easiest way to do this trick is to have the new Web page open in its own full-sized browser window. Nearly nothing to it: Just add the attribute `target="_blank"` to the anchor tag.

The `target` attribute isn't necessary for the e-mail link, which automatically opens a new message window in your e-mail program.

The following command opens a page containing additional pictures in a new browser window (you might want to include the instructions to close the window to return to the listing description on the page of pictures):

```
<a href="http://www.yourisp.com/pictures.html"
        target="_blank">Click here for additional
        images (close the new window to return to this
        page)!</a>
```

Connecting thumbnails and larger images

If you have multiple detailed pictures of your merchandise and don't want to load them all in your listing, you can create small versions (called *thumbnails*) of your images and make them into links to larger images. That way, your customers only have to wait for the detailed images to load if they really want to view them. Chapter 7 gives you the skinny on how to create a thumbnail image from a larger one.

The two images need to have different names, but to makes things easy on yourself, give the images similar names. If the full-size image name is *widget.jpg*, make the name of the thumbnail image *widget-tn.jpg* to help you remember which is which.

After you have the two images (the full-size version and the thumbnail), linking between the two is as simple as linking from an image as described in the section "Making a Hole-in-One: Linking to an Image" earlier in this chapter. The only difference is that instead of the hyperlink leading to another Web page, it links directly to the location of the larger image. The following command shows how to link your images:

```
<a href="http://www.yourisp.com/image.jpg" width="400"
        height=300" border="0"><img src="http://
        www.yourisp.com/thumbnail.jpg" width="40"
        height=30" border="0" /></a>
```

Don't forget to explain in the text that clicking the thumbnail images will display larger, more detailed pictures. Your customers don't know to click the thumbnails if you don't tell them — and why let all your intricate commands go to waste! Including a note that the browser Back button gets back to the item page is also a good idea.

Rollovers and other fancy tricks

You can find many other linking tricks to use — such as having the font color change when the cursor goes over it — but some people find such features either distracting or confusing. Remember, you want to keep your listings simple and easy to read. Any time your customer spends figuring out how a link works is time not used to make a purchase!

Chapter 6

Brewing JavaScripts (Not the Starbucks' Kind)

. . . .

In This Chapter

▶ Figuring out JavaScript advantages

▶ Finding JavaScript scripts you can use

▶ Counting down to a special date

. . . .

*J*avaScript commands are powerful, but don't be overwhelmed by the thought of adding them to your listings. As with Cascading Style Sheets and HTML, JavaScript commands change the way a page is displayed on the Internet. JavaScript can be a little more complicated, but with the information in this chapter — and yeah, okay, a bit of work — you can include some JavaScript in your listings and reap the rewards. For example, you can make your listings more informative, easier to view, and a snap to navigate. Call it *pampering the customer.*

In this chapter, you find out how to add helpful JavaScript routines to give your listing viewers special messages that change as the auction progresses. We also show you how to use JavaScript to keep your images safe from capture, and to locate — and insert in your listings — scripts that are ready-to-use (and free, too). We think it's just as important to let you know what you can't do as well as what you can, so we'll outline the JavaScript no-no's for eBay listings.

Knowing What You Can Do with JavaScript

JavaScript, which was originally developed by the Netscape company, is simply an extension of HTML. Where HTML allows you to change the look of a page and the way text and images are displayed on a page, JavaScript gives you even more control over the information that your page displays. With JavaScript, you can direct the browser to perform one of a set of actions based on criteria that can be different each time the page is viewed, such as the displaying a message based on the current date and time — we've included a countdown timer at the end of this chapter that you can use to do just that! A few items you can accomplish with JavaScript include

- **Displaying different text or images** based on the current date or other criterion (such as the browser that's used to view the listing).

- **Changing the appearance or the actual content of text or images** based on the position of the mouse on the page. For example, you can have a different caption display underneath an image based on which portion of the picture the mouse cursor hovers over.

- **Displaying a message box** based on a left- or right- click of the mouse. Later in the chapter (in the section "Disabling right-click functions"), we show you a sample script that disables the common options displayed when a user right-clicks on a Web page.

Don't confuse Java*Script* with Java. *Java* is an actual computer programming language that has very powerful features, but requires a separate program (a Java compiler) to work on a Web page. Specifically, the programmer creates a file of commands, and this compiler converts the Java commands into a sort of mini-application (called an *applet*), which is then saved in another location to be included as part of the Web page when it is accessed. Most of us never need to learn how to write code in the Java language, thank goodness!

Finding Ready-to-Use Scripts

The great community that makes up the Internet gives you access to free graphics, animated images, backgrounds, and a myriad of other things you can use to spruce up your listings. Not surprisingly, you can find many Web sites offering JavaScripts that you can use for free. In most cases, the authors ask only that you be sure to retain the script *comment lines,* notes tucked in-between lines of code that give them credit for writing the script.

Searching for scripts online

To find these freebies, point your Web browser to your favorite search engine, search for **free JavaScript,** and prepare to be inundated with a multitude of Web sites to choose from. On these sites, you'll find free scripts that perform a wide variety of functions, such as

- **Telling time** via JavaScript clocks, calendars, and timers.
- **Scrolling single- or multi-line messages as if they were on a stock market ticker display.**
- **Dressing up a page** with special effects, such as randomly changing colors, for your status bar, backgrounds, or on-screen text.
- **Adding interest and movement** with image slideshows and galleries.
- **Playing up on-screen activity,** such as highlighting a link on mouse-over or adding a mouse cursor effect that changes an image that the user sees when the mouse cursor passes over it.

Figure 6-1 shows the results of incorporating a script that uses an image map and the location of the mouse cursor to change the caption displayed underneath the image.

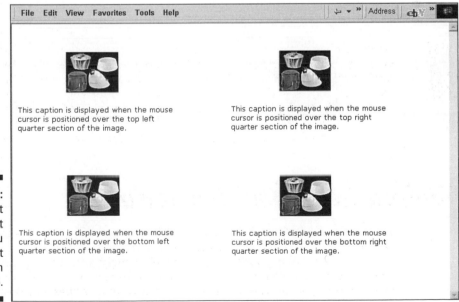

Figure 6-1: Here's what you get when you add a script that uses an image map.

The more movement, animation, and special effects you add to your listings, the slower the page will load. All these fancy features can also be distracting — and can slow down the entire computer, so use them judiciously, and only if the value they provide outweighs the potential side effects.

Copying free scripts for your own use

After you find a script that you want to use, follow the instructions at the free JavaScript site to get the script onto your computer (so that you can actually use it). Getting the script's code may be as simple as copying and pasting from the Web site, or you may need to download a file to your computer using the instructions that are available on the site. After you have the script you want to use saved as a file on your computer, the next step is to incorporate it into your listing.

You usually place scripts within your listings by opening the file on your computer where the script was saved, copying it, and then pasting it in your listing description. For scripts that don't display a specific image or text, the script can be pasted at the very top of the description. If the purpose of the script is to display an image or text, it should be placed in the exact location where you want the image or text. As with HTML commands, the JavaScript commands themselves don't display on your pages — just the results of the commands.

JavaScript, like HTML, behaves differently in different browsers. Be sure to view the results of any script you use in your listings. Try it out in the most popular browsers to ensure that the resulting display looks the way you designed it — and that it works.

Some of the flashy tricks you can do with JavaScript — like mouse cursor trails — can annoy your customers. As with everything else we discuss in this book, remember that fancier isn't always better!

Making Sure Your JavaScript Is Allowed in Listings

Certain JavaScript (or HTML) commands are potentially malicious to the end user — there are bad guys out there who would just *love* to make your computer do things for them automatically — so eBay doesn't allow the use of such commands on its site. These forbidden fruits include commands that

✔ **Drop or read a cookie on any eBay page,** including item listing pages.

✔ **Redirect the users from eBay to a page on another site.** For example, scripts such as the *replace* script that send a user to another auction site would, understandably, be prohibited.

✔ **Automatically call remote scripts and pages,** such as JavaScript `includes` or `iframes`, which could be used to emulate an eBay page for nefarious reasons, such as collecting personal information.

✔ **Change Windows Registry entries,** or otherwise write to another's computer hard drive. Commands like these could introduce major system problems for your customers, innocently or not!

✔ **Create automatic *pop-ups,*** or separate windows that appear unexpectedly and obscure the window that the user is actually trying to see. An exception to the no-pop-up rule is the type of link that opens in a new window when clicked — and gives the user a way to close it.

✔ **Automatically load any binary program on another computer.** eBay makes an exception for Flash content — the only reasons we can come up with to load a program on customers' computers wouldn't be for their benefit.

✔ **Automatically overwrite any area on the listing outside of the item description area.** eBay doesn't want you to inadvertently (or purposely!) cover up any content it generates; eBay considers all information it provides to be important to your customer.

To view the most current restrictions for both HTML and JavaScript on eBay, check out the eBay Help info at

```
http://pages.ebay.com/help/policies/listing-javascript.html
```

Handy Scripts for Any Listing

We often include scripts in our listings; disabling the right mouse-click is one and a countdown clock is another. You can add either of these scripts, or others that you find online, to your listing by copying the script and then pasting it at the top of your listing description.

Both of the scripts that we commonly use — and other helpful scripts we've run across — are available to download from Marsha's Web site at

```
www.coolebaytools.com/javascripts
```

Disabling right-click functions

One of the first tricks new Internet users discover is that depressing the right button on their mouse when viewing a Web page allows them to quickly and easily pop up a list of commands. And it doesn't take them long to figure out that right-clicking an image gives them an option they can select to save that image to their computer. With a short JavaScript incorporated into your listing, you can disable customers' access to the functions that pop up when they right-click your listing. The idea here is to prevent the less-than-scrupulous from making off with your image and using it for their own purposes (say, to sell some other similar item).

When placed right at the beginning of your listing description, the following script will keep viewers from using the right-click menu to save your product images for their own use. Figure 6-2 shows the pop-up message that readers see in place of the menu.

```
<script language="JavaScript">
<!--
var message="Sorry, that function is
          disabled.<br><br>Contents & Graphics Copyright
          2005 Marsha Collier - this Art Work is NOT
          Public Domain, and should NOT be taken from
          this site.";
///////////////////////////////////
function clickIE4(){
if (event.button==2){
alert(message);
return false;
}
}
function clickNS4(e){
if (document.layers||document.getElementById
          &&!document.all){
if (e.which==2||e.which==3){
alert(message);
return false;
}
}
}
if (document.layers){
document.captureEvents(Event.MOUSEDOWN);
document.onmousedown=clickNS4;
}
else if (document.all&&!document.getElementById){
document.onmousedown=clickIE4;
}
```

```
document.oncontextmenu-new Function("alert(message);return
          false")
// -->
</script>
<script language="JavaScript1.2">
function disableselect(e){
return false
}
function reEnable(){
return true
}
//if IE4+
document.onselectstart=new Function ("return false")
//if NS6
if (window.sidebar){
document.onmousedown=disableselect
document.onclick=reEnable
}
</script>
```

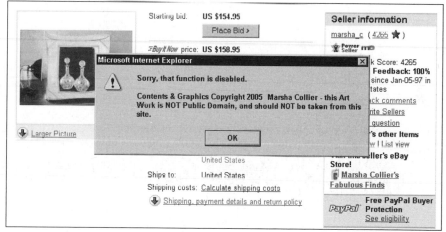

Figure 6-2:
Shoppers
see this
message
when they
right-click
Marsha's
listing.

You can customize the message that appears for your listing viewers by
replacing the following `message` variable with your own text:

```
"Sorry, that function is disabled.<br><br>Contents &
          Graphics Copyright 2005 Marsha Collier - this
          Art Work is NOT Public Domain, and should NOT
          be taken from this site."
```

After all, Marsha's message isn't in the public domain, either. (Friendly reminder.)

Disabling the capability for a customer to use right-click functions will not harm their computers — or necessarily keep an experienced user from capturing an image. This JavaScript function just makes the capture a little more difficult, and serves as (yep) a friendly reminder.

Although customers might right-click a listing page to capture an image, that isn't always the only reason. They might want to print a page, go back to a previous page, add a page to their favorites, and so on. So keep in mind that receiving a pop-up message — instead of the expected behavior — might frustrate some customers enough to keep them from continuing to browse your listings.

Displaying a countdown message

If you want to encourage customers to make a quick buying decision by displaying a countdown to a specific date, you can use a script to get that effect; it's just a little more complicated than the right-click disabler. Whatever the date you choose to be your target — whether it's a specific holiday, the end of a sale, or a special event — this script displays an appropriate message based on the current date when the page is viewed. Follow these steps (on a computer running Windows XP) to add the countdown and customize it for your listing:

1. **Choose Start⇨All Programs⇨Accessories⇨Notepad, or open your simple text editing program of choice.**

2. **At the top of a blank page, type the following script commands (or copy and paste the script from** www.coolebaytools.com/javascripts**).**

```
<script language="JavaScript">
//simple countdown script
var leadupdays=" the end of our Clearance Sale! Don't
      wait -- make your purchase today!"
var ontheday="Final Clearance Sale Day!"
var months=new
      Array("Jan","Feb","Mar","Apr","May","Jun","Jul
      ","Aug","Sep","Oct","Nov","Dec")
```

```
function countdown(yy,mm,dd){
var today=new Date()
var thisyear=today.getYear()
if (thisyear < 1000)
thisyear+=1900
var thismonth=today.getMonth()
var thisday=today.getDate()
var todaystring=months[thismonth]+" "+thisday+",
     "+thisyear
var targetstring=months[mm-1]+" "+dd+", "+yy
var difference=(Math.round((Date.parse(targetstring)-
     Date.parse(todaystring))/(24*60*60*1000))*1)
if (difference==0)
document.write(ontheday)
else if (difference>0)
document.write("Only "+difference+" days left until
     "+leadupdays)
}
//target date formatted (yyyy,mm,dd)
countdown(2006,01,31)
</script>
```

3. **Type your changes to customize the script for your listing.**

   You can change the following elements in this script after pasting it in your description:

   - **The** `leadupdays` **variable,** which contains the end of the message that viewers see on any date leading up to the target date. The message you put in this variable appears after the phrase *Only xx days left until.*

   - **The** `ontheday` **variable,** which contains the message that appears on the day you're counting down to.

   - **The** `countdown` **function** (in the next to last line of the script) that defines the actual target date you're counting down to, as in `countdown(2006,01,31)`. The previous line is a comment (designated by the // at the beginning of the line) and it's there to remind you how to format the target date by entering the year first, then the month, and then the day. All these are numeric and have leading zeros where necessary.

   These dates appear in this script as follows:

April 1, 2006	`countdown(2006,04,01)`
Christmas Day 2007	`countdown(2007,12,25)`
January 31, 2006	`countdown(2006,01,31)`

Figure 6-3 shows the message (displayed in a framed table) three days before the target date, and Figure 6-4 shows the very same page, with no scripting changes, on the actual target date.

 4. **Choose File⇨Save As to save your completed template.**

    The Save As dialog box appears.

 5. **In the Save In drop-down list, choose a location where your count-down script is readily available for use when creating your listing descriptions; type a logical name for your script in the File Name text box.**

 6. **Click Save to save your script.**

 7. **To add the script to a listing description, open the file. Copy the script, and paste it at the location in the listing description where you want to display the message box generated by the countdown script.**

The date used for the computations in the countdown script is the current date, taken from the computer belonging to the person viewing your listing. Obviously, if the date on that computer is incorrect, the viewer won't see the proper message. Placing a note above the message stating — in a jesting manner, perhaps? — that the message is for entertainment purposes only should avoid any misunderstandings with a customer if their computer date isn't set properly or they have turned off JavaScript in their browser.

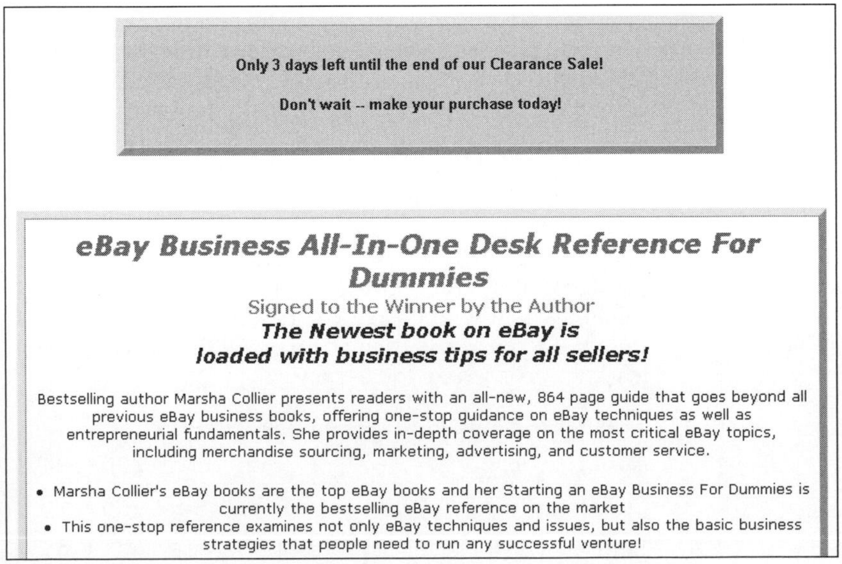

Figure 6-3:
The count-down script message with three days to go.

> Only 3 days left until the end of our Clearance Sale!
>
> Don't wait -- make your purchase today!

> ### eBay Business All-In-One Desk Reference For Dummies
> Signed to the Winner by the Author
> ***The Newest book on eBay is loaded with business tips for all sellers!***
>
> Bestselling author Marsha Collier presents readers with an all-new, 864 page guide that goes beyond all previous eBay business books, offering one-stop guidance on eBay techniques as well as entrepreneurial fundamentals. She provides in-depth coverage on the most critical eBay topics, including merchandise sourcing, marketing, advertising, and customer service.
>
> • Marsha Collier's eBay books are the top eBay books and her Starting an eBay Business For Dummies is currently the bestselling eBay reference on the market
> • This one-stop reference examines not only eBay techniques and issues, but also the basic business strategies that people need to run any successful venture!

Final Clearance Sale Day!

eBay Business All-In-One Desk Reference For Dummies
Signed to the Winner by the Author
**The Newest book on eBay is
loaded with business tips for all sellers!**

Bestselling author Marsha Collier presents readers with an all-new, 864 page guide that goes beyond all previous eBay business books, offering one-stop guidance on eBay techniques as well as entrepreneurial fundamentals. She provides in-depth coverage on the most critical eBay topics, including merchandise sourcing, marketing, advertising, and customer service.

- Marsha Collier's eBay books are the top eBay books and her Starting an eBay Business For Dummies is currently the bestselling eBay reference on the market
- This one-stop reference examines not only eBay techniques and issues, but also the basic business strategies that people need to run any successful venture!

Why are some eBay businesses booming while others bomb?
Marsha Collier knows the answers, and she's packaged them neatly in these nine self-contained minibooks that cover every facet of running a successful eBay business. Your business will blossom with

Figure 6-4:
The count-down script message on the big day!

Don't display critical information via any script that is dependent on a setting on the user's computer — fancy stuff and important information should never be put together!

Chapter 7

Embedding Images for Flash and Effect

In This Chapter

▶ Getting your pictures the right size

▶ Making sure to cover all the angles

▶ Inserting a picture in your listing

▶ Optimizing listing-page download speed

A picture is worth a thousand words, or so the old saying goes. And when we're selling items online, it's an important saying to keep in mind. Having a picture — usually more than one — along with your listing description is essential if you're going to make sure that potential buyers know everything they need to make the decision to purchase your merchandise.

In Chapter 4, we cover the mechanics of the HTML commands you use to actually place the images in your description. This chapter covers some concepts you'll need to keep in mind when getting your pictures ready for use in your listing. We've been taking listing pictures for many years, and we still routinely need to tweak our images before they're ready to use on eBay. In this chapter, we share what we've found out about making your images the optimum size and clarity for viewing online, while keeping them small enough to download quickly. And that means we also have to indulge in a little bit of techno-babble, but stick with us because we do explain how to have your images show what they need to — nothing more and nothing less.

Sizing (and Resizing) Your Pictures

Part III gives you the scoop on how to get the best pictures of your merchandise. Whether you use a digital camera or a scanner, you may often find that the picture you end up with is too big to use with your eBay listing. The image might take up too much of your computer screen because it has too many *pixels* (the dots that make up the picture). Or the image file might take up 500 K — or more! — and take an eon to load. (We recommend that you keep the size of your eBay image files around 50 K instead.) If you notice one of these problems, then you probably have both. And to correct either problem (screen hogging or file bloat), you need to resize the image.

Most digital cameras and scanners come with an image-processing program. We encourage you to learn how to use the basic features of this program; it has what you need for cleaning up your pictures before you use them in your listings. The most useful functions help you *crop* and *resize* pictures that are too big:

- ✔ **Cropping** is trimming off unnecessary areas around the edges of a picture. For example, if you have a picture of a lamp that you are selling, but discover your daughter peeking in on the left side of the picture, you'll want to remove that little "extra" from your image before using it in your listing. We give you step-by-step instruction on how to crop an image in Chapter 16.

- ✔ **Resizing** is making a big image smaller — or vice versa — so you can see what it is but still have room for everything else on-screen. Although digital pictures are rarely too small, re-taking a too-tiny picture is our usual recommendation. You probably want to resize your picture if it is larger than 400 x 300 pixels (the recommended size for an image on eBay). See Chapter 16 for step-by-step instructions on how to resize a photo.

If your image-processing program has a *resample* function in addition to *resize,* then resampling is the better choice. When the program shrinks a picture by resizing, it simply removes pixels to bring the image down to the new size. If the original size is 800×600 and the new size is 400×300, every other pixel is discarded. If the same picture is resampled, however, the computer actually analyzes the surrounding pixels and determines which pixel is the more logical one to remove. This selective process retains the closest reproduction of the original image for a crisper, clearer result.

Every time you save a picture in JPEG format, it's compressed all over again, in order to make the final size of the file as small as possible without losing much of the clarity of the image. Be careful when editing pictures that you intend to save in this format. If you save an image multiple times, each save takes away just a little of the sharp edges in the picture; eventually the image quality gets sketchy and muddy.

For sharpest clarity, try this formula: When resizing or resampling your photos, make the new size evenly divisible into the old. For example, If your original image is 1200 pixels by 900 pixels, a good size for the resized image would be 400 pixels by 300 pixels. This will result in exactly one in every three pixels being kept for the new, smaller image. If you select a new size of 500 × 375, one pixel will be kept for each 2.4 pixels in the original image, resulting in rougher edges throughout.

Zooming in on your subject

In Chapter 13, we talk about zooming in on the subject when taking your pictures, but when *processing* your pictures, zooming takes on a whole new meaning. Almost any image-processing program you decide to use will have a Zoom function. When you use this handy-dandy little feature to zoom in (for a closer look) or out (for an overall look) at your image, you have much greater control over its details.

Keep this in mind when using your program's Zoom function: Even though the picture on your screen *appears* larger (or smaller, as the case may be), the actual size of the image has not changed. For a true size change (say, for an image you want to save and display later in your listing), use the resize or resample function as noted in the previous section.

Before saving an image you've changed, make sure that the Zoom ratio displayed in the toolbar of your image-processing program shows the current viewing ratio as 1:1. A one-to-one ratio means the image you're viewing is the actual size of the image that will be saved.

Maintaining your aspect ratio

When resizing your picture, you see one of the following options preceded by a check box:

> Constrain proportions
>
> Maintain aspect ratio
>
> Preserve ratio

These options all do the same thing. Whichever one's on-screen, make sure that its check box is checked (selected) before you resize your image. Otherwise the newly resized image will be distorted in height or width (funhouse mirrors, anyone?).

Maintaining the aspect ratio actually makes an image easier to resize. When you select this check box, you enter either the new height or the new width — and the computer calculates what the other dimension should be, based on the original height and width. If the original image is (say) 1200 × 900, you designate that the aspect ratio should be maintained, enter the new width of 400, and let the computer figure out that the new height will be 300.

More than you ever wanted to know about dpi, ppi, pixels, resolutions . . .

If you read avidly about digital images and printers (and who doesn't?), you see the terms *dpi* (dots per inch) and *ppi* (pixels per inch) bandied about. Trade secret: These measurements actually have no effect on the size of the images displayed on your computer screen. Instead, they're all about how sharply the details show up.

The dpi specification is normally used only when referring to printers; it describes how many dots of ink (per inch) can be printed on a page. A *dot* is an actual, tiny drop of ink; a *pixel* is the electronic equivalent — a lit-up "dot" in an on-screen image. If you look closely at a printed image, you can usually see the individual dots that make up a picture. Your eyes usually ignore individual dots and smooth them together.

An image displayed on a computer screen is completely different than one printed on a piece of paper, for more than the obvious reason. An image on a piece of paper is the size that it is, forever and ever. An image on a computer screen, however, can be many different sizes, based on the display settings of the screen. A 19-inch monitor screen — like a 19-inch television — is measured on the diagonal from corner to corner. The actual display area is approximately 15 inches wide by 12 inches high. However, the size of the screen is only one part of how text and images are displayed. The *resolution,* or degree of sharpness of displayed text or images, also comes into play.

The power of pixels on-screen

By tweaking the number of pixels used to create an on-screen image, you can give the image its best possible look on the widest range of monitors. So finding the highest possible resolution (that still lets the image load quickly) means paying some attention to computer hardware. You define resolution for a 19-inch monitor, for example, by making settings through the computer's operating system; these tell the monitor to display Web pages at resolutions ranging from 640 × 480 pixels (lower) to 1280 × 1024 pixels (higher).

What these measurements mean, in essence, is how large and how clear your image can be. At lowest resolution, an image is made up of 640 pixels (or dots) spread from left to right across the screen, and 480 pixels from top to bottom. The highest resolution uses 1280 pixels left to right, and 1024 top to bottom. Okay, please stop yawning; wrestling with screen resolution is how you get images that are right-sized for your eBay listings. Here's why:

✔ **The higher the resolution of an image, the sharper it is within its patch of precious on-screen space.** But all monitors are not created equal. If you choose a resolution that's too high, some of your customers' monitors will have to use too much screen space to show your image, or won't be able to show it at all. (More about that in a minute.)

✔ **All those resolution numbers affect what your customer actually sees.** eBay recommends an image size of 400 × 300 (that's pixels, of course, not inches). On a 15 × 12-inch screen set at its lowest resolution (640 × 480 pixels), the image would show up as 9.375 inches wide and 7.5 inches tall — and take up approximately 2/3 of the height and width of the screen. On the same monitor set at the highest resolution (1280 × 1024), the image would appear approximately 4.7 inches wide and 3.5 inches tall, about 1/3 of the height and width of the screen. That's a big difference!

Table 7-1 shows how much of the available screen space a 400 × 300-pixel image covers at different resolutions.

Table 7-1	Display Sizes (Width × Height) for a 400 × 300-Pixel Image on a 19-inch Monitor	
Screen area in pixels	*Image size in inches*	*Required percentage of display area*
640 × 480	9.4″ × 7.5″	62.5% × 62.5%
800 × 600	7.5″ × 6″	50% × 50%
1024 × 768	5.9″ × 4.7″	40% × 40%
1280 × 1024	4.7″ × 3.5″	31% × 29%

So what happens when the images you want to put on-screen are too big? Even more of the display space is used! Table 7-2 shows what happens when the image's pixel size increases by 50 percent in both directions — making the image 600 × 450 pixels.

Table 7-2	Display Sizes (Width × Height) for a 600 × 450-Pixel Image on a 19-inch Monitor	
Screen Area in Pixels	*Image Size in Inches*	*Required percentage of display area*
640 × 480	14.1" × 11.25"	94% × 94%
800 × 600	11.25" × 9"	75% × 75%
1024 × 768	8.8" × 7"	59% × 59%
1280 × 1024	7" × 5.3"	47% × 44%

Getting your pixels right on eBay

Many of us like to keep up with the latest technology, and so we upgrade to at least 19-inch display screens. But we might forget that many computer users still have 15-inch monitors — with an actual display area no more than 12 inches wide by 9 inches high. This scrunches up the area available for displaying the images in your eBay listings. For example, Table 7-3 shows the percentage of space used by that eBay-recommended image size of 400 pixels wide by 300 pixels.

Comparing this table with Table 7-1 (for a 19-inch display) shows that although the percentage of display space used is the same, the image is smaller.

Table 7-3	Display Sizes (Width × Height) for a 400 × 300-Pixel Image on a 15-inch Monitor	
Screen Area in Pixels	*Image Size in Inches*	*Required Percentage of Display Area*
640 × 480	7.5 × 5.6	62.5 × 62.5
800 × 600	6 × 4.5	50 × 50
1024 × 768	4.7 × 3.5	40 × 40

Very few users set their monitors' display resolution to 640 × 480 (the lowest available), but many use 800 × 600, so we recommend that you design and scale your listings and images using this resolution as the baseline. This means that all your images should be smaller than 800 × 600 (as that would fill up the screen), and we recommend no larger than 600 × 450.

Placing Your Pictures for Maximum Effect

Although it isn't the most important aspect of your description, the picture of the item you're selling is a big part of the first impression it makes. No surprise that the position your pictures take within a description can make a huge difference in ease of viewing the information about the item. Keep the following in mind:

- ✓ **If the item image is wider than it is tall,** centering the picture above the text describing the item is appropriate.

- ✓ **If the item image is taller than it is wide,** placing it on the left (or right) side of the description text is better.

Placing your images according to these general guidelines helps to keep the image and the description together on-screen when your customer views your listing. See Figure 7-1 for an example of both placements.

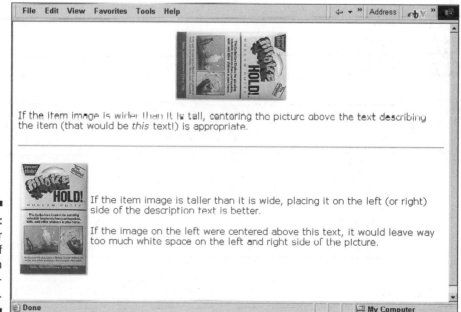

Figure 7-1:
Proper placement of figures with the descriptive text.

If your image is just about as wide as it is tall, then placement of the picture with respect to the text isn't as crucial. You just want to avoid forcing your customer to scroll up and down too much to view both image and text.

 Always use the one-free-picture option that stores an image with your item listing on eBay. This image can be the same one you embed in your description, or a different image. This way, if eBay is having problems displaying pictures stored on its server, odds are that your own picture-hosting service won't be having the same problems at the same time (and vice versa). Thus an image of the item you're selling is always available.

Embedding the Image in Your Listing

eBay gives you the option to add pictures to your listings, but if you have a place to host your own images (Chapter 15 tells you how to find an image host), you can embed one or more images directly in your listing — without paying any additional fees!

An image can be embedded anywhere within your listing with the help of the img (Image) HTML tag. This particular tag is one that stands alone — that is, it has no need for a closing tag. The / just before the ending > (shown in the follow HTML command) is a signal that the tag closes itself.

```
<img src="http://www.yourisp.com/yourimage.jpg" />
```

Selling Up with Multiple Pictures

Selling items online is, without a doubt, much different from selling the same merchandise in a brick-and-mortar storefront. One major difference is that your customer can't pick up the item to view it more closely, or to look at the bottom or inside. But here's the next best thing: to offer potential buyers a look at multiple pictures of your item.

Take a main picture that shows the entire item, but also take pictures of the back, sides, top, and bottom. Close-up photos can also be important. Here are some item-specific examples; if you are selling

- ✔ **A painting:** Take a close-up picture of the artist's signature. Apply this concept to any artwork you have for sale, including pottery, sculpture, prints — or signed first edition books.

- ✔ **Silver:** If the silver piece has a maker's mark, take a close-up of the mark itself.

- ✔ **A designer dress:** Make sure to take a close-up of the tag that shows size, fabric content — even laundering instructions!

As with other aspects of your listing, put yourself in the position of a potential buyer. What parts of the item for sale would you like to see in detail?

Make sure that the entire surface of the item is visible in your picture(s). If you zoom in too close on the item and leave out some of the edges, your buyer might think you're hiding something.

With multiple pictures of your merchandise, placement of the images in your description can become either simpler (or, for that matter, more complex) depending on the size of the images. If the pictures all have similar widths, stacking them along the left or right side of your description might be the most appropriate placement — just be sure to place the appropriate text for each image right next to it.

Choosing a Main or Dominant Photo

So you've followed our instructions and taken multiple pictures of your item — there will be one that stands out as the main (dominant) photo. This image might be an overall picture of the item or a close-up of its most important element.

Emphasize this main photo in your listing. If you use eBay Picture Services, this picture will be the first picture your customers encounter — and thus will be the one displayed at the top of the listing. When you design the layout of your description, this picture should be the primarily placed image, usually centered at the top, so that it is the first thing seen by your customer when viewing the listing.

Saving Space with Thumbnails

One major problem with putting multiple images in your listing is how long it takes to download them from the Internet. The longer customers have to wait to see your item information, the greater is the chance that they'll get impatient and move on to another seller's item. One way to avoid this situation is to use *thumbnails* — small images your customers can click to see larger versions.

If you have more than two or three images in your listing, we recommend using thumbnails that give your customers access to photos with greater detail if (and only if) they want to see the details.

Selecting the Gallery image

When you list an item for sale at eBay, you have the option of paying a small additional fee for a Gallery image. The Gallery image is a thumbnail photo, automatically created by eBay, of a specific photo you designate when creating your item listing. The Gallery image appears to the left of your listing title in search and category results — and, by virtue of this location, gives potential customers an additional incentive to choose your listing to view in more detail. If you have an eBay Store, the Gallery image appears to the left of the item title on your Store category pages, which gives customers an experience similar to catalog shopping.

The Gallery image is a useful marketing tool that provides greater visibility for your merchandise. Choosing the correct photo for the Gallery image can have a significant effect on its value as a marketing device — and can help you get the biggest bang for your buck when you use this feature.

Don't automatically select the main picture of your item as the Gallery image; that particular photo might be completely ineffective when reduced to eBay's standard thumbnail size (80 pixels wide by 60 pixels high as of this writing). Do choose an image that, when reduced, will be easy to view and will catch your potential customer's eye.

Creating thumbnails in two steps

Chapter 5 explains why you would link thumbnail images to larger images — primarily to reduce the amount of time required to download your listing. You can create your own a thumbnail image simply, in either of two ways — crop the photo to a much smaller size or reduce the entire photo to a small size (100 ×100 pixels works well) — and save the resulting picture to a separate file.

When you're deciding how to create thumbnails, keep in mind that a direct reduction in size can make the thumbnail image detail so small that it's unrecognizable. Customers who can't make head nor tail of your item could get frustrated and skip looking at it — or, if you require that they always click through to the larger image, there goes the reason for using the thumbnail in the first place.

Figure 7-2 shows an example of an effective original image linked to a thumbnail image.

Figure 7-2:
Here's an original image to which a customer can link via a thumbnail.

When you create a thumbnail image, we suggest using a two-step process that involves both *cropping* and *resizing* (an earlier chapter section — "Sizing (and Resizing) Your Pictures" has how-to details). With your picture open in an image-processing program, follow these steps:

1. **Crop the image to eliminate extraneous detail and avoid a too-cluttered thumbnail.**

   For example, if you're selling a matching set of jewelry (necklace, earrings, and bracelet), crop out the bracelet, earrings, and neck chain and leave just the pendant, which shows up well in a thumbnail.

2. **Resize the cropped image to scale it down to a smaller size, usually 100 × 100 pixels.**

The original photo that's displayed when you click the thumbnail still retains all the detail and the overall context. But the thumbnail image you create with this process makes a clearer initial impression for your potential buyers. Figure 7-3 shows the image from Figure 7-2 after it has been (first) cropped and (second) resized.

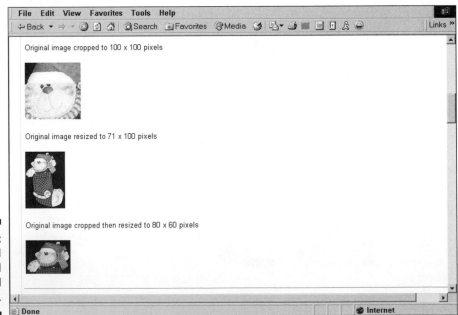

Figure 7-3:
Cropped and resized thumbnail image.

If you need a lot of detail in your photos and wind up with image files larger than the recommended maximum of 50 K — but find that a thumbnail image simply doesn't provide enough detail — don't despair. A standard-size image can be linked to a larger, higher-resolution photo in just the same way you'd link a thumbnail to a standard image. In either case, you provide more information only when it's requested by the customer.

Offering a larger view

When you use thumbnail images in your listing, you need to include the HTML coding that links each thumbnail to an alternative image (as described in Chapter 5). Using HTML, you can set up this link to allow your customers to click the thumbnail image and display a larger version of the picture, whether in the current window or in a new window. If the image opens in a new window, be sure to provide instructions on how to close the window and return to your listing (many such temporary windows include a Close button).

When you make a thumbnail image into a link, your customers' cursors will change when passing over the thumbnail, indicating that they can click it. But don't assume that they'll notice this nifty feature. In your listing text, be sure to include a message that the image is clickable; mention it more than once if necessary. You want to make it easy for your customers.

Chapter 8

Plumping Up Your Description

· ·

In This Chapter

▶ Painting the walls of your online store

▶ Installing fixtures and shelving

▶ Determining how detailed to make your description

· ·

*H*ere, as in other chapters, we ask you to compare the online selling experience with that of selling similar merchandise in a storefront. Imagine an empty store, ready for you to move in and start selling your items. You have (at least) four empty walls, nothing on the floor, and lots of wide open space. First, you might consider painting the walls and installing some carpet. Shelving or some type of display case is next, to exhibit your product attractively. The type of shelving or cases you choose depends on the size and shape of your merchandise.

The purpose of furnishing your storefront is to give your customers a comfortable, efficient shopping experience. We've all walked into a store where there was so much stuffed into every nook and cranny that locating anything in the mess was an overwhelming task. Likewise, an item listing that has text and photos scattered haphazardly on the screen without any breaks, headers, or divisions can make your online customers' shopping trip equally hairy.

So here we shift the focus: Previous chapters give you multiple ways to enhance what's in your item descriptions, this chapter shows how to present the item, using HTML to create a repeatable structure for your listing that effectively displays your wares. In particular, we get you started creating the proper online *fixtures* — such as horizontal rules and tables, the virtual equivalent of shelves and display cases for the merchandise in your listing.

Filling In the Background

Just as you might paint (or otherwise decorate) the walls of your brand new storefront, you might also fill in the background of your listing with color, a picture, or a logo. More important than selecting a specific color or image is remembering this main rule: The background must enhance — not overwhelm — the item description. As Figure 8-1 shows, if the background is what the customers notice, then it is too bright, too bold, or too detailed!

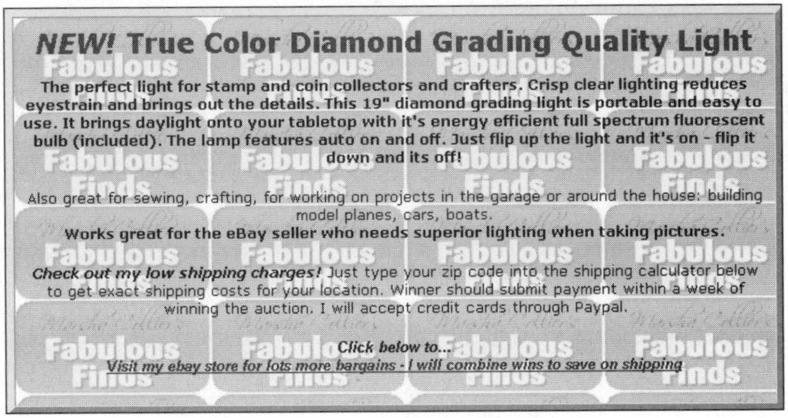

Figure 8-1:
The text
is over-
whelmed
by the
background!

The background should complement, but not compete with, your text description. Figure 8-2 shows how much better a muted background looks.

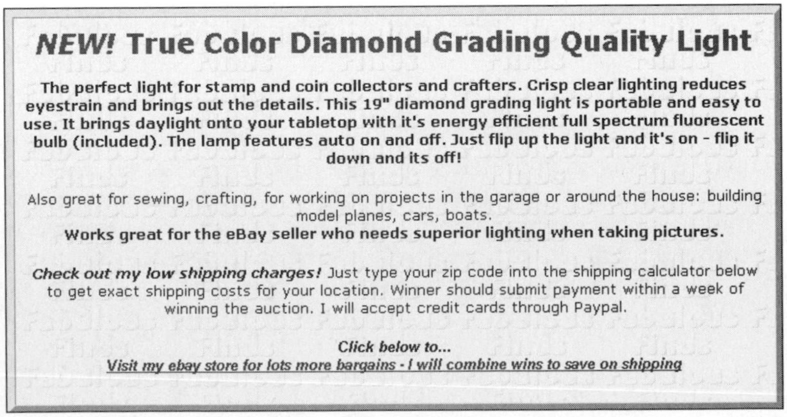

Figure 8-2:
A subtle
back-
ground that
enhances
without
over-
whelming.

Also consider the following points when you're choosing a listing background:

- ✔ **Coordinate your colors:** Keep in mind the colors that appear in your item pictures. If the usual background color in your product images is (say) a teal green, the colors you choose for your auction template should probably be in the blue and green neighborhood, and avoid the red or yellow palette.

- ✔ **Use color and images that identify you:** As we discuss in Chapter 4, creating a unique template that establishes a "brand" for you and your merchandise is a good marketing technique. The background color becomes just a part of your entire color scheme.

- ✔ **Don't automatically dismiss white:** A distinctive background color (or image) isn't the be-all and end-all for an effective listing template. We've seen some very effective listings that use a plain white background as part of the color scheme. If the standard background color in your item photos is a crisp, clear white that melds with the standard white background of listing pages, it can help make the items in your photos quite eye-catching.

The easiest way to change the background color in your listing is by placing the entire description in an HTML table and defining the color with the `bgcolor=` attribute of the `table` command. (Figure 8-3 shows this technique in action.) Follow these steps to put a colorful background on your listing description:

1. **Type the `table` command at the start of your listing description.**

   The command looks something like this:

   ```
   <table width=100% bgcolor="color"><tr><td>
   ```

   And its components do the following:

   - `width=100%` gives you a column width that uses the entire width of the display screen.

   - `bgcolor="color"` sets the background to the color you specify; just put the right code in place of the word *color* shown here.

   Check out Marsha's Web site (www.coolebaytools.com) for a chart to help you with the color codes to use in the `bgcolor=` attribute. You'll also find sample HTML and CSS coding you can use to create simple background colors, textures, or images.

   - `<tr><td>` are the two commands which define table rows and table columns. In this case, we have the simplest of tables with only one row and one column. Stay tuned; we have an example of one row and two columns coming up!

2. **Follow the opening** `table` **command with your formatted listing-description text.**

   Check out Chapter 4 to find out about HTML text formatting.

3. **At the end of your listing text, type the tags that close the** `table` **command and turn off the background color.**

   The closing command looks like this:

   ```
   </td></tr></table>
   ```

Figure 8-3:
A background color applied using the `table` command.

NEW! **True Color Diamond Grading Quality Light**

The perfect light for stamp and coin collectors and crafters. Crisp clear lighting reduces eyestrain and brings out the details. This 19" diamond grading light is portable and easy to use. It brings daylight onto your tabletop with it's energy efficient full spectrum fluorescent bulb (included). The lamp features auto on and off. Just flip up the light and it's on - flip it down and its off!

Also great for sewing, crafting, for working on projects in the garage or around the house: building model planes, cars, boats.
Works great for the eBay seller who needs superior lighting when taking pictures.

Check out my low shipping charges! Just type your zip code into the shipping calculator below to get exact shipping costs for your location. Winner should submit payment within a week of winning the auction. I will accept credit cards through Paypal.

Click below to...
Visit my ebay store for lots more bargains - I will combine wins to save on shipping

Use the following commands to use an image as the background rather than a simple color. (If you decide to use an image, make absolutely certain that the image is light and unobtrusive so it doesn't overwhelm your description text.)

```
<table width="100%" cellpadding=20 cellspacing=0 border=1
        background="http://www.yourdomain.com/yourimage
        .jpg">

<tr><td width="100%">

Your text description goes here.

</td></tr></table>
```

Should you decide to use an image — perhaps your logo — as a background in your listing, make sure that it is subtle! Otherwise your listing could easily become unreadable, and if your potential customers can't read the listing, they'll take their business elsewhere!

Arranging Stuff by Nesting Tables

In Chapter 7, we explained the importance of providing multiple images of your items so your customers have all the information that's pertinent to their buying decisions. But where you place the images with respect to the text that describes them is also important.

Have you ever noticed how some people manage to have a photo perfectly aligned to the right or left of their descriptions? It's really not that difficult to do — just add a few HTML commands to the description (the tags themselves won't show up on-screen — just the results they create).

For example, Figure 8-4 shows a listing with a picture on the left of an item description. (By the way, when the full version of this auction ran on eBay, with the kind cooperation of the people on *The View,* we raised over $1,000 for UNICEF!)

Figure 8-4: A listing using nested tables to put the picture on the left.

"The View" Cast Autographed Coffee Mug

Signed by
Joy Behar
Star Jones
Barbara Walters
Meredith Vieira

All you fans of *The View*, this is your chance to own a coffee cup autographed by all four stars of the show. The proceeds from this auction will be donated to UNICEF. The winner will be announced on ABC's *The View* TV show on Monday. We'll be checking this auction live on the show on Wednesday, April 23rd, 2003 with Marsha Collier, the author of *"eBay for Dummies"*.

Shipping will be via Priority Mail. Credit cards are accepted through PayPal.

The HTML coding for the listing shown in Figure 8-4 looks like the following listing. (The code that does the job is bolded here so you can easily pick it out, but there's no need to bold HTML code when you use it.)

```
<table align=center cellpadding=8 width="80%" border=7
        cellspacing=0 bgcolor="White">
<tr><td>
<center><font face="VERDANA,HELVETICA,ARIAL"
        color="crimson" size=5>
```

```
<b>"The View"<br>Cast Autographed<br>Coffee
        Mug</b></font><p>
<img width=250
        src="http://images.auctionworks.com/viewmug.
        jpg">
</td>
<td>
<center><font face="VERDANA,HELVETICA,ARIAL"
        color="crimson" size=3>
<b><i>Signed by</i><br><b>Joy Behar<br>Star
        Jones<br>Barbara Walters<br>Meredith Vieira</b>
</font><p>
<font face="verdana,arial,helvetica,sans serif"
        color="Black" size=2>
<b>All you fans of <i>The View</i>, this is your chance to
        own a coffee cup autographed by all four stars
        of the show. The proceeds from this auction
        will be donated to UNICEF. The winner will be
        announced on ABC's <i>The View</i> TV show on
        Monday. We'll be checking this auction live on
        the show on Wednesday, April 23rd, 2003 with
        Marsha Collier, the author of <i>"eBay for
        Dummies"</i></b>.</font><p>
<font face="verdana,arial,helvetica,sans serif"
        color="Black" size=1>
Shipping will be via Priority Mail. Credit cards are
        accepted through PayPal. </font>
</center></td></tr></table>
```

When you have multiple-item lots (or multiple images of a single item), you can use several of these tables, nested within one surrounding table, to place pictures and text exactly where you want them. Table 8-1 shows you all kinds of HTML codes that format, align, and strategically arrange your item images and descriptions.

Table 8-1	Basic HTML Codes to Use for Listings	
Text Code	*How to Use It*	*What It Does*
`<b></b>`	`<b>eBay tools</b>`	**eBay tools** (bold type)
`<i></i>`	`<i>eBay tools</i>`	*eBay tools* (italic type)
`<b><i></i></b>`	`<b><i>eBay tools </i></b>`	***eBay tools*** (bold and italic type)
`<font color= red></font>`	`<font color=red> ebay tools</font>`	Selected text appears in red. (This book is in black and white so you can't see the color here.)

Text Code	How to Use It	What It Does
`<font size=+1>` `</font>`	`<font size=+3>` `eBay</font> tools`	**eBay tools** (font size normal +1 through 4, increases size *x* times)
` `	`eBay tools`	eBay tools (inserts line break)
`<p>`	`eBay<p>tools`	eBay tools (inserts paragraph space)
`<hr>`	`cool eBay<hr>tools`	cool eBay ─────── tools (inserts horizontal rule)
`<h1></h1>`	`<h1>eBay tools</h1>`	**eBay tools** (converts text to headline size)

Code for Lists	How to Use It	What It Does
`<ul><li>` `</ul>`	`<ul><li>I accept` `<li>PayPal` `<li>Money Orders` `<li>Checks</ul>`	I accept · PayPal · Money Orders · Checks
`<ol><li>` `</ol>`	`<ol><li>I accept` `<li>PayPal` `<li>Money Orders` `<li>Checks</ol>`	I accept 1. PayPal 2. Money Orders 3. Checks

Linking (Hyperlink) Code	How to Use It	What It Does
`<img src>`	`<img src="http://>` `www.`*yourwebsite.* `com/`*imagename*`.jpg"`	Inserts an image from your server into the description text
`<a href=  >`	`<a href= http://` `www.`*yourwebsite.* `com/shippinginfo.` `htm>`	When selected text is clicked, the user's browser goes to the page you indicate in the URL
`target=_blank`	`<a href= http://` `www.`*yourwebsite.* `com/shippinginfo.` `htm target=_blank>`	When inserted at the end of a hyperlink, it opens the page in a separate browser window

(continued)

Table 8-1 *(continued)*

Table Codes	How to Use It	What It Does
`<table border>`	`<table border=4>`	Puts a border around your table at a width of four pixels

`<table>`
`</table>`
	`<table>`
	sample text
	`</table`
		The `table` command must surround *every* table

`<tr></tr>`
 	
`<td></td>`
	`<tr><td>`*text*`</td>`
	`<td>`*text*`</td></tr>`
	`<tr><td>`*text*`</td>`
	`<td>`*text*`</td></tr>`
		Table row `<tr>` must be used with `<td>` table data to end and open new boxes
		
		text text
		text text

Deciding When Enough Is Enough

In this and preceding chapters — and we're not done yet — we show you many ways to fancy up the description in your listings. Your mission (should you choose to accept it) is to pick which enhancements to use. Do yourself (and your customers) a favor: Don't try to use all the bells and whistles in one single listing. A garish, hard-to-read description will, at best, frustrate the readers — and at worst, drive them away to purchase the item from another, more tasteful seller. Check out this book's color insert for an illustration of this point.

The amount of effort — research, development, and testing — you put into plumping up your description should be directly related to your potential for profit-making on the sale of the item. If you have only one item and its expected sales price is less than $20.00, spending hours crafting an intricate listing description is a less-than-optimal use of your time. But if you have tens — even hundreds — of a single item, spending a little time creating an easy-to-read listing is worth the investment. Besides, if you have a deep inventory of the merchandise, you'll be using the listing for a long time, so making it attractive will be easier on *your* eyes, too!

As with many other aspects of selling online, consider what methods you would use in a storefront to market each of your products. If you're only selling one type of item — and lots of it — you showcase the product in a carefully decorated area of the store; a single item, on the other hand, could go on a shelf without much thought, effort, or money spent on the display — unless that item has a high dollar value, of course (say, Dorothy's red shoes or Toto's basket). In that case, you'd spend more time and resources to direct your customers' attention to the item. Apply these same theories to marketing your online merchandise.

Chapter 9

Adding Some Bells and Whistles

· ·

In This Chapter

▶ Using multimedia as a listing enhancement

▶ Not alienating your customer with unwanted sights and sounds

▶ Locating products that help you add bells and whistles

· ·

*B*ells, whistles, animation, audio, video . . . the multimedia options available for sprucing up your listings are infinite! But they can also be an embarrassment of riches. In this chapter, we go over many of these options — and show you how to go about adding them (tastefully!) to your listings.

Any extras you add to your listings have some looming pitfalls. The first is that the more complexity you introduce in your listings, the greater the potential for a problem with the page displaying properly. Additionally, the multimedia approach can significantly increase the amount of time it takes for your listing to load. The longer the wait, the greater the chance that your customer will get tired of waiting (or get annoyed with unwanted details or frills) and go elsewhere to make the purchase.

Warnings aside, you may have a really good reason to include a video or audio clip in a listing. For example, if you're selling a 78 RPM record, the best way to show off the quality of the sound reproduction is to provide a clip of what the recording actually sounds like — including all the pops and hisses. Or if you have a working robot, a video clip of it actually doing what it does would be invaluable. Because the advantages of including bells and whistles may outweigh the potential pitfalls, we show you the best way to link to audio and video clips, or animations in your listings.

Animating Your Graphics

Animated images can be eye-catching for eBay shoppers, but (for the sake of your sales — and okay, as a public service) consider all the facts about the impact of including animation in your listings. For example, offering shoppers a slideshow is an effective way to display multiple images of your merchandise. But don't use this feature without understanding that *every one* of those multiple images still has to be downloaded *before* the slideshow can begin. In effect, the only real advantage to using a slideshow — versus displaying all images right in your listing — is to reduce the amount of screen space taken up by the images. Best solution: Make the slide show optional, as shown in Figure 9-1.

We strongly suggest that you avoid including animated images if they're unrelated to your merchandise. That is, when you list your jewelry for sale, don't include an image of a jaguar doing the jitterbug just because you think it's cute and funny. That said, you may decide that an animated graphic is the very thing to liven up some of your listings. For example, if you want to sell Olympic memorabilia, an animated image of a speed skater zooming across the top of your listing may differentiate your listing from the masses of listings out there. To include an animated graphic in your listing, you can use the same HTML command that you use for a static (nonmoving) image, as follows:

```
<img src="http://www.yourwebsite.com/animation.gif" />
```

In this command, `http://www.yourwebsite.com/animation.gif` is the location on the Internet of the animated graphic image you're adding to your listing. For more details on including images in your listings, see Chapter 7. And check out Figure 9-1, which shows a listing that offers customers the opportunity to view a slideshow of product images.

It's wise to approach the use of animation with some trepidation. Besides the obvious potential for annoying your customer, there is a small danger that if your animation uses high contrast or flashing images, it can cause seizures in users who have photosensitive epilepsy. If you decide to use animation, be sure that the look is smooth — not flickering — and that the images change at a slow speed.

Click here for the slideshow.

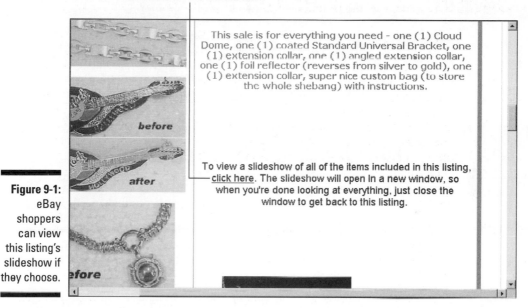

This sale is for everything you need - one (1) Cloud Dome, one (1) coated Standard Universal Bracket, one (1) extension collar, one (1) angled extension collar, one (1) foil reflector (reverses from silver to gold), one (1) extension collar, super nice custom bag (to store the whole shebang) with instructions.

To view a slideshow of all of the items included in this listing, click here. The slideshow will open in a new window, so when you're done looking at everything, just close the window to get back to this listing.

Figure 9-1:
eBay shoppers can view this listing's slideshow if they choose.

Playing Some Music

Sometimes providing a sound clip for your customer might help convince them to purchase your merchandise — especially if you sell (say) music boxes, CDs, or dolls that sing. Any of these items make good candidates for providing small sound files (recorded from the item itself) in your listing — but make sure the customer has the option to listen to them or not.

(How to suggest this tactfully? Oh well.) *Please don't* include a continuously looping recording of your favorite song as background music for your listings. Another inadvisable use of audio is including a song that is related in some way to your merchandise. Honestly, a rousing patriotic march won't provide additional information about the political buttons you have for sale — nor will a lullaby be the focal selling point for your handmade baby items. Customers who get clobbered with unwanted sound are less inclined to buy.

When you want to include an appropriate sound file in your listing — to be played on demand — use the following HTML command:

```
<a href="http://www.yourisp.com/youraudiofile.wav">Click
         here</a> to listen to the music!
```

Yep, it's just an anchor link to an external file location — where you uploaded the audio file. You can put this link anywhere you'd like in your description.

Telling Your Story with Speech

Lately, we've noticed a rash of listings that "talk" to us. Although an overbearing speech can be as irritating as unwanted music, you might want to include a brief sound bite to emphasize a specific feature of your listing, a special sale, or your terms and conditions. Avoid including a message that repeats over and over; this alone can make an otherwise-acceptable recording into a nuisance that drives your customer out the door!

If you are using a product that offers computer-generated speech, be sure to listen to the recording before you include it in your listing. We've heard some programs that don't pronounce the words properly, and others that have an annoying sound quality.

Any information presented to the customer as an audio file must also be included in your listing text because some shoppers either don't have speakers or don't routinely leave them turned on.

Streaming Video to the Bidder

Streaming video is becoming more and more "visible" — not so much in terms of visual clarity (though that's usually fine), but rather as a prevalent capability on the Web. Recently NBC has begun making its nightly news broadcasts available online in streaming video format. This probably doesn't mean we'll all start watching television on our computers, but it is an indication of how common streaming video on the Internet has become.

As with sound clips, providing a video clip for your customers might sometimes help convince them to purchase your merchandise. If you're selling (say) a video you produced yourself, a robot, a doll that walks and talks — any of these would be candidates for putting small video files in your listing.

As you can imagine, audio and video files are more than one hundred times the size of still images. Rather than requiring large files to be downloaded prior to viewing (or listening), streaming media technology is the best solution. When audio, video, or both are streamed, they are retrieved in compressed form and viewed as they arrive on the viewer's computer. This is accomplished by a player, which is either integrated into the browser being used, or an additional program which starts up when the media starts to download. Most computers come with one or more media players already installed. Should you decide to use streaming media, one of the factors to keep in mind is whether it is capable of being played by the most common of the media players on your customers' computers.

Finding Third-Party Solutions

New vendors that supply methods for providing rich media content are joining the market with the speed that you'd expect from any growing industry. For example, you can find software and services that help you add just the right amount of multimedia flair, give customers the information they need to be fully informed about your product, or add sound, streaming video, and functionality to your listings. (We're still not sure how we'll feel about aroma-vision — though it might work if you're selling designer fragrances!)

When you, as a seller, become a buyer for such a product or service, eBay provides the Solutions Directory. It's a handy place to locate and compare third-party providers in addition to products developed or acquired by eBay itself.

To access the Solutions Directory, go to http://solutions.ebay.com or take the following steps:

1. **Click the Site Map link at the top of any eBay page.**

2. **Find the Selling Tools area (about halfway down the page in the center column).**

3. **Click the eBay Solutions Directory link.**

   The Solutions Directory, as shown in Figure 9-2, appears.

When you've reached the main Solutions Directory page, you find a list of main categories of solutions — any of which you can browse by clicking the link for the category title. You can also use the search box at the top of the page, and look for providers of solutions by typing in keywords. For example, you can type **audio** or **video** in the search box and click the Search button to retrieve a list of related solutions.

Figure 9-2:
The eBay
Solutions
Directory.

Checking credentials of solution providers

Whether you browse a solutions category or a search results page (as shown in Figure 9-3), you can compare the list of solutions. Note that when the Search Results page first appears, the solutions are sorted in order by Solution Title. To change the order in which they are displayed, just click any of the column headers (such as User Rating).

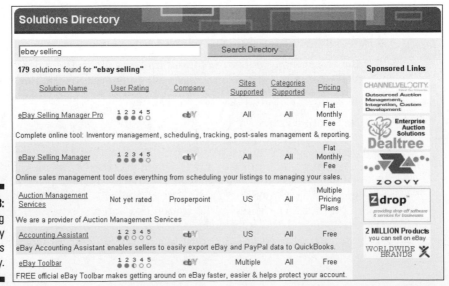

Figure 9-3:
Browsing
the eBay
Solutions
Directory.

Clicking any of the solution titles takes you to a listing details page where you find more information about the third-party solution, including:

- **Company Name**

- **Sites Supported,** for example, US, Canada, Australia (eBay country-specific sites)

- **Categories Supported,** which is a list of the main categories on eBay where the solution can be used

- **Platforms Supported,** such as Web Application or Client Application - PC

- **Detailed Description** of the product or service that outlines the exact details of the service, its benefits to you (the seller), and the features the company feels are the most important to their customers

- **Pricing Details**

- **User Ratings,** which are similar to feedback ratings for buyers and sellers on eBay, are displayed at the bottom of the listing details page for each third-party solution.

Accommodating the visually impaired

Throughout this book we've warned against overusing graphics, color, animated graphics, and other fancy enhancements that add nothing to the information about your merchandise for sale, but (too easily) add the potential for irritating your customer. Another thing to keep in mind while designing your listings is that some of the visitors to your pages might be visually impaired in some way. Even if it's just the "long-arm" syndrome that aging baby boomers are beginning to experience (holding the fine print at arm's length), keeping your listings easy on the eye — and not assuming that others see in the same way you do — is a good habit to develop.

Here are a few things to keep in mind about visual limitations when designing your listings:

- Colorblindness is not always limited to the inability to distinguish between red and green — other colors may be affected by the condition as well.

- Yellow text is often difficult to read, even when displayed on a dark background.

- The use of a special browser that renders Web pages into either Braille or speech due to the complete inability of the user to see pages distinctly.

- Small text can be difficult to read — and the older the user, the bigger the segment of the population affected by this problem.

- Users may have disabilities such as dyslexia that prevent them from reading or comprehending text properly.

Limiting the use of graphics and other bells and whistles in your listings not only reduces load time for all your customers, but may also prove less stressful and distracting to the average person (as well as the visually impaired).

The eBay Certified Provider icon that you find in the listings in the Solutions Directory and on many of the third-party provider's Web sites does not mean that the company sporting the icon is in any way approved or recommended by eBay. This mark simply means that eBay reviews the company's claim to ensure that it can provide eBay members with services and solutions to grow their eBay businesses. Among other criteria, participating companies must have extensive experience with eBay, pass a strict certification exam, and provide a number of proven customer references — which eBay checks before granting certification.

Figure 9-4 shows the solutions detail page for eBay's Selling Manager product.

Figure 9-4:
eBay Selling
Manager
product-
description
page.

Note the comment eBay displays at the top of every User Rating page: "User Ratings are shown with most-recent comments first. Each comment is attributed to its author who takes full responsibility for the comment. If you have any questions or concerns about a particular comment, please contact the author directly by clicking on the author's User ID and then clicking the contact member link." As with transactional feedback on eBay, the reputation of the person leaving a comment is almost as important as the comment itself.

Letting buyers silence the bells and whistles

Any audio or video solution you add to your listing should be optional for the customer and be provided in a streaming mode if at all possible. That is, any time you include audio or video in a listing, give your potential customers the option of *not* listening or viewing. Customers can view your listings in many different ways — and places — which raises the possibility that audio or video would be an unwelcome intrusion. (Think: Employees browsing your store from their offices during lunch hour, or a mother whose children are napping, may want to keep things quiet.)

So as you're evaluating a product that supplies any multimedia content, check the product specifications to make sure your viewers can easily turn off the multimedia elements supplied by the product. If you can't tell whether the product has this capability, ask the product's provider this essential question when evaluating their service and deciding whether to add it to your arsenal of eBay selling tools.

It's possible that some of your customers might have their computers' sound turned off (for any number of reasons), so be sure that any information you include as either a sound or video clip is *also* included in the text of your listing.

Part III
Turning Pictures into Dollars

In this part . . .

One of the reasons we wrote this book was to demystify the photography process. So we do that in this part. And perhaps we go into a bit more detail than you really need right away, but we know you want your pictures to be, uh, picture-perfect (or is that *picturesque?*). To that end, we tell you about the lighting, tools, and techniques you need to prepare images that show off every item's good side. We also offer advice on handling the digital files after you get that great picture. What we won't do is fill your head with lots of jargon and unnecessary manual adjustments; you just find out how to take good pictures that picture your goods right — and sell them.

Chapter 10

Choosing and Knowing Your Camera

In This Chapter

▶ Spending the fewest dollars possible

▶ Discovering the magic of digital cameras

▶ Figuring out what the gizmos do

▶ Working the buttons

*Y*our digital camera is the heart of your eBay operation (okay, maybe your computer is the heart, but this book is about photography and HTML, so give us a little leeway here). Without quality photos, your listings end up blah and unattractive. You need alluring pictures to catch the eye of the buyer.

Your pictures tell the story of your item, and if the item looks off-color or out of focus, odds are it won't seem as appealing to your prospective customers. Retailers — those who know you're an eBay seller — will play on your goal of taking appealing photos — and if they think you're not savvy about digital cameras, they may steer you toward an omnifunctional, complex (and did we mention, *pricey?*) model.

Reading this chapter sets you straight, and helps you save time and money when you choose and use your digital camera. The decision's not that hard; don't let an overzealous salesperson talk you into spending unnecessary bucks. You can buy a simple camera that allows minor adjustments. You accomplish the rest of the photography magic with the proper setup (and we tell you about setting up in Chapter 13).

Deciding How Much to Spend

Thinking about your target price and how much you want to spend is nice; in theory. If you're anything like us, once you're faced with an array of cameras (which tend to look all the same — even after first glance) you start to get picky and look for the one with the most horsepower — or options in this case. Remember that for eBay photography more horsepower is purely unnecessary. If you'd *like* to spend $500 on a camera, you may, but you'll be using only a fraction of the camera's abilities for your eBay pictures. You can find a perfectly suitable camera for your online photography needs for under $150. You can use a high-dollar camera for family photos, but a basic one is all you need for eBay.

Soon-to-be-big-time sellers, just starting out in an eBay business (with no experience on the site), seem compelled to go out and buy the most expensive digital camera with scads of megapixels (more about those in a minute). Maybe that's a macho thing — but realistically, it's overkill. For eBay images, there are a few important (and some merely desirable) features to look for when you're shopping for a digital camera. Here's our short list:

- **Optical versus digital zoom.** *Zoom* is the feature you need to get close-ups when you photograph smaller or more detailed items in the macro setting (say, the fine inlay on that banjo you're selling).

  - *Digital zoom* is the latest hocus-pocus from the camera industry. It simulates what happens when you shoot moving pictures with a camcorder and zoom in, enlarging a picture in much the same way as image-editing software: It centers the focus over half the focal plane (the camera's focusing area), and uses software interpolation (computer magic) to enlarge the picture — which may make your image slightly fuzzy.

  - *Optical zoom,* on the other hand, harkens back to the fine lenses used in traditional photography. No software tricks here, just old-fashioned glass and light: Optical zoom is produced through magnification from the camera's lens, using the camera's internal lens optics to produce a vivid picture. Professional photographers spend big bucks on lenses, and the zoom lens is one of the most important. Select a camera with the highest optical-zoom value you can afford.

  Figure 10-1 shows one place to look to find out whether your camera has optical zoom.

  If you've used a regular single-lens reflex camera, you might find it useful to note that a 3x optical zoom gives you results equivalent to what you'd get from a 35mm to 105mm zoom lens.

Figure 10-1:
The camera company shows you the difference in zoom.

🖛 **Megapixels.** A *megapixel* is a unit of measurement reflecting resolution when the number of pixels is equal to or greater than one million. For example, multiply the active horizontal by active vertical pixels in a full computer display (1280 × 1024) and you get 1,310,720 pixels — basically a 1.3-megapixel image!

The more megapixels, the more detailed your image will be. Your images can be enlarged without losing precious detail. Fun, but not always practical for eBay image photography; we *don't* need 'em (mega-megapixels, that is). Here's why: If you use a high resolution, multi-megapixel image on eBay, it will either look huge on your listing page (taking up the entire screen), or the file size will be so pixel-bloated that it could take several minutes for the image to load. No point in showing a high-res image to customers who have already moved on.

For online use, all you need from a camera is 800 × 600 pixels because the average computer display is incapable of taking advantage of more pixels.

🖛 **Power Supply.** When you're picking out your camera, be sure to check into the length of time the camera's battery will hold a charge. The last thing you want is to run out of juice at the wrong moment. Even though you may adore having a huge LCD on the back of the camera for image preview, those things burn power like there's no tomorrow! Consider the following:

- Look for a camera battery with at *least* three hours of photo-taking time.

- Keep a spare battery on hand.

  Marsha likes to keep a Lithium CR-V3 battery (which substitutes nicely in many cameras for the two AA batteries) in her purse so she'll be prepared if her camera battery runs low while she's on the road. CR-V3s seem to last forever!

- Invest in a charger and rechargeable lithium ion batteries.

We recommend that you get rechargeable backup batteries for all your cameras. These batteries last a long time and are worth the cost of investment.

✔ **Memory storage.** Many cameras have up to 10 megabytes of internal memory. This means you can store up to that amount, without using any external removable storage media. You retrieve images held in memory with a hard-wired connection to your computer. Most cameras also have removable media.

Your computer may have appropriate slots for inserting and reading media, but you may also need an external media-reader if your computer isn't so outfitted. Consider it as the equivalent of a teeny disk drive for the little cards; you insert 'em into the reader to transfer the data into your computer. You can buy a new USB reader on eBay for as little as $20.00 — and various removable storage media (as illustrated in Figure 10-2) are currently available:

- **Floppy disks:** Sony has a line of Mavica cameras that save images to a regular 3½-inch floppy disk. After taking your pictures, you just remove the floppy and put it into your A: drive. Voilà! The pictures are available to your computer for copying to a directory on your hard drive, cropping, and uploading.

- **CompactFlash memory card:** This is a small medium, slightly smaller than a matchbook. There are also readers for a laptop's PCMCIA slot. CompactFlash cards come in different sizes, holding from 16MB to 2GB of memory capacity.

- **Secure digital card:** The smallest incarnation of mini-storage is the secure digital card, an amazing little piece of technology in a postage-stamp size — and also one of the most durable. It's encased in plastic, as are the CompactFlash card and the Memory Stick, and it uses metal connector contacts (rather than pins and plugs like other cards) — making it less prone to damage. These cards can be set to hold up to one gigabyte, but more commonly hold 256 to 512MB.

- **SmartMedia cards:** A SmartMedia card — slightly smaller than a Compact Flash card — is very thin and has no plastic outer case. It's only used in a few brands of digital cameras (such as Olympus). SmartMedia cards come in different data sizes, and hold from 8MB to 128MB.

- **Memory Stick:** This tiny media card is about the size of piece of chewing gum and as long as an AA battery. The Memory Stick — a Sony device used in most Sony products (cameras, PCs, and video recorders) — can now hold as much as 2GB of memory. One of the great things about a Memory Stick is that it can be used in numerous devices.

- **Mini CD, CD/RW and DVD:** These mini-optical discs hold tons of images for eBay, as much as 185MB. You can read them right in your computer's CD or DVD reader. If you look at the disc platter of your computer's CD or DVD drive, you'll notice a smaller round indentation. This is to hold the mini-disc format.

You may find that you use more than one type of medium with your digital camera. And because you can record any type of digital data on these removable media, you may find other uses for them. For example, when you want to back up files or move larger files from a desktop to a laptop, you can transfer them via your digital media. Simply copy the files from your desktop computer onto the medium (say, a Sony Memory Stick), plug the medium into the port or adapter on the laptop, and copy the files.

Figure 10-2: There's quite a variety of digital media available to store your images.

✔ **Tripod mount:** Have you ever had a camera hanging around your neck while you're trying to repackage some eBay merchandise that you've just photographed? Or perhaps you've set down the camera for a minute and then can't find it? Avoid this hassle by using a tripod to hold your camera. Tripods also help you avoid the blurry pictures that result from a shaky grip on the camera. To use a tripod, you need a *tripod mount,* the little screw hole that you see at the bottom of some cameras. (The upcoming section gives you some tips on how to find the right tripod.)

✔ **Macro-setting capability or threading for a lens adapter:** These features will come in handy if you plan to photograph coins, jewelry, or small, detailed items. A camera's *macro setting* enables you to get in really close to items while keeping them in focus. Usually the macro mode can focus as close as 1 inch and as far away as 10 inches. A small flower icon in the camera's menu normally signifies the macro setting. A threaded lens mount is an alternative that enables you to screw in different types of lenses to give the camera macro-focus capability.

The average camera's *focal length* (focus range) is from 3 feet to infinity. If your camera says its macro-focus range is set at 5.1 inches, it means you can't focus it clearly on an object any closer than 5.1 inches. Macro pictures require a steady hand; any vibration can blur your image. Some of the newest hot-shot, high-dollar cameras have a feature called *image stabilization*, which automatically compensates for the shakiest of hands.

✔ **White-balance setting:** Most eBay digital photographers set the camera's white balance to Auto and hope for the best. Look for a camera that allows you to *adjust* the white balance. (This can be a bit tricky, so we show you how to make this adjustment later in the chapter.) Keep in mind that different manufacturers use different presets. The list of options can include settings for incandescent lights, twilight, fluorescent lights, outdoor, indoor, or shade. All these lighting situations have different color temperatures. It's worthwhile to take the time to play with the various white-balance settings of your camera in the different places where you normally photograph eBay merchandise. While you're experimenting, always take notes on the settings you use; that way, you can identify which ones give you the truest colors in your digital images.

At the end of the day, we recommend that you buy a brand-name camera. Marsha uses a Sony Mavica FD92 mounted to a Cloud Dome (an apparatus that diffuses light, see Chapter 14 for how to use it) for jewelry and coin pictures. She also keeps a Nikon CoolPix 3200 around for shooting images of . . . well . . . just about everything else. It turns out that her Sony Mavica DSC-H1 is far, far too much camera for eBay images. The FD92 may be outdated, but it has all the bells and whistles needed for eBay photos (that is, not too many). It stores images on a Sony Memory Stick or on a floppy disk, which are simple to pop out and insert into the computer.

AUCTION ANECDOTE

An oldie-but-goodie Mavica . . .

Marsha just got off the phone with one of eBay's top sellers. She asked him what kind of camera he uses for his eBay product photography. Sheepishly, he replied that he uses several cameras from the early Sony Mavica FD series. He was using the almost-antique FD73 model (vintage 1999) with a 10x optical zoom. Marsha countered that she loved her FD73, recommended it to everyone, and finally sold it to another eBay seller who *really* wanted one. Marsha recommended that camera in her books as the best until she snapped up the Mavica FD92, which came out in 2001. This model is almost ideally designed for online photography. Here are some of the features:

Resolution: 1.3-megapixel CCD, 1472x1104

Zoom: 8x optical, 16x digital

Media: 3.5" Floppy Disk and/or a Memory Stick

Auto Contrast Detect, Auto focus: 9.8" to infinity

Macro Auto focus: 1.2" minimum

Computer connection: Connects with Macs and PCs via an included USB cable.

All this, plus the FD92 has a crisp, 2.5-inch color LCD screen for previewing images, a rechargeable InfoLithium battery, and a quick battery charger.

Marsha still uses her Mavica, and keeps it permanently attached to her Cloud Dome for capturing macro images. (See Chapter 14 for more on the Cloud Dome tabletop photography studio for jewelry and tiny items.) How convenient is it that you can store up to 30 pictures (in Web resolution) on a floppy disk and then pop the disk into your computer to transfer the images without cables or messing with software? And if your computer has no floppy disk drive, you can use the camera's memory-stick slot with a Sony Memory Stick (which holds so many photos that Marsha has never filled it up!).

When budget is also a factor in the purchase decision (and when isn't it?), savvy eBay shoppers find deals on lower-resolution cameras (3 megapixels or less). Because much of the world's population is upgrading to mucho-megapixel cameras, the displaced — but still perfectly good — low-resolution cameras show up for sale on eBay for a pittance. (We bet you could find a camera that fits your needs right now on eBay for considerably less than $150.) You can be right there to snap up the deals! And remember that many professional camera stores also sell used equipment.

Checking Out the Important Parts

Strangely (or not so strangely), digital cameras are pretty much the same from manufacturer to manufacturer. Take a look at Figure 10-3, which shows you two of Marsha's cameras. Notice that several gizmos on the cameras seem to be the same — whether the camera is a Nikon or a Sony.

Many of the buttons are self-explanatory (*Shutter button = push here to take picture*), while others are a bit more esoteric. Figure 10-3 shows a sampling.

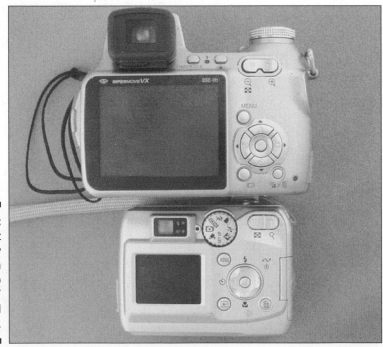

Figure 10-3: Check out the similarity between these two cameras' gizmos and buttons.

Marsha's lovely mannequin Midge models a beautiful dress. Check out those wicked shadows (left photo) that appear on the wall when you use straight floodlights. Such lighting affects the background of the image and puts harsh shadows on the apparel. By using wings or panels (the poor man's photographer's umbrellas; see Chapter 12), you can smooth out the lighting and get a much more pleasing appearance (right photo).

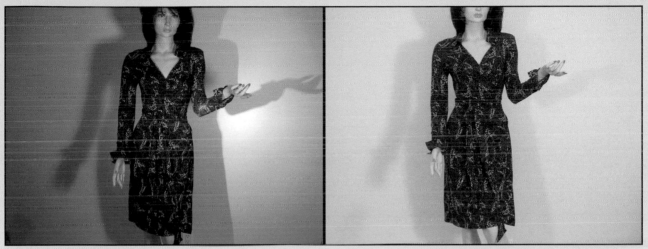

Photo taken with straight floodlights.   Photo of Midge taken with diffusion panels (wings).

This charming Toby jug was photographed twice: once with regular floodlights and once in a photo tent. Notice how the photo tent knocks out glare and gives you a good look at the item. When Patti saw these pictures, she thought the floodlight version made ol' Henry appear to be smirking. See how lighting can affect your images?

Photo taken with regular floodlights.   Photo taken in a photo tent.

Here's a colorful little teapot that Marsha plans to sell on eBay; of course, she wants the color to look just right in the listing. Without filtering the floodlight to remove glare, Marsha took several pictures with different types of light bulbs.

An incandescent bulb with ambient (also incandescent) room light.

A compact fluorescent bulb.

Halogen Bright White PAR 20 mini-floodlight.

Believe it or not, the White Balance was set to automatic — on a brand new, state-of-the-art digital camera! Just look at the variance in color you get with different light sources (see Chapter 12 to get your light right).

GE Reveal bulb.

5000°K True Color lamp.

Full-spectrum compact fluorescent 5500°K (CRI 93).

The photos on the next four pages were not retouched by image-editing software. These jewelry and coin images were shot in the same lighting with and without a Cloud Dome. (*Note:* Marsha turned off the camera's flash and may have used additional lighting.)

Images shot without the Cloud Dome.

Notice Marsha's reflection in the necklace!

The differences are striking! Notice how using the Cloud Dome smooths out the images: no glare, no burnout, no harsh edges, and no unwanted reflection. Chapter 14 shows how to take pictures with the Cloud Dome.

Images shot with the Cloud Dome.

Rhinestones and coins benefit from the diffused light of the Cloud Dome. The images on this page show hot spots (no Cloud Dome used here!).

The Cloud Dome helps you get truer images with marvelous detail.

Varying the colors and fonts you use can be an attractive way to highlight important information or soften the look of your listings. But color and variety used unwisely can drive buyers away. Just check out the figures on this page. The top figure presents a glaring example of bad color and font choices. The bottom figure demonstrates a more conservative approach (we're the masters of understatement), but results in a listing that a buyer could actually read. Refer to Part II for guidance on using HTML to dress up (but not overdress) your eBay listings.

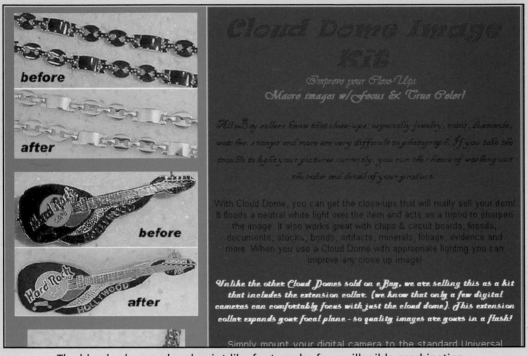

The blue background and script-like fonts make for an illegible combination.

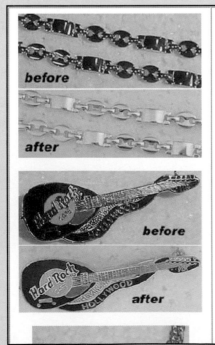

Cloud Dome Image Kit
Improve your Close-Ups:
Macro Images w/Focus & True Color!

All eBay sellers know that close-ups -- especially jewelry, coins, diamonds, watches, stamps and more -- are very difficult to photograph. If you take the trouble to light your pictures correctly, you run the risk of washing out the color and detail of your product. With Cloud Dome, you can get the close-ups that will really sell your item! It floods a neutral white light over the item and acts as a tripod to sharpen the image. It also works great with chips & circuit boards, fossils, documents, stocks, bonds, artifacts, minerals, foliage, evidence, and more. When you use a Cloud Dome with appropriate lighting, you can improve *any* close-up image!

Unlike the other Cloud Domes sold on eBay, we are selling this as a kit that *includes* the extension collar (we know that only a few digital cameras can comfortably focus with just the Cloud Dome). This extension collar expands your focal plane -- so quality images are yours in a flash!

Simply mount your digital <u>camera</u> to the Standard Universal bracket, set the Cloud Dome on the extension collar, and take your pictures. **This sale is for one (1) Cloud Dome, one (1) coated white Standard Universal Bracket, one (1) extension collar with instructions.**

Ah, much better! The listing still sports some variety, but is quite easy to read.

Most digital cameras have the following dials and switches:

✔ **Zoom toggle:** These two buttons, generally placed toward the top of the camera (as shown in Figure 10-4), function very simply: Press one side and the camera zooms in (gets closer); press the other side, and the camera zooms out (gets further away).

Figure 10-4: The zoom toggle works pretty intuitively.

✔ **Optical viewfinder:** Just as on a trusty old (and we mean old) Brownie camera, you have the option of viewing your subject through a viewfinder versus using the LCD screen. If you've ever tried to look at an LCD screen in sunny, bright conditions, you'll know the value of alternative viewing. LCDs are rendered pretty useless in the sun; they just aren't bright enough for accurate viewing.

✔ **Mode dial:** Here's a look (in Figure 10-5) at magically quick tool that enhances your control over your camera. You can choose from a plethora of settings that make your camera do technical magic — for example, portrait mode for taking pictures of your loved ones and fireworks mode for taking images of nighttime fireworks exhibitions — although (sadly) very little of this fun stuff is useful for eBay purposes (where generally you just set your camera on auto and shoot). Have fun with the various modes when you take your trusty camera out for a walk — or on vacation!

✔ **Control button:** The control button (sometimes more than one) is usually a quick toggle for five basic functions. Pressing in the center usually finalizes your selection from among these:

   • **Flash control:** Here you click to force the flash to go off (whether or not the camera thinks it should) or to turn off the flash. Having that kind of sayso is often useful when you're trying not to wash out details with too much light.

- **Macro photography:** You can only zoom into your item so far with the toggle buttons, but when you push this button to set the Macro mode, you may be able (depending on your camera) to zoom in your focus as close as a couple of inches — accurately!

- **Self-timer:** Yawn. Use this when you have the camera set on a tripod and want to jump into the image with your spouse before the shutter goes off.

- **Image review:** Shows you the last image you shot, putting it in the LCD screen for quality review.

- **Menu selectors:** Thought you caught us stumped, eh? Well, yeah, there are only *four* buttons or directions on this control — but then there are the menus. When you select the Setup mode from the Mode dial (or another button on your camera that might say *Menu*), you can use these buttons to make selections and go up or down the menus.

Figure 10-5:
Here's a look at Sony and Nikon mode-dial features. Check out the subtle differences.

Making the Magic Setting(s) for Quality Images

I know, I know, you don't have a good picture unless it's in focus. We'll give you that. But in our experience, focus isn't the biggest issue that eBay photographers have to face. Often a photographed item is masked with too much shadow or washed out by too much light (we help you resolve both these excesses in Chapter 12). The complexity of producing accurate colors in your photos can easily become the more dreaded issue.

Never fear! Chapter 14 shows you how you can control color reproduction in special situations. But before diving into that topic, consider: You can turn to one simple-to-set control — White Balance — to improve color right away. The good news is that most digital cameras have one.

White balance

White balance is sort of the digital equivalent of a good laundry detergent — it makes sure your whites stay white instead of turning yellow — and that helps keep the other colors vibrant. Take a look at our color insert to see the results of setting the white balance in a product photo. You'll notice that taking photos with particular light bulbs (and *no other* ambient lighting) alters the colors of the resulting pictures. Table 10-1 outlines how different types of lighting will affect your images.

Table 10-1	Image Color as Affected by Light
Type of Light	*Results During Exposure*
Daylight	Turns out white (about the best you can get)
Cloudy	Sets a blue/gray cast on everything
Fluorescent light	Tinges everything a nasty bluish
Incandescent bulb	Casts the entire photo in reddish-yellowish ickyness

Most top-name cameras will have a setting to cover all the lighting situations listed in Table 10-1. These settings work very well, but you have to remember to set up your camera *for each shooting session.* (You can find the instructions for making these settings in your camera's manual, or online.) We've had success with all modes except Incandescent. That yellow cast from regular lighting is a bear to get rid of. If you use regular light bulbs in your lights, we suggest counteracting the "incandescent yellows" by using a full-spectrum white-light bulb (such as the GE Reveal) or a halogen-type bulb.

Your camera may also have an "auto" (automatic) White Balance (WB) setting. This setting will work *sometimes* — when you have perfectly balanced lighting for your items (sadly, we can't claim that positive experience). If you really want best results, set the white balance manually. It's usually as easy as pressing the right button to let the camera's computer take a look at the ambient lighting and make its own adjustments.

Chapter 11

Outfitting Your Studio

A bad workman blames his tools — we've certainly heard that time and again. Coincidentally, blaming the tools is also a common phenomenon amongst eBay sellers who just can't get a decent photo. Personally, we feel the problem stems from laziness — on two fronts. Some sellers don't take enough time to get the picture quality that's necessary to display their items. Nor do they take the time to set up their pictures properly before shooting — for example, shooting a picture of a crystal vase against a white backdrop (versus a black one) makes the vase to blend totally into the background and prevents the viewer from seeing any details.

Simple, small things, such as props and backdrops, can help you build a good informal photo studio. But don't go nuts thinking that you need to outfit your studio all at once — that's an ongoing venture (at least it is for us — we add items continually) over many years. A well-stocked studio for shooting online photos stays current with the latest "tricks of the trade." This chapter lets you in on the details of the essential equipment and accessories you need — and how to use them.

Storing Your Studio Equipment

We realize that the entire population of eBay sellers may not have as much room as Marsha does for her eBay photo studio. At least that used to be the case. Marsha used to have an entire room set up just for prepping the merchandise and shooting the pictures. Now most of that room is filled with shelves of merchandise for eBay — but, oops, that's a different book!

Letting the chips fall where they may

The wonderful (and demanding) thing about having an eBay business is that you need to be ready for anything. True entrepreneurs often find themselves in a situation where they can make money selling something that's outside the realm of their usual items. For example, we just heard of one such instance from a fellow eBay-seller friend and his wife. They usually sell random electronics and computer parts, but they recently came upon a box of old casino chips while visiting a local estate sale. Their listing reads, "We acquired this and many other rare casino chips from an estate sale of an 82-year-old woman. The chips were stored in a dry basement in a covered box and were apparently there since the early 1940s."

Being true eBay entrepreneurs, these sellers have two eBay User IDs: one for their regular business and another for buying and selling the oddball items they come across. But more to the point of this story is that they fortunately had a wide array of tools available in their photography studio, so they were able to produce a fine photo (shown in the sidebar) of this prized vintage casino chip.

The bidding started at $9.99 and ended seven days later at $39,345.00. A record price for a single casino chip!

Most sellers don't have a lot of space for a permanent studio — so making efficient use of the space you have is the name of the game. At the very least, keep all the supplies for your eBay photo studio in a few boxes that you can conveniently access at a moment's notice (no, that doesn't mean stored in the rafters of the garage). That way, when you want to start shooting pictures in the dining room, you can pull out whatever you need from your prepackaged boxes.

Many photography and lighting products sold on eBay come with their own storage boxes, so stowing these items is fairly easy. I suggest that you package your portable photo studio into several labeled boxes, broken down in the following manner:

- Lighting and tripods
- Cloud Dome
- Lighting panels and/or tents
- Props (backgrounds, risers)
- Cleaning supplies
- Apparel kit (items you use only when you photograph clothing)

If, due to lack of space, you wind up having to shoot on a usually cluttered kitchen counter or desktop (where you've shoved aside your paperwork and/or cat food), be sure to acquire and use an inexpensive *photo stage,* such as an infinity board — which you can see pictured in Figure 11-1 and (no surprise) you can find for sale on eBay pretty easily.

Stocking Up on Studio Essentials

At the outset, we want you to know that we're as cost-conscious as anyone (especially Marsha, who has been known on occasion to be outright cheap). In this chapter, we list some items that would help you prepare your online photo studio for almost any eventuality. But let's not be chintzy about it. Many other current books suggest that you put together temporary studio props out of cardboard and light filters out of cut pieces of shower curtain. By and large, if you're serious about your online business, skip the duct-tape solutions.

There are good reasons to purchase substantial, quality products for your photo studio:

- ✔ **Durability:** Products designed for a photo studio (even if they are entry-level and not top-dollar) are less likely to get crumpled and trashed.

- ✔ **Suitability:** Products made for a real photo studio are probably made so they won't catch on fire from your lights (a significant benefit).

- ✔ **Resale value:** Studio equipment maintains its value while you use it. Although this may be the least important reason to furnish your studio with quality products, if you decide that this business isn't for you, you can always resell your photo studio equipment to someone else.

In general, don't buy everything all at once! The exception is, of course, that rare deal you might find on complete kits — or if you buy a whole used photo studio from another seller who may be retiring from the online selling game (although we can't imagine who might consider retiring)!

Getting the basics

Besides a camera, an effective photo studio needs several basic pieces of lighting and background equipment — fortunately, they're pretty straightforward and aren't that hard to find. If you're selling particular types of merchandise, you may need, say, a mannequin to display clothing or an easel to display artwork. If you sell a variety of items, then you can use all such extras you can lay your hands on. Marsha is a bit of a gadget freak; her photo studio seems to sprout new ones all the time — Cloud Domes, tripods, light panels — to make photo-taking easier.

Be sure to double-check with your tax person, but in most cases the money you spend for photo-studio equipment becomes a write-off for your profitable eBay business.

There are really only two things you can't do without — besides your camera — in your photo studio:

- ✔ **Lights:** You need a floodlight with a reflector — and something to hold the light in place — either a clamp or a traditional light stand. No need to spend big bucks here, although it's best to use lights designed specifically for photography (lights made to illuminate a garage for nighttime automotive work are not exactly what you need).

   You can also use a small tabletop true-light lamp for illuminating smaller items. Be sure your bulb is rated at least 5000 K, where *K* stands for *Kelvin*, a measurement of light's color temperature. See the sidebar, "Checking out the Kelvin (K) rating" for more on this aspect of lighting.

✔ **Backgrounds/backdrops:** Here's where you use your imagination. A backdrop can be almost any solid-color surface (whether painted or draped) that provides a contrasting background for your image photography. Remember, your goal is to show the product — not lay out a museum piece. The only thing you want a picture of is your item; a clean, solid surface behind it makes the item easy to see but doesn't call attention to the background. Here are some suggestions:

- Backgrounds come in many shapes and sizes. You can get paper, fabric, or use a portable plastic photo stage for smallish items.

- In professional photo-talk, *seamless* is a large roll of 3-foot (and wider) paper that comes in various colors and is suspended and draped behind the model and over the floor so the model seems to be floating in infinity — and is instantly the center of attention. Photographers also drape seamless over tabletop shots, or use fabrics such as muslin instead.

- We recommend using wrinkle-free backdrops in neutral colors — such as white, light gray, "natural," and black — for photographing your merchandise. That way, the color of the paper or fabric doesn't clash with or distract from your items.

For taking a picture anywhere, indoors or out, a portable photo stage is a valuable tool. It's made of a textured plastic made to be set in a curved shape; the stage rests on any surface and permits you to take a clean picture without any extraneous stuff in the background. You can use a photo stage to achieve an infinity look by curving the background under the item, as shown in Figure 11-1. Best of all, you can store it flat on a bookshelf until you need it next.

Figure 11-1:
An item being photographed on an infinity background.

Checking out some common setups

Take a look at Figures 11-2 through 11-4. They show you several of Marsha's photo setups — and as you can see, she's about ready to photograph nearly anything that comes her way.

The original home photo studio (shown in Figure 11-2), is a super beginner's setup. It has a black backdrop, a white backdrop (pictured), and can be set up anywhere in the house. In the background, notice the light-diffusing device for specialty photos such as macro jewelry shots (Marsha uses a Cloud Dome quite a bit for that these days).

Figure 11-2:
Marsha's
original
eBay photo
setup.

Figure 11-3 shows another option: a pure white photo cube, lit with either small clamp lights (shown) or with tall floodlights. A photo cube works well for finely detailed and collectible objects — as well as any other object that will fit in it. Using a translucent white fabric cube, you can fully illuminate your item without glare, harsh shadows, or detail burnout!

In Figure 11-4, you can see how to change a photo setup to accommodate large items by placing Lite-Wings(r) light panels on tall *floodlights* (regular lights inside hemispherical aluminum reflectors, mounted on adjustable stands). With a setup like this, you can get close to the same effect as you get when using a Cloud Cube on a table — but for much larger items! Traditionally photographers used expensive, umbrellalike reflectors for this purpose — but the umbrellas required special mounts for the light stands, and the Lite-Wings attach simply with Velcro.

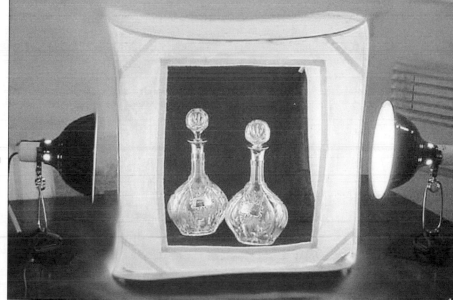

Figure 11-3:
Using a photo cube on a dining-room table to photograph antiques.

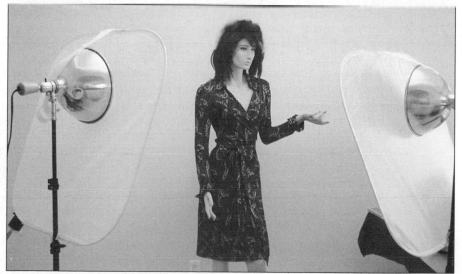

Figure 11-4:
Flood lights illuminating Midge, Marsha's mannequin and star of many an auction.

Checking out the Kelvin (K) rating

You can get some good buys in true-color light bulbs on eBay. Such lights usually have a Kelvin rating of 5,000 or higher. *Kelvin* (K) is the standard unit used to measure color temperature, or the degree of warmth or coolness of a light source. Higher Kelvin temperature produces fuller color spectrum in the light. The higher the K, the bluer — or cooler — the light appears. The lower the K, the more red light is present, and the warmer the lamp appears. Take a look at the following chart; it gives the various Kelvin ratings for common everyday light sources.

Kelvin Temperature Rating (Degrees)	Light Source
1200 K	Candlelight
2680 K	40W incandescent lamp
3000 K	Studio lamps
3200 K	Sunrise/sunset
3400 K	Tungsten lamp
5000 K	Electronic flash and standard daylight (also designated by the symbol D50, which stands for "Daylight 5000 K")
5500 K	Midday sun
7000 K	Lightly overcast sky
8000 K	Hazy sky

Adding on Other Valuable Equipment

The basics are great, but (as with any venture worth doing right), there will always be things you can add to your arsenal of tools to improve your pictures. We're constantly adding new stuff to our photo studios (most recently, Marsha's new set of risers — gotta love those gadgets). All professionals have a bag of tricks, and you might find that the tools in this section are more than you thought you'd need for photographing your items.

Good photographs can help sell your merchandise, so to take this part of your business seriously. If you sell only one type of item, you won't need such a varied selection of photography tools, but you should have the basic photo setup and a few extras.

Tripod

A *tripod* is an extendable aluminum stand that holds your camera. Look for one that has a quick release so that if you want to take the camera off the tripod for a close-up, you don't have to unscrew it from the base and then screw it back on for the next picture.

The legs should extend to your desired height, lock in place with clamp-type locks, and have a crank-controlled, geared center column so you can move your camera up and down for different shots. Most tripods also have a panning head for shooting from different angles. You can purchase a tripod from a camera store, or on eBay for as little as $25.

Power supplies

If you've ever used digital cameras, you know that they can suck the life out of batteries faster than sugar through a five-year-old. A reliable, consistent power supply is a must. You can keep the power flowing in a couple of ways:

- ✔ **Rechargeable batteries:** Many specialists on eBay sell rechargeable batteries and chargers. Choose quality Ni-MH (nickel metal hydride) batteries because this kind, unlike Ni-Cad (nickel cadmium) batteries, has no memory effect. That means you don't have to totally discharge them.

- ✔ **Lithium-ion batteries:** Lithium batteries are the longest-lasting and lightest batteries available, but they're also expensive. Or at least they were. Then some smart cookie figured out a way to put two batteries into one unit; considerably cutting the price. This new battery can average 650 photos before you have to change it. The CR-V3 is a new kind of battery that takes the place of two standard AA batteries. It is also available in a rechargeable form, thereby extending the life even further (and reducing your battery budget significantly).

If your eBay photo studio includes a camera on a tripod (and it should — basics, right?), then you can use a good old-fashioned AC adapter (you know, it's the one that plugs into the wall) to generate low-cost power for your battery-powered studio gadgetry. Just be sure to get one that's compatible with your devices.

Props — for example, a mannequin

To take good photos, you need some props. Although you may think it strange that a line item in your accounting program will read *props,* they do qualify as a business expense. (Okay, you can put it under *photography expenses — props* just sounds so Hollywood!)

How often have you seen some clothing on eBay from a quality manufacturer, but just couldn't bring yourself to bid more than $10 because it looked like it had been dragged behind a car and then hung on a hanger before it was photographed? Could you see how the fabric would hang on a body? Of course not. But take a look at Figure 11-5 — *that* dress looks simply fantastic, darling!

Figure 11-5:
Midge the
Mannequin,
modeling for
a successful
eBay sale.

If you're selling clothing, you'd better photograph it on a mannequin. If you don't want to dive right in and buy a mannequin, at least get a body form to wear the outfit. Just search eBay for *mannequin* to find hundreds of hollow forms selling for less than $20. If you sell children's clothing, get a child's mannequin form as well. The same goes for men's clothes. If worst comes to worst, find a friend to model the clothes. There's just no excuse for hanger-displayed merchandise in your auctions.

Marsha got her mannequin "Midge" at a department store's liquidation sale in Los Angeles — and paid all of $25 for her. Well, okay, maybe her face is a little bit creepy (the solution is often to crop her head out of the photos), but she has a great body — and everything she wears sells at a profit. Many stores upgrade their mannequins every few years or so. If you know people who work at a retail store, ask when they plan to sell their old mannequins; you may be able to pick one up at a reasonable price.

Display stands, risers, and more

Jewelry doesn't photograph well on a human being. Most people's hands and necks aren't exactly works of art (that's why there are professional "hand models" and such). Your item will look a lot better when you display it on a stand (see Figure 11-6) or a velvet pad.

Figure 11-6:
Various risers and stands can be used to improve your pictures.

If you're selling a necklace, display it on a necklace stand (or photograph it flat using a Cloud Dome — the ultimate light-gadget for jewelry — see Chapter 14). Marsha bought her necklace-display stand from a manufacturer but had to wait several months to receive it. Apparently, this type of quality display stand is made to order, so a more economical way (in both time and money!) to search for a stand is — you guessed it — on eBay. (You'll get it sooner and probably cheaper.)

Risers can be almost anything stairlike that you use to prop up your item to make it more attractive in a picture. If your riser isn't all that attractive, put it under the cloth you use as a background. Keep a collection of risers and propping materials in your photo area so they're always close at hand.

You wouldn't believe what the back of some professional photo setups look like. Photographers and photo stylists think resourcefully when it comes to making the merchandise look good — from the *front* of the picture, anyway! Throughout years of working with professional photographers, we've seen the most creative things used to prop up items for photography:

- **Bottles of mercury or (better yet) sand:** Mercury is a heavy liquid metal. A photographer Marsha once worked with used little bottles of this stuff to prop up small boxes and other items in a picture. But mercury is a poison, so we suggest you do your propping up with small bottles (prescription bottles work well) filled with *sand*.

- **Museum Gel or Quake Hold:** These two products are invaluable when you want to hold small objects like jewelry at unnatural angles for a photograph. (They're like beeswax and clay, but cleaner.) Quake Hold is used by the leading museums in earthquake territory to keep valuable artifacts from careening off the table when the inevitable earthquake occurs. The clear version, Museum Gel, is often difficult to remove from items; we recommend using Quake Hold instead for your eBay items.

  A single packet of Quake Hold (that much will last you nearly forever) is only about $6. Although plain old clay is a cheaper alternative, it can leave grease spots on paper and fabrics.

- **un-du:** If your items have stickers or sticker residue on them, the gunk is bound to show up in the picture — and your customers won't be too thrilled with sticker goo on their items. Squirt on a little un-du on the sticker area and use the included (and patented!) scraper to remove the sticky stuff and bring back the shine. un-du is getting hard to find, so we've used old-fashioned lighter fluid to accomplish the same task. (*Please* be careful if you try that!)

- **WD-40:** Clean your item's plastic or cellophane with WD-40 (no kidding); unbelievably, it takes off any icky smudges. Just spray a tiny bit on a paper towel, and use the paper towel to polish the plastic surface. Don't spray right on the article — it's an oily mixture and you don't want accidental stains on the surrounding cardboard.

Almost any cleaning solution can help your items (sometimes even a little 409), but use these chemicals with care so you don't damage — or destroy — the item while cleaning it.

✔ **Kneaded-rubber art eraser:** Keep one around to clean off small dirt smudges on paper items. Use it just the way you did in school: rub, rub, rub then brush off the dirt.

✔ **Clothespins and duct tape:** (You know . . . the stuff that holds the universe together.) These multipurpose items are used in many photo shoots in some of the strangest places. For example, If your mannequin is a few sizes too small for the dress you want to photograph, don't pad the mannequin; simply fold over the dress in the back and clamp the excess material with a metal clamp or a bunch of clothespins. You can also use a small piece of duct tape — or, better, gaffer's tape — to hold the fabric taut. (You can find the magic non-sticky, non-glossy gaffer's tape at theatrical supply stores — or inquire at your local television station and find out where it gets its supply.)

Software

You're also going to need some photo-editing software to use on your computer to touch up your images. We love the Fast Photos program because it's quick to master and easy to use, but in Chapter 16, we show you some other excellent software packages — and show you how to use them.

Chapter 12

Getting the Right Light (Or the Light Right)

In This Chapter

▶ Flashing your subject — or not

▶ Learning about bulbs

▶ Deciding what lighting works for you

▶ Setting up the lights

*L*ighting is the key to quality pictures. As you've probably already discovered, it can also be your greatest challenge. These days, even the least expensive digital camera can deliver enough quality to take great pictures. The problem we really have is with the lighting, and here's the long and short of it:

✔ Lighting is what brings out the best in your item. Look at any catalog. When a shopper is looking at merchandise that they can't touch or look at up close, they must have a good photo to look at to discern the quality of the item at hand. If you don't show the details in your item, chances are your item won't sell for the highest amount possible.

✔ Lighting can be as simple as your daughter holding a flashlight on your item in a fully lit room to pick up extra detail while you take the picture. (Maybe that sounds clumsy, but Marsha has lived this scenario — and sometimes a simple solution works best.)

Marsha's philosophy of eBay photography

High-end digital cameras bristle with settings, for many technical reasons that pro photographers appreciate. The dazzling array of controls for aperture, shutter speed, and such are for using the camera in manual mode instead of automatic. With study and practice, you can make some amazing works of art with your digital camera. If you want to play with all those buttons — when you have buckets of time — great. But we're running a business here . . .

Read this paragraph several times until you commit its message to memory. Your eBay photography objective is to take the best images humanly possible; *in the shortest period of time.* And the goal of this book is to help you do that. Too many eBay sellers spend their time shooting works of art. A work of art is something that is supposed to last forever. These pictures are supposed to last for seven days. You take them to sell your item and then you disposed of them.

Here's the one rule to follow when photographing items for eBay: *Take the best picture you can and move on to the next item* so you can list all the items for you have for sale without taking forever. Period.

What's the best way to shoot for eBay? Assembly line (Henry Ford had it right). Have everything assembled in one area and the process can go smoothly and quickly. This sidebar establishes the mindset, and this chapter tells you how to prepare your lighting to get the best picture for the least effort.

Chapter 11 tells you about light temperature and basic lighting setups — the building blocks for planning your photographic lighting. In this chapter, we show you the tools and types of lighting available, and describe how to best use them. You'll never really have to worry about photography's geeky technical side if you follow the recommendations in this book. And we strongly encourage you to read and digest the sidebar "Marsha's philosophy of eBay photography" to grasp the mindset that will help you crank out the right photos.

Using the Flash

The most basic, easiest way to light your pictures is with your digital camera's built-in flash. It's bright; usually color-balanced, and will illuminate your subject. A snap (so to speak), right? Well, as is often the case in life, the most obvious answer isn't always the best. Using your camera's flash can often *flash out* important small details in your image by hitting them with too much light (take a look at Figure 12-1 for a typically awful example). That sudden burst of light can also cause some wildly nasty shadows. Hmmmmm. Is your flash even worth using? Well, yes and (mostly) no.

Figure 12-1:
Notice how
the detail in
the fabric is
washed out
by the flash.

A digital camera's flash has several possible modes, and here are the ones that affect your online images.

✔ **Auto flash.** Cameras today are pretty smart. They know when you need a flash and when you don't — at least they *think* they're that smart. With this mode on, you relinquish all judgment to the little chip inside your camera. This means there's a good chance that you'll lose detail in the shadow areas and your highlights will flash out.

✔ **Forced flash.** When you set your camera in this mode, the flash will go off when you take a picture — even if you're shooting in bright sun and the camera wouldn't ordinarily think you need a flash. Oddly enough, that may be just when you *do* need a flash — overly bright outdoor light can often cause wicked shadows. By setting the flash to go off, you use it as a fill, illuminating shadowed areas to make a more detailed picture. Forced flash can be a friend when shooting your pictures in bright sun.

✔ **No flash.** This is the mode you'll use most often. Although camera makers try to make flash units that compliment your pictures, nobody can anticipate every possible lighting situation. If you've set up special lighting, the flash might only get in the way. Also, if you skip using the built-in flash, you can control a bit more of what appears in the picture.

Seeing the Light about Light Bulbs

Wow. Was this whole topic an education for us! We used to think that to illuminate our picture setups, all we needed was a light (remember the flashlight stunt a few paragraphs back?). But all light is not the same; the type of light source you use can have considerable impact on how the image of your item affects a potential customer. The sidebar "How hot is that look (in degrees Kelvin)?" takes a look at why.

Once you've soaked up the available enlightenment in this chapter, you'll be able to select bulbs for your photo lights quickly and correctly every time. We checked out many light bulbs and here's what we learned.

Getting warmer with incandescent bulbs

Incandescent bulbs are your standard light bulb as invented by Thomas Edison. Choosing would be simple if there were only one kind of incandescent bulb, but there's quite a variety.

 If you've ever wondered what's special about "tungsten" bulbs, the answer is — not much. Tungsten is in nearly all incandescent bulbs; it's the filament that glows white-hot when the electricity passes through. No surprise that only about 10 percent of the light they produce is in the visible spectrum — most of the energy they give off is in infrared (that is, heat)! That's why bulbs are often called "hot" lights (we talk about "cold" lights later on).

The average light bulb will last about 750 to 1,000 hours with normal usage. The heat the electricity generates causes the tungsten filament to evaporate and deposit bits of itself on the glass (ever notice the black spots on an old light bulb?).

How hot is that look (in degrees Kelvin)?

For a photographer, the Kelvin scale measures how "cool" or "warm" a light source appears. Color temperature isn't a matter of whether a light source will scorch your hand, but rather, what happens to the *color* of the light at different levels of energy. Any object will emit light if heated enough; a black metal, for example changes color as it's heated from a cold black to a white-hot state; as the actual temperature increases, the color shifts from red (getting hot) to orange to yellow (hotter) to white, and finally to a blue-white at its hottest. But *color temperature* actually turns that value upside-down, essentially evaluating light in terms of its esthetic effect: light from the red/orange/yellow side of the spectrum is described as "warm" — and light at the violet/blue end is referred to as "cool." In practical terms, incandescent light sources provide a "warmer" look than you get with the "cool" (very blue-white) light of standard fluorescents.

You can find variety in incandescent bulbs (Figure 12-2 shows you an assortment of incandescent bulbs — going from standard to blue photoflood):

✔ **Standard bulb:** The plain-vanilla, cheap-as-dirt bulb that you can buy at the average grocery store is probably the worst choice to illuminate your pictures. If you have taken online images with regular bulbs, you may have noticed that your pictures have a yellow tinge. That tinge takes a lot of tweaking (and time) in an image-editing program to remove. Not good. Not good at all.

✔ **Professional photoflood bulbs:** As an incandescent bulb deteriorates over time, it loses brightness — which is something a professional photographer can't waste time with. Photoflood bulbs are rated in actual Kelvin temperatures, and are guaranteed to maintain the light for the life of the bulb. Photoflood bulbs burn at 250 or 500 watts and can be purchased for under $5 each. They also come in a blue tint to produce a variety of daylight similar to the light you'd get at 3,200 or 4,800 degrees Kelvin. (The problem with those bulbs is that they can be rated for as short a life as 3 hours of guaranteed color temperature.)

Speaking of temperature, those babies burn incredibly hot! Remember that 90 percent of the bulb's energy goes into heat — and we're talking about a 500-watt bulb! Eeeyow! When you put these in the stock floodlights, the aluminum reflectors also get very, very hot. To be honest, we've found that we don't go near most bulbs for at least an hour after turning them off. When attempting to remove any light bulb, use a paper towel to grasp it; never touch a potentially hot bulb with your fingers!

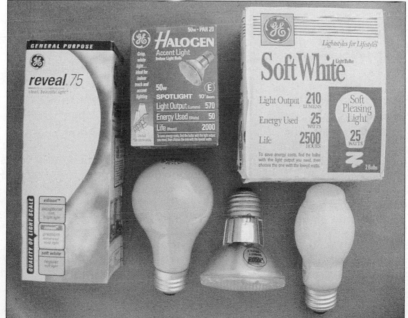

Figure 12-2:
The variety of incandescent light bulbs can be dizzying.

Table 12-1 shows the standard types of photoflood bulbs.

Table 12-1	Photoflood Bulb Types		
Bulb Type	*Watts*	*Color*	*Color Temperature*
BBA	250W	white	3400°K
BCA	250W	blue	4800°K
ECA	250W	white	3200°K
ECT	500W	white	3200°K
EBV	500W	white	3400°K
EBW	500W	blue	4800°K

✔ **General Electric Reveal bulbs:** This is a new and revolutionary type of bulb that's physically color-corrected, using the element neodymium in the glass to filter out the standard bulb's yellow rays. If all you can get hold of is a standard bulb, the GE Reveal is your best bet for your images. It casts a very nice white light and, if you adjust your white balance just once, you should get some very good online images.

This is a satisfactory and very cost-effective solution. You can buy a four-pack of GE Reveal bulbs for under $5, and GE projects their standard life at 1,000 hours.

Cooling it (the light, that is) with fluorescent bulbs

This is a horse, er *bulb*, of a different color. A florescent bulb is the "cool" version of the light bulb; it emits much more light than heat. Common fluorescent lamps are the long, tubular kind usually installed in offices, kitchens, and convenience stores. They're cheap to operate, but they're also the worst lights to use to illuminate your images (note that we're not referring to compact fluorescents — that's an entirely different kind of light). Unless your camera's white-balance control has a very accurate fluorescent setting, your images may come out with an annoying sparkly-greenish-blue tinge. There is no camera on the market today that can reproduce colors correctly under standard cool white fluorescent lighting. Just don't use it.

One reason you get such lousy color from a florescent light is the way it works: When current travels through a filament that goes from end to end of the glass tube, it bothers the heck out of inert gases in the tube (argon and a small amount of gaseous mercury) until they give off photons of ultraviolet light. The UV light (which normally just hangs around the "cool" end of the color spectrum being invisible) reacts with the white phosphor coating of the bulb to produce bright, visible light.

✔ **Compact fluorescent (CF):** These bulbs are an economical answer to the standard incandescent bulb. Many of the compact fluorescents have a standard, medium-size, screw-in base so they can be used in light fixtures that normally take incandescents. Figure 12-3 shows an assortment of these super CF bulbs.

The energy in compact fluorescents goes directly into light, so you can have a way lower-wattage bulb that will produce a brighter light. For example a 13-watt compact fluorescent bulb can be equivalent to a 60-watt incandescent bulb. It also lasts six times as long and uses less than a quarter of the energy.

When these new designs were introduced in the early 1980s, they revolutionized lighting. A variation on the fluorescent tube, compact fluorescents work the same way, only the tube has been made smaller and folded over in a way to make them fit into spaces designed for incandescent bulbs.

Figure 12-3: Compact fluorescent bulbs come in quite a variety, and often come in true-light versions.

From the reports we've read on the Internet, when it comes to compact fluorescent (and especially *full-spectrum* compact fluorescent) bulbs, you really get what you pay for. Bulbs that cost a bit more will be truer to their color rendering and color temperature, and will last as long as they claim.

✔ **Full-spectrum compact fluorescent bulbs:** Here's what we use for our picture-taking. The full-spectrum light output closely matches natural daylight. To achieve natural, balanced sunlight indoors, the light from these bulbs has to contain a full spectrum of color — including the infrared and ultraviolet wavelengths.

One example is the Sunwave Compact fluorescent reading light (in Figure 12-3, it's the one on the far right). The bulb was developed with a special phosphor blend that guarantees full-spectrum color. It will screw into any medium size screw-in base, and has a CRI of 93, 5500° K. It only uses 30 watts and gives brightness equal to a 150W bulb. They also have a 10,000 hour life. Yes, they're expensive. But they save you a ton of time by shining the "right light" on your items.

Our tech editor replaced all the bulbs in her office with full-spectrum compact fluorescent bulbs. By using them, she calculates that she can save $40.61 over the life of the bulb. Her electric bills have gone down, and she doesn't have to worry about the "color" difference of the over-head bulbs when shooting pictures in her office. Table 12-2 gives you a look at the potential savings estimate.

Table 12-2 Estimated Savings with Compact Fluorescent Bulbs

What You're Measuring	Compact Fluorescent	Incandescent
Bulbs needed for 10,000 hrs. of light	1	10
Bulb cost (sale price)	$19.99	$7.50 (10 x $.75)
Energy cost for 10,000 hrs. of light*	$18.40	$72.00
Total Cost	$38.39	$79.00
Total Savings	$40.61	

*Calculated at $.08 KWH for electric power.

✔ **Halogen bulbs:** These bulbs are the modern version of Edison's incandescent bulb, and they last longer — 2,250 to 3,500 hours. The ones we've used for eBay photography are PAR 30. They feature a *parabolic aluminized reflector* (PAR) to improve the focus of the light, which makes them look like baby-size floodlights.

These amazing little wonders (second from the right in Figure 12-3) give off a crisp, very bright, white light — and they maintain their light output over time without fading with age, as incandescents do. Because of this reliability, most automobile headlights are halogen now.

Halogen lamps also use the tungsten filament (encased in a quartz envelope) in a mixed krypton/xenon/halogen gas environment. (In the PAR type, the halogen lamp is encased in an outer glass bulb). The halogen gas performs a unique task; it actually recycles the tungsten as it deteriorates and the high heat redeposits it back on the filament, meaning the bulb will last way longer! They average 2,500 to 3,000 hours.

A few warnings to heed should you plan on using halogen bulbs:

- **They run hot.** Don't use them in proximity to paper, cloth or other combustible materials that can catch fire from the heat of the bulb.

- **They can break.** Some halogen bulbs are very fragile. Do not drop, crush, bend, or shake them.

- **Skin oil damages them.** Never touch a regular Halogen bulb with your bare hands. Oils from your skin can lead to breakage or shorten the life of the lamp. Use cotton gloves or a lint-free cloth for installation and removal.

- **They stay hot after you turn them off.** Not only should you never touch the lamp when it's on, but also keep (gloved) hands off for awhile after you've turned off it — it's still hot enough to cause serious burns.

Color Rendering Index

Aside from the color-temperature measure, there is one other standard measurement for artificial lighting: the Color Rendering Index, or CRI. The CRI is used by manufacturers of fluorescent, metal-halide, and other non-incandescent lighting equipment to describe the visual effect of the light on colored surfaces. It shows how a light source can affect the appearance of an object's colors — and how well any subtle variations in color shades are revealed. The higher the CRI rating is, the better its color rendering ability. To put it another way, a low CRI causes colors to appear washed out (and perhaps even take on a different hue); a high CRI makes all colors look natural and vibrant.

CRI describes the extent to which an artificial light source can render true color. True color, as seen by natural outdoor sunlight has a CRI of 100. The higher the CRI of the light source, the "truer" the color it renders.

Here are some typical CRI indexes:

Warm White fluorescent tube	55
Cool White fluorescent tube	65
Daylight fluorescent	79
Cool White fluorescent	86
100-watt incandescent	100

Now that you've had a close look at color temperature and Kelvin ranking, you should be an expert. Next time you see an ad like the one for the true-color task lamp (shown here), and you see the phrase *95 CRI 5000° K*, you'll know what it means. (It means you've got a rocking bulb for taking pictures: nice and bright and full-spectrum).

When removing Halogen bulbs, try to hold them only by the edges and be sure to protect your hands from the heat. Again, give bulbs at least half an hour to cool before attempting to change the bulb.

Setting Up Your Lighting

Your lighting setup will be a highly personal thing; it depends on not only your personal preferences, but also on what you sell. Not to worry: Here's where we lay out the different types of items and suggest a reasonably priced lighting setup for each.

The one universal thing about all your lighting arrangements is the position of your bulbs. You can get a bit fancier (depending on what the item needs to show it to best advantage), but your basic setup should be consistent: Camera in the center, positioned in front of your item, with two floodlights at a 90-degree angle from each other, as in Figure 12-4.

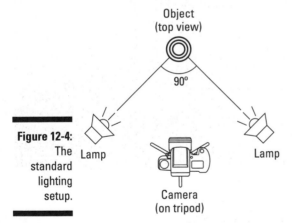

Figure 12-4: The standard lighting setup.

If you don't have two lights, another standard setup (pictured in Figure 12-5) uses just one. If you have more than two, you can also combine the arrangements shown in Figures 12-4 and 12-5 into an outstanding setup for your images.

If you don't have (or don't want to deal with) big floodlights because all the items you sell are small, you can use a couple of compact-fluorescent true-color flip lights with a photo stage, as pictured in Figure 12-6.

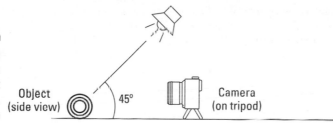

Figure 12-5:
Adding a little light from above.

Object (side view)   45°   Camera (on tripod)

Figure 12-6:
A simple, basic setup for small items, using a photo stage.

Shooting jewelry and coins

When it comes to really small items like jewelry and coins, we recommend the Cloud Dome. Taking pictures with a Cloud Dome isn't difficult — and you can set it up anywhere. For the most natural lighting (and to add just enough shadow), set the Cloud Dome near a window and use the ambient light. If you need additional lighting, you can use flip lights (mentioned earlier) along with your Cloud Dome. (For more information on the Cloud Dome, visit the manufacturer's Web site at www.clouddome.com.)

To take a picture with the Cloud Dome, follow these steps:

1. **Attach your camera to the bracket on top of the Cloud Dome using the camera's tripod mount.**

2. **Select a background for your item: plain white paper, frosted Plexiglas stands, black velvet, or whatever gets the look you want.**

3. **Arrange your item against the background, or put it on a riser, or both.**

4. **Center the dome on top of your object.**

5. **Set your camera to macro mode and turn off the flash.**

6. **View the item through your camera's LCD screen to see whether your item needs additional lighting. If it does, add that light!**

You are now ready to take a nicely lit photograph.

Using light cubes, panels, and umbrellas

A super advantage of these photo accessories is that you can get the benefit of true-color white light without using special bulbs. When you shine a light through a high-quality, pure-white fabric, it changes the quality of the light and you get a near-perfect picture — often the first time. Figure 12-7 shows the result of using a light cube to photograph a collectible item. Depending on what we're shooting, we use different backgrounds in the cube. We find that white or light gray is best for most items, and black (inside the cube) is good for making glass and crystal stand out.

Figure 12-7:
A light cube diffuses and brightens the light, preventing burnout and shadows.

Using a mannequin for apparel shots can be a challenge (no offense, Midge) because it's so hard to light every part of the apparel properly. The same problem crops up when you have to lug your lights outside to take pictures of a car's interior: Direct lighting will produce some really nasty, unwanted shadows. But if you attach light-diffusing panels to your floodlights, you have a cheap, safe way to spread your light around just right. Figure 12-8 shows an eBay fashion photo taken with these panels.

Figure 12-8: Midge the Mannequin is showing her age, but with the correct lighting, her outfit looks swell.

Umbrella-style diffusers are the true professional solution for diffusing light, but they're expensive. By and large, you can simulate them well enough by using the panels, the light cube, or by even by attaching a 12-inch-by-12-inch *diffusion gel filter* (available at your photo dealer, or on eBay for a couple of dollars) to your floodlight. Nothing fancy needed here; a clothespin works fine (as in Figure 12-9). You can also do this with a piece of translucent shower-curtain plastic — but be careful not to get it too close to your lights, especially if you're using special bulbs that throw off a lot of heat. You don't want to burn down the house when you're taking picture!

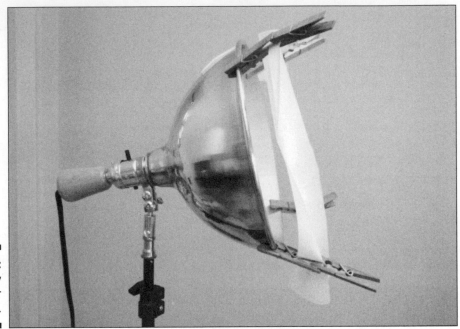

Figure 12-9:
A temporary
diffuser for
floodlights.

Remember, good lighting is the key to good pictures — and *consistent* good lighting can save you time. After you've set up your lighting — if at all possible — *leave it alone* until you finish a large group of pictures. Setting up once and taking pictures of similar-size items can make your image assembly line move much faster!

Chapter 13

Setting Up Your Pictures

• •

In This Chapter

▶ Creating a "clean" image

▶ Setting up your item for the shoot

▶ Avoiding some common photo-goofs

• •

*T*his is the part that always amazes us: Why is it that people feel that they need to add things to "decorate" the listing of their item for sale? Just check eBay. Every day you can see hundreds of item's images overshadowed by the seller's desire to "doll up" the picture.

Those items rarely get the highest price they deserve. Why? Because the purpose of our online images is to clearly show the item for sale — not to create an Ansel Adams work of art.

Clean, clear pictures will get you high bids and fast Buy It Now sales. Period. No question. No argument. You can decorate your listing with some nice HTML (that's what the rest of this book is all about), but your pictures need to be no-fooling-around representations of your merchandise.

It's easy to talk the talk, but take a look at Figures 13-1 through 13-4 for proof of the pudding. They show you some examples from listings with impeccable illustrations.

Figure 13-1:
Austrian
seller
Muederjoe's
image
clearly
shows this
set of vin-
tage crystal
glasses.

Figure 13-2:
NobleSpirit
is selling a
Vintage
Mark 999 die
cast engine
circa 1952,
and provides
several
excellent
pictures.

Figure 13-3: Seller *evanp* also uses several pictures to show the details. Here are three of six used in the listing.

Figure 13-4: *piecesofthe past-al* sells exquisite Swarovski crystal beads — note his watermark on the image.

Here's a quick list of really good reasons to use well-made digital images in your auction pages:

- If you don't have a picture, potential bidders may wonder whether you're deliberately hiding the item from view because you know something is wrong with it. Paranoid? Maybe. Practical? You bet.

- Fickle bidders generally don't even bother reading an item description if they can't *see* the item. (Must be all those years of TV, right?)

- Taking your own pictures shows that you have the item in your possession. Many scam artists take images from a manufacturer's Web site to illustrate their bogus sales on eBay. Why risk being suspect? Snap a quick picture of the real thing!

- Everyone's doing it — and in this one case (whatever your mom used to say), that's a good reason to do it too. I hate to pressure you, but digital images are the custom on eBay; if you're not using them, you're not reaching the widest possible number of people who would bid on your item. From that point of view, you're not doing the most you can to serve your potential customers' needs. Hey, fads are *driven* by conformity. You may as well use them to your advantage.

You can successfully use a scanner to get quality images of many paper items. I use mine as a quick way to get those images up and online — and it works like gangbusters!

Getting the Cleanest Image Possible

Setting up your merchandise isn't always an easy proposition. I often use Quake Hold or clay to balance an item so I can get a special angle to display in the listing.

You may need to shoot your item from several different angles to show it fully — not only to show off its hallmarks, but also to acknowledge its chips and flaws. The more you show, the better!

Point-and-shoot may be okay for a group shot at a historical monument, but illustrating your listing is a whole different idea. Remember the importance of setting the White Balance for your images, and set it every time you begin a merchandise photo session.

Checking your white balance

Nope, this isn't about untangling errant sheets in the washer. The *white balance* is when a camera adjusts itself to the ambient light so it can give accurate and true color-rendition to the image of your merchandise. As I recommend, you need to have a camera that can perform a custom white balance adjustment. If it can't, you probably won't be able to capture very accurate colors — especially if you're taking pictures of your items against a white background. Adjusting the white balance is incredibly crucial because if it isn't adjusted you'll likely end up with all kinds of color variations. Your camera will have a list of presettings you can select — usually including incandescent, twilight, fluorescent, sunlight, cloudy daylight, and shade — all of which have different color temperatures. (For more about color temperature, see Chapter 11.)

If your camera's white balance has a manual setting, you should use it to get the best quality of white balance reading. Study the manual to learn how to set up your camera to perform a custom white-balance calibration. Here's how it generally goes:

1. Set up your picture and when everything is ready to go (including lighting), focus your camera on the merchandise.

2. Get a piece of white paperboard and put it next to the item.

3. Focus your camera on the center of the white board. If focusing is a problem, you can put a business card next to the white board and focus on the writing that appears on it — and remove the card prior to performing the calibration.

Using the Timer shooting mode

Sometimes it's very difficult to focus on an item — especially if your camera is in macro mode — unless you hold the camera very, very still. Keeping your camera still while shooting your picture will yield the best results. That's easy to *say* — but all I have to do is try to hold the camera steady, and my hands start to shake like I'm in an earthquake! Luckily my new Sony camera has and "anti-shake" feature, but most cameras in use now don't. Anything you can do to lessen camera shake will improve the quality of your image.

Tripods, copy stands, or even stacks of books may come in handy here as firm, hands-off places from which to aim your camera at the item you want to shoot. But there's also the matter of tripping the shutter without jiggling the camera . . .

This is where you can use your camera's timer! (See, it has uses other than giving you a chance to jump into the family Christmas card picture — after you've composed and focused the shot on your spouse's nose, of course.) Mount your camera on a tripod or on a Cloud Dome, select the Timer mode, and take the picture. Your camera will delay taking the picture for approximately ten seconds after you activate the timer. Plenty of time to get out of the way.

Here's a trick that will work for some cameras: When you want to speed up your camera's timer, tap the shutter button twice. Depending on the camera, this move *may* drop the countdown timer to two or three seconds. The countdown duration can also be selected in the shooting menu (consult your camera's documentation to see how to access that menu).

Shooting for Online: Dos and Don'ts

When it comes to capturing the best pictures for your listings, there's nothing like a few basic photographic guidelines. Here are some that can give you noticeably better results:

✔ **Do** take the picture of your item outside, in filtered daylight, whenever possible. That way the camera can catch all possible details and color. If you can't take your images during the day, use a good set of floodlights, mounted on clamps or stands.

✔ **Do** consider investing in quality studio tools: a photo stage, a Cloud Dome, a photo cube.

✔ **Don't** use fancy backgrounds; they distract viewers from your item. Put small items on a neutral-colored, nonreflective cloth; put larger items in front of a neutral-colored wall or curtain. You'll crop out almost all the background anyway when you prepare the picture on your computer before you upload the image.

✔ **Do** avoid getting yourself in the photo by shooting your pictures from an angle. If you see your reflection in the item, move around till you "disappear," focus from right there, and try again.

One of my favorite eBay pictures featured a piece of fine silver. Now, silver and reflective items are hard to photograph because they reflect everything in the room in their reflection — and when the lady selling the piece on eBay had her husband take the shot, there he was. She got around it with a little humor, explaining (in her item description) that the man reflected in the silver coffeepot was not included in the final deal! To avoid having this problem reflect oddly on you (sorry about that), take pictures of silvery objects in a photo cube.

✔ **Do** use extra lighting. You can do this by using your camera's Flash mode judiciously (see Chapter 12), or with extra photo lighting on stands. Use extra lighting even when you're taking the picture outside; the idea is to put some *fill light* on the item to make shadowed spots easier to see.

✔ **Don't** get so close to the item that the flash washes out (overexposes) the image. The easiest way to figure out the best distance is by trial and error. Start close and keep moving farther away until you get the results you want.

✔ **Do** take two or three acceptable versions of your image. You can choose the best one later on your computer.

✔ **Do** take a close-up or two of detailed areas that you want buyers to see (in addition to a wide shot of the entire item), if your item relies on detail.

✔ **Do** make sure that your items are clean. Cellophane on boxes can get nasty-looking, clothing can get linty, and all merchandise can get dirt smudges. Not only will your items photograph better if they're clean, they'll sell better, too.

✔ **Don't** get carried away and spend too much time on any one picture (unless the item will be selling for thousands of dollars). Remember that *time is money!*

✔ **Do** make sure that you focus the camera; nothing is worse than a blurry picture. If your camera is a fixed focus model (it can't be adjusted), get only as close as the manufacturer recommends. Automatic-focus cameras measure the distance and change the lens setting as needed. But just because a camera has an autofocus feature doesn't mean that its pictures automatically come out crisp and clear. Low light, high moisture, and other factors can easily blur an image. Double-check the picture before you use it.

Some eBay creeps, whether out of laziness or deceit, steal images from other eBay members. They simply make a digital copy of the image and use it in their own auctions. This is not only rude, but unethical (you put the work in, and besides, the copied image doesn't represent their actual items). This pilfering has happened to me on several occasions. To prevent picture-snatching, you can add your user ID to all your photos. The next time somebody lifts one of your pictures, it has your name on it. If you're familiar with adding HTML code to your auctions (and you should be by the time you finish reading this book), check out the simple Java code on our Web site (www.coolebaytools.com) or in Chapter 6 that you can use to insert in your auction descriptions to prevent scurrilously lazy users from stealing your images.

Lifting another seller's photos is against eBay's rules, so be sure to report the photo-thieving seller to eBay's Security Center at

```
http://pages.ebay.com/securitycenter/
```

Avoid using incandescent or fluorescent lighting to illuminate the photos you take. Incandescent lighting tends to make items look yellowish, and fluorescent lights lend a bluish tone to your photos. One exception is *GE Reveal* incandescent bulbs, which throw a good natural light. Halogen lights give a nice bright white, but they also have a tendency to get very hot! (For more about why light works this way, have a squint at Chapter 12.)

Patti & Marsha's Gallery of Horrors

This section shows you a bunch of big-time don'ts. We've seen images like these all over eBay at one time or another.

Horror #1

Figure 13-5 shows a nice item, but the picture suffers from two major flaws:

- **A glare from the camera's flash shows in the cellophane on the item.** You can avoid the glare-spot by turning the item slightly at an angle so the flash bounces away from you rather than back at the camera.

- **The price sticker is smack on the front of the item.** Often eBay sellers buy things for resale that already have stickers in place. Be a pro and use a commercial product (see Chapter 11) to remove stickers.

Figure 13-5:
Glaring
errors here!

Horror #2

Don't dress your picture with props to decorate the scene. Your photo should be a crisp, clean image of the product you're selling, and only that. Figure 13-6 shows a common eBay seller mistake: What a cute teddy — but what are we selling here?

Figure 13-6:
. . . and
you're sell-
ing what?

Horror #3

I never knew how much colorful upholstery people had in their homes. I've
seen items photographed on plaid, floral, and striped fabrics (see Figure 13-7).
It's a distraction from your item. Don't do it.

Figure 13-7:
Nice sofa!
What's that
thing doing
sitting on it?

Horror #4

I'm sure the item in the box shown in Figure 13-8 is desirable, but who can make that judgment without seeing the item? Take the item out of the box. If the box is a crucial part of the deal (as in collectibles), be sure to mention that the box is included in the sale.

Figure 13-8:
Peek-a-boo.
I can't
see you.

Sometimes *not* removing an item from the box (to maintain its status as *mint* or *new*) is an important selling point. If you can't open the box without ruining the value of the item, pull in for a macro close up and photograph the item at an angle so that your lights won't glare on the cellophane or other packaging. When you have a quantity of the item, bite the bullet and open one up for demo purposes. A good picture gets you higher bids, and perhaps that loss of one item will be made up by the higher bids on the sales with good pictures.

Horror #5

Can you say *close-up?* Figure 13-9 shows a common error made by many sellers: The item is adrift in the wide-open spaces. Use the zoom on your camera to fill the frame with a full picture of your item. Draw your camera close to the item so the prospective customer can see some detail. Don't just rely on cropping the picture in an image editing program; that only makes the image smaller.

Figure 13-9:
Pay no
attention to
the object on
the carpet.

Chapter 14

Special-Situation Photography

*U*nfortunately, all items are not the same under the lights: You are going to have to make some special accommodations when it comes to photographing certain types of items. It really is a drag for those of us who will sell anything and everything on eBay; we have to have a bit more knowledge (and tools) to keep ahead of the competition that sells in each category. We'll go over a few of the more common tricks of the trade.

Marsha has been selling on eBay since 1997, and thought she was pretty good at showing off and selling her wares. But then she purchased a small lot of Morgan silver dollars to resell. No problem. She figured she'd just take her standard digital picture and sell away. Oops, not so fast. The first pictures of the coins bore only the slightest resemblance to the actual coins. The digital pictures made the beautiful silver coins look gold! Eeyow!

Then came her next challenge: photographing some silvertone and goldtone costume jewelry. The setup — with its perfect positioning, beautiful lighting, and black velvet jewelry pads — looked stunning. The pictures *should* have been perfect. But NO: Silvertone looked gold, and goldtone looked silver. What's the deal?

The deal is lighting — specifically, the need for ambient lighting. Marsha used to work with catalog photographers who took pictures of jewelry, and she remembered the elaborate setup they used to produce the sparkling images you see in the ads. Okay, maybe most of us can't recreate the experts' silk tents, minimalist lighting, and multiple light flashes per exposure — but we can still set up for some great-looking images that do justice to our wares. That's why this chapter shows you how to diffuse, and how to take advantage of the ambient light you have at home.

Photographing Jewelry and Coins

The first time we all figure out that there must be a "trick" to photography is when, as sellers, we try to photograph coins or jewelry for online sale. The novice photographer is, for the most part, totally floored in this situation. Several things become apparent right away:

- It's almost impossible to photograph any form of metal in its native color — silver looks gold — and gold looks silver.
- It's impossible to photograph the patina (finish) of any metal accurately.
- Gems will often look muddy and pearls will often white out.
- Detail in coins may be too strong or too light to show up to best advantage.
- You may have horrendous shadows.

And that's the short list of why this type of photography will challenge even the most seasoned eBay photographer. So this chapter offers a few fixes, ranging from the most economical (and unfortunately *still* the most difficult), to the expensive. At that end of the spectrum, you wind up investing in a serious piece of equipment — but at least the equipment will last you forever.

Take the pictures outdoors

I know this is going to sound kind of hokey, but most "necessity is the mother of invention" solutions *are* hokey, so bear with me. Here are the prehistoric-and-cheap-outdoor-photo-studio details:

1. **Go outside in bright sunlight with your item and a white piece of cardboard to use as your background.**

2. **Arrange your items on the cardboard so they're ready to photograph.**

3. **Have a friend hold an old white sheet (the older and thinner, the better) between your item setup and the sun.**

   That way the sunlight has to travel through the sheet, which cuts down on direct sunshine, diffuses the light, and cuts out harsh shadows. (If you don't have a friend to help out, tie the sheet to something stable and drape it over your shoulder — yes, Marsha has actually done this — then *hold really still* while the shutter clicks . . .)

4. **Turn off your camera's flash and take the picture in the ambient light illuminating your item.**

With any luck, you'll find that the thin-old-white-sheet a fast, cheap way to filter the sunlight and reduce the glare and shadows. This system really does work, but we guarantee after doing it long enough, you're gonna want to upgrade!

Scanning the small stuff

We know that it's hard to believe, but even as a beginner, you can actually scan your items on your scanner — and get good images you can use! Scanning an item is far faster than taking the time to set up, take the picture and download it to your computer. Marsha scans a good many of her paper items (and more) in her HP All-In-One that sits on the side of her desk. The All-In-One is her copier, fax, scanner and part-time printer — and it was purchased for about $200. She used to do all her coins and jewelry that way, but found she was spending a bit too much time in her image-editing program to get 'em to look right, and that's a no-no for a Power Seller. She still uses the scanner now and then — mainly because it's easy! If it fits on the scanner — she'll try to scan it first rather than taking a picture.

Figure 14-1 shows you a quick and easy scan that was taken of an expensive gold metal belt. It's amazing how well it turned out.

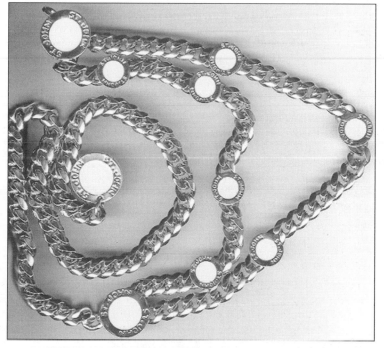

Figure 14-1:
You can
even clearly
read the
manufac-
turer's
hallmark.

Next is a picture from auctions by Cardking4 on eBay. This is a proof set of coins. They are encased in plastic (which is why they look a tad hazy). If you took the picture with improper lighting, it would be a nightmare — considering the amount of glare you'd get from the plastic case!

Figure 14-2:
A 2004
United
States Proof
Set clearly
still encased
in plastic.

Figure 14-3 shows a coin in a paper holder that's been scanned — we think it illustrates the coin adequately!

Figure 14-3:
A scan of a
vintage
American
coin.

Here are the steps you need to follow for scanning:

1. **Clean your scanner glass. Magnified on a scanner, nothing looks grosser than a hair or an icky piece of dust.**

2. **Cover your now-clean scanner glass with a plastic page protector from the office-supply store. Any piece of crystal-clear plastic will do — the point is not to scratch up the glass.**

3. **For jewelry, use a jeweler's cloth to bring the piece to it most shining glory. *Please* leave the coins alone — cleaning only brings down the value!**

4. **Arrange your jewelry or coins on the scanner (over the plastic protector).**

5. **Before you bring down the lid, place a small object on the glass so as to wedge the scanner in an open position so the cover doesn't squish your layout.**

6. **Lay a background over your item and a cloth to prevent light from leaking in around the side.**

We know this seems like a huge hassle, but it really isn't. You'll get some perfectly good images to use in your listings.

Although scanning works well, you still may have problems in getting the right colors. So if you're in the coin or jewelry business in earnest, it's time to climb up to the next step.

Going pro with the Cloud Dome

Ambient light, light that occurs naturally, is the best light for photographing many types of items (especially shiny items). Problems start when you use flash or flood lighting alone (without a Cloud Dome) for pictures of metallic objects, Common lighting problems that affect the quality of your photographs include shiny spots from reflections (off walls and ceilings), washed out areas from the glare of the lights and loss of proper color.

Enter the Cloud Dome to offer your at-home photos the ability to take advantage of natural, ambient light. The Cloud Dome looks like a giant bowl that you place upside-down over the object you want to photograph. This bowl evenly diffuses ambient room light over the surface area of the object. This way, you can produce quality digital images in average room lighting.

A fellow eBay University instructor introduced Marsha to the Cloud Dome — it's an amazing tool. You can purchase the Cloud Dome and its accessories at many professional camera shops, from the Web site at `www.clouddome.com`, or (you guessed it) on eBay.

Shooting pictures with the Cloud Dome

The Cloud Dome looks like a giant inverted salad bowl with a camera mount attached. Figure 14-4 shows a Cloud Dome being set up to photograph jewelry. Follow these steps to take a picture with the dome:

1. **Attach your camera to the Cloud Dome's mount with the lens positioned so that it peers into the hole at the top of the dome.**

2. **Place your item on top of a contrasting background.**

   See the sidebar "Tips for taking Cloud Dome pictures," later in this chapter for ideas on choosing a background.

3. **Place the dome with camera attached over your item.**

4. **Check the item's position through your camera's viewfinder or LCD screen.**

   If it's not in the center, center it. If you feel you still need added lighting to bring out a highlight, position another lamp outside the dome.

5. **Focus your camera and shoot the picture.**

Figure 14-4:
Taking a picture with the Cloud Dome.

The ideal subjects for Cloud Dome photos

Many items benefit from being photographed through a Cloud Dome, especially:

✔ **Jewelry:** We've found that taking pictures with the Dome keeps the gold color gold and the silver color silver. Also, using the Cloud Dome helps your camera pick up details such as engraving and the metal surrounding cloisonné work. It also gives pearls their unique luster and soft reflection, as in Figure 14-5. Much of the detail that the Cloud Dome helps capture can be washed out when you apply enough light to take the picture without it.

Figure 14-5:
A pair of lustrous pearl earrings.

✔ **Gems and stones:** We've seen some beautiful pictures taken of gems and stones with the Cloud Dome. You may also want to focus a floodlight or lamp on the outside of the dome for extra sparkle. Take a look at Figure 14-6: on the left is a lovely ruby-slippers pin photographed under the Cloud Dome. On the right is the same pin, taken without the dome — notice the glare.

Figure 14-6:
Notice the benefit of using ambient light.

✔ **Coins and stamps:** The Cloud Dome allows you to hold the camera steady for extreme close-ups — and when you photograph coins, it helps you leave out any coloration that is not on the coins. For small detailed items such as coins and stamps, the Cloud Dome helps you achieve sharp focus and true color.

✓ **Holographic or metallic-accented items:** If you've ever tried to photograph collector cards, you know that the metal accents glare and the holograms are impossible to capture.

Also, the glossy coatings confuse the camera's light sensors, causing overexposed highlights. Check out the before-and-after images in Figure 14-7 and see how clear the hologram on the credit card appears after shooting through the Cloud Dome.

Figure 14-7:
A hologram,
before
and after.

✓ **Reflective objects:** Items like silverware — or even computer chips — reflect a lot of light when lit properly for photos. The Cloud Dome diffuses the light so that the pictures become clear. Check out the before and after in Figure 14-8.

Figure 14-8:
Computer
chips,
before and
after
shooting
with the
Cloud
Dome.

Selling Fashion through Pictures

A simple truth of eBay: Nothing gets less bids than a photograph of a pair of jeans (or a dress) folded up on a table (or hanging on a hanger). Take a look at Figure 14-9 and look at the Gallery thumbnails. Notice which dresses look desirable and which seem less so. (Some droop from hangers — but that cocktail party dress looks like it's *already* at a party!)

☐		TRACY REESE RED DRESS SIZE 2 LIKE NEW		$14.50	3
☐		BOMBShell RED Wiggle Vintage 80s Cocktail Party DRESS 8		$14.97	1
☐		byergirl Red dress size 5		$4.99	-
☐		Girl Sz 4T NWT Lydia Jane Dress Valentines Red Hearts		$12.99	1
☐		Grace Chinese Dress Evening Gown Red 36 NR (FZD13801)		$0.01	-
☐		Semi formal dress size 3 (small) brilliant red		$2.00	1

Figure 14-9: Searching for fashion on eBay.

Gathering fashion photography tools

Photographing fashion *right* takes a little time, but the right tools make the project easier. Here's a list of some of the items you'll need when photographing clothing.

✔ **Mannequin body double:** You don't want to deal with supermodels and their requirements for non-fat, sugar-free vanilla lattes, so you have to find someone who will model the garments and not give you any grief. Figure 14-10 pictures faithful mannequin Midge, who has sold lots of dresses on eBay for Marsha.

Tips for taking Cloud Dome pictures

Surprisingly, there's very little learning curve to using a Cloud Dome. (Hey, how about those simple steps? Doesn't get much simpler than that.) What may take you more time is discovering the tips and tricks that help you achieve professional-looking results. Not to worry: Reading this section will kick-start your discovery process. While that's going on, here are a few things to keep in mind when taking photos with the Cloud Dome:

✔ **Focus, focus:** Due to the focus limitations of many of today's digital cameras, we found it best to use the Cloud Dome with the extension collar (often sold along with the dome), which allows you to put your camera 17 inches away from the item you're photographing on a flat surface.

✔ **Close-ups:** When attempting *macro* (extreme close-up) photography, the Cloud Dome

holds your camera still while shooting the picture. If you prefer, after you've centered your item, stand away use your camera's self-timer to take the picture.

✔ **Fine upstanding items:** If your item is vertical and doesn't lend itself to being photographed flat, use the optional angled extension from Cloud Dome, which allows you to shoot the item from an angle instead of from the top. An angled collar is also sold separately, or in a package deal with a Cloud Dome.

✔ **Keeping background where it belongs:** When selecting a background for your item, choose a contrasting background that reflects the light properly for your item. Make it a solid color; white is always safe and black can add dramatic highlights.

Figure 14-10: Midge modeling a vintage fur (photo was cropped before listing).

Full-body mannequins can be purchased on eBay for about $200. Marsha bought Midge the Mannequin from a local store that was updating their mannequins. Major department stores often liquidate their display merchandise in auctions, so keep your eyes peeled in your local newspaper for auctions of store fixtures.

Keep in mind that you needn't spend a mint on a brand-new model. If your mannequin is used and has a few paint chips — so what?

Following are some less expensive alternatives to a mannequin:

- **Molded body form:** Before you decide to jump in with both feet, you might want to try using a *hanging* body form. These are molded torsos that have a hanger at the top. You can find molded styrene forms on eBay for as little as $20. If you decide to stay in the apparel-vending business, you can always upgrade to a full-size mannequin.

- **Dressmaker's adjustable form:** You can also use a dressmaker's form to model your eBay clothing. The best part about using these is that you can adjust the size of the body to fit your clothing. You can often find new or good-condition used ones on eBay for under $100.

✔ **Vertical photo lights on stands:** Check Chapter 12 to get the lowdown on lighting your apparel. Here's a quick description of what you need. To light your merchandise, you'll do best to invest in some floodlights — and to prevent glare you could use some diffusing elements. You don't have to spend a mint, but (as you'll see when you start taking pictures), the little flash on your camera just can't bring out the really good parts of your apparel.

You may want to prevent the flash on your camera from going off altogether when you take pictures of clothes; too much light coming from the front will wash out the detail in the fabric.

✔ **Clothespins:** To fit your clothing on the mannequin, use clothespins to take up any slack in the garment (be sure to place the clothespins where camera won't see them). Before you think I'm crazy, I'll have you know that clothespins were used in almost every apparel photo that I've participated in. Think about it: The clothing you're selling will come in different sizes and may not always hang right on your mannequin.

Cleaning and pressing essentials

Before you photograph your clothing items, make sure each one imparts the image you want your buyers to see. For example, remove any loose threads and lint that may have accumulated on the fabric.

Have the following items handy to help you with the cleaning and pressing chores:

🖛 **Garment rack:** When you unpack your merchandise from the carton it was shipped in, the items can look pretty ragged. And if you've purchased some hanging merchandise and it's in tip-top shape, you'll want to keep it that way. Hanging the merchandise on a garment rack (see Figure 14-11) keeps it fresh-looking so it looks great when you get ready to ship.

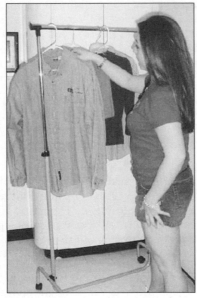

Figure 14-11: Garment rack, with clothes to list on eBay.

🖛 **Steamer:** Retail stores, clothing manufacturers, and drycleaners all use steamers. Why? Because steaming the garment with a steam wand is kinder to the fabric and takes wrinkles out in a hurry. Steam penetrates the fabric (not crushing it, as does ironing) and seems to make the fabric look better than before.

Steaming is also five times *faster* than ironing — and not as backbreaking — which is why it's truly the professional's choice. Steaming garments is a breeze; see for yourself in Figure 14-12.

A handheld travel steamer will work well enough if you're selling only one or two apparel items a month — and that's fine for beginners, but the time can add up. While a professional-style steamer gets a garment done in a minute or two, you might have to work on the same garment with a travel steamer for 15 minutes to get usable results. If you're thinking about selling any significant quantity of clothes on eBay, then a professional-style, roll-base steamer is what you should look for.

Figure 14-12:
Kristy helping Marsha with steaming for eBay!

As Marsha says, "I use a Jiffy Steamer that I've had for quite a while. (I even bought it on eBay and got a great deal.) It's the same kind they use in retail stores, only slightly smaller."

✔ **Dryel:** This is a popular, reasonably priced, home-dry-cleaning product you use in your dryer. Dryel can be used with almost any type of garment (be sure to double-check the packaging before you use it). After going through a Dryel treatment, clothes come out of the dryer sweet and clean. The starter kit even comes with a spot remover. You can buy Dryel at your local supermarket.

According to eBay rules, all used clothing must be cleaned before it's sold on the site. Even if the vintage garment you have up for sale is clean, it can always benefit by a roll in the dryer with Dryel. New garments, too, benefit; Dryel removes any smells that have clung to the garment during its travels.

✔ **Spot cleaners:** We recommend that you use spot cleaners only if you know what you're doing. Some really great ones out there will remove a small spot, but you'd best practice on items that you're *not* selling first.

Turning Cars into Dollars

Cars can turn into quite a few dollars. Based on sales in the first quarter of 2005, $12.9 billion- (that's with a *b*, followed by *nine zeros*)-worth of merchandise sold in a year on the eBay Motors site. Is that huge enough to make you want to sell a vehicle? We'd think so, but photographing cars for eBay auctions is a bit . . . involved. Typically a successful vehicle auction shows at least ten pictures of the vehicle:

- ✔ Pictures of the car from all four sides
- ✔ The driver's-side interior through open door
- ✔ Passenger's-side interior with open door
- ✔ Driver's side of the vehicle from the back seat
- ✔ Close-up of the dashboard
- ✔ Back-seat photo taken from the front seat
- ✔ Pictures of tires and fenders (make sure that all are visible)
- ✔ All documentation that comes with the car
- ✔ Picture of the engine

Take your pictures outside, on a nice sunny day. A car is one thing that looks good *with* a reflection! To see what we mean, take a look at these shots (Figures 14-13 through 14-16) of a used Chrysler Town and Country Van sold by e.vehicles. They're fine examples of some types of images you'll need if you're going to sell a car successfully on eBay. You can see why John Rickmon, the owner of e.vehicles, has been making a good living selling automobiles on eBay for many years — as these pictures attest, he really knows his stuff!

Steaming hot tips

Keep these tips in mind when steaming the clothes you sell on eBay:

- ✔ Always keep the steam head in an upright position so the condensation inside the hose drains back into the steamer.
- ✔ Run the steam head lightly down the fabric.
- ✔ Don't let the steam head come directly in contact with velvet or silk; otherwise you may spot the fabric.
- ✔ Steam velvet (or any fabric with a pile) from the reverse side.

- ✔ Hang pants by the cuff when steaming.
- ✔ Heavy fabrics may respond better to steaming from the *underside* of the fabric.
- ✔ When you're through steaming your clothes for eBay, try steaming your mattresses and furniture. Steaming has been proven to kill a majority of dust mites and their accompanying nastiness.

Figure 14-13:
A nice long
shot of the
vehicle.

Figure 14-14:
Check out
those seats.

Figure 14-15:
Nice
dashboard!

Figure 14-16:
Look — it's
got a clean
engine!

These pictures sold the van for over $8,500.00 in seven days — with a starting bid of $100!

Pictures in your listings make a huge difference. Be sure to treat your picture-taking as the serious enterprise that it is. Once you've got our methods perfected, you should be whizzing through your shoots — taking only minutes for each listing!

Chapter 15

Getting the Pictures from Your Camera to eBay

*W*e know that some of you may look at this chapter and wonder why we wasted the space, but we also know two of the most common questions we hear:

"How do I get my pictures up on eBay?"

and

"How do I get my pictures out of my camera?"

So if you've ever asked yourself those questions, look to this chapter for the answers. Not only do we guide you step by step — until you're an expert uploading your pictures to eBay — but we also advise you on best practices for storing and safeguarding any pictures you take.

A good way to start developing your picture-handling skills is by understanding how your camera stores its images. And then you'll recognize that storing your images in the camera is a waste of precious picture-taking space. But never fear; this chapter shows you how to get those pictures out of your camera, store them on your computer, and safeguard your artistry with regular appropriate backups.

Finding the Pictures in Your Camera

As we discuss in Chapter 10, digital cameras can store your images on various types of removable media. The industry refers to these media types as *flash media.* Why, you ask? We hear that the *flash* part has something to do with how quickly the media can be erased, but we advise you to just hum along and go with it. To recap the media types, you can find Smart Digital, Secure Digital, Memory Sticks, Compact Flash, DVDs, and floppy disks all used in digital cameras. And you also discover that the storage media comes in lots of sizes — all the way up to 1GB (gigabyte) of storage space!

Your camera's manufacturer decides which media type your camera takes but the size of the storage space you choose is up to you. Most newer cameras also have an internal memory where they can store images. So you've got plenty of ways to store pictures and three ways to retrieve them. We go over your options, one by one.

Your camera names your images in a random manner — and in a language that makes sense only to your camera. The language dubs your images with names like *MVC-015F.jpg* or *DSCN0237.jpg,* and odds are that those strange names will make recognizing your images of choice difficult (to say the least). So getting the images onto your computer where you can view them — and rename them into something more sensible — becomes quite important.

Retrieving images from your camera's memory

Surprisingly, some digital cameras can even store your pictures without removable media! Marsha (who's been known to be a bit ditzy at times) bought a new Nikon digital camera and started snapping away happily until she realized when hadn't inserted a memory card! Yikes, had she lost all her images? Nope, most of the newer cameras have their own internal memory that can hold many images in temporary storage. This memory is also useful when you want to do some in-camera photo editing. (See Chapter 16 for info on how to do this.)

You can transfer images held in your camera's internal memory to your computer through a direct cable connection. In some cases, the camera has a docking station (as is the case with the Nikon Cool-Station or the Kodak EasyShare).

Kodak has been the leader in offering cameras that depend on a docking station to retrieve the images (see Figure 15-1). With its cameras, Kodak includes its own EasyShare software, which makes downloading and editing images in one place uber-easy. The camera dock connects to your computer and allows you to download pictures with the push of a button. Once the images are on your computer, you can edit and rename them easily.

Figure 15-1:
Kodak's
snappy
EasyShare
V530 has a
docking
station that
also allows
you to view
a slide show
of your
images and
download
your images
quickly.

Older digital cameras come with a cable that connects directly to your computer's USB port. When you connect your camera and computer via the cable, your computer treats the camera as if it were a hard drive. You can then pull up a folder window and download the images as if you were copying files from one drive to another. EasyShare software works on PCs or MACs. On a PC running Windows XP, the process goes something like this:

1. **Right-click in your computer's My Pictures folder and selecting New⇨ Folder from the resulting menu.**

2. **Type a logical name for your new folder (something like** My Camera**) when prompted and click OK.**

3. **Plug your camera's cable into the computer's USB port.**

   If you're lucky, your computer has the USB port on the front. After you make the connection, your computer should confirm that a new device is attached to your computer and will ask what you'd like to do, as shown in Figure 15-2.

4. **Click a folder that selects your camera as a device. When you see the memory folder in your camera (the folder's name depends on the type of camera you have), select the option to Open Folder and View Files.**

   Selecting this option allows your computer to access the memory in your camera.

We prefer to view the files in a folder before doing anything to them — and we suggest this strategy for preparing to transfer your image files because it's as a good way to organize them prior to transferring!

5. **Click individual files, Ctrl+click to select multiple files, or Ctrl+A to select all files in the folder.**

6. **Drag the selected file or files over to the My Camera folder on your computer.**

   Alternatively, you can right-click and choose Copy from the resulting menu to copy all the highlighted files. Then right-click on your My Camera folder and choose Paste. In either case, the images files will be copied to your computer.

Figure 15-2:
When you connect a new device (such as a camera or media card), your computer asks what you want it to do.

You can create subfolders in your My Camera folder to store images from different photo shoots. You can also (as we do) have separate folders — with names like *Jewelry, Shoes,* and *Collectibles* — for storing your sales items by category.

Mounting the flash media card

To retrieve the digital pictures from your flash media, you first need to find the media in your camera. Think back to where you found a tiny trap door in your camera — the one you opened when you put the media card in the camera in the first place. When you've scratched your head a few times and found the trap door, open it and remove the media card, as shown in Figure 15-3.

Figure 15-3:
Removing a
teeny-tiny
256MB card
from
Marsha's
camera.

When you pull out the camera's media card, you've got a handful of pictures in a tiny piece of plastic. What to do now? If your computer doesn't have a bay of media card readers, you may need to go out and buy a media reader. A *media reader* is a small, portable device that sports slots for many types of flash media (as shown in Figure 15-4). If you need to buy one, we recommend that you get a media reader that reads as many different media types as possible. That way, when something goes wrong (you know it will) and the new camera you have to buy uses different media, your media reader can still have you covered.

After you find a place to stick the card that will permit your computer to read it, stick it there, and a small window — similar to the one shown in Figure 15-2 — should pop up. You can follow the same procedure to extract files from the camera's media card as you would for getting pictures from the camera's memory (see the section "Retrieving images from your camera's memory," earlier in this chapter). Unless your camera comes with some fancy downloading software, the procedure to copy images onto your computer works the same in either case.

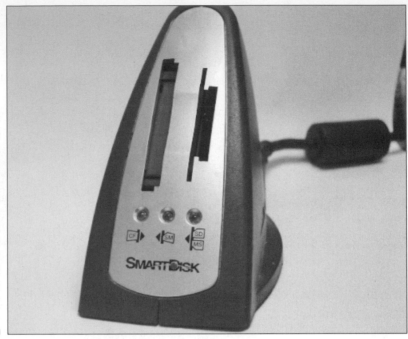

Removing the media

No, you don't just yank the camera's media card out of your computer when you're through copying over the files. (Okay, we admit to doing so several times ourselves. But we felt awful about it.)

 If you don't follow your computer's unmounting procedure, it's very possible that you can mung up the files on your media card so the pictures residing on it become unreadable — potentially a very, very bad thing. You never know when you might need a backup copy of an image — which you won't have *until* you backup your images elsewhere (for instance, on a CD).

 For Windows XP users, it's best to look in the lower-right corner of your taskbar at the bottom of your screen to find a small icon like the one shown in the margin. If you don't see this Safely Remove Hardware icon, click the chevron-shaped icon to reveal your hidden icons. When you see the right one, follow these steps:

1. **Right-click the Safely Remove Hardware icon.**

   A small list (such as the one shown in Figure 15-5) appears.

2. **Click to highlight the media you want to remove.**

   Your computer will chug and grind a bit, and soon a bubble appears to let you know it's okay to remove your flash media.

3. **Remove the media from your computer's slot and insert it back in your camera's little trap door.**

Figure 15-5:
Selecting
which
media you
want to dis
connect in
Windows XP.

| Safely remove USB Mass Storage Device - Drives(H:, I:, J:, K:) |
| Safely remove USB Mass Storage Device - Drive(G:) |
| Safely remove hp psc 2400 series (DOT4USB) |
| Safely remove Oxford Semiconductor Ltd.   OXFORD IDE Device   IEEE 1394 SBP2 Device - Drives(P:, O:) |

Uploading Your Images to a Server

Unless you use eBay's Picture Services (see the upcoming section, "Uploading your picture to eBay"), you will need to upload your images to a server somewhere on the Internet. By doing so, your images will have an address, or URL, which you insert into your HTML coding or on eBay's sell your item form. This address allows the eBay Web site to display the picture in your listings. To get such an address for your pictures, you have several options:

✔ **Your ISP (Internet service provider):** All the big ISPs — AOL, AT&T, Road Runner, and Earthlink — give you space to store your Internet stuff. You're already paying a monthly fee to an ISP, and you can park pictures there at no extra charge.

✔ **An image-hosting Web site:** Web sites that specialize in hosting pictures are popping up all over the Internet. Some charge a small fee; others are free. The upside here is that these specialized sites usually have uploading software built in, which makes them extremely easy to use.

✔ **Your server:** If you have your own server (those of you who do know who you are), you can store those images in your own home base.

To many eBay users, uploading pictures to space provided by their ISPs seems to remain a major mystery. And so many users are still convinced that they have to pay for an image-hosting service — but that's rarely the case these days.

Using your free ISP space

Most major ISPs give you a minimum of 5MB of space to put a personal home page on the Internet. You can usually store your images for your eBay sales there — unless your provider has some strict rules about not doing that (it's a good idea to check first).

Name size does matter

After you get your digital images onto your computer, you might want to take a quick look at them and then name them appropriately. You can also use this quick-look time to delete the truly awful pictures with those random, letter-and-number-based nightmare names before you rename the keepers. Go to the folder that holds your images, and if you're using Windows XP, choose View⇨Filmstrip to get a display similar to the one shown in the sidebar figure.

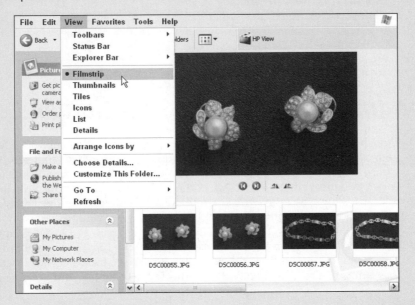

Viewing your images in the filmstrip mode gives you a good idea of how they came out.

Going with our *For Dummies* philosophy of naming a subfolder with the category of the items in it, we usually name our images so we know exactly what the image portrays — without having to open it. For example, we might name the image in Figure 15-3 *pearl_cz_ earring.jpg*.

Here's an important thing to keep in mind: Some file-naming conventions apply specifically to files that will be used on the Internet. Although your computer (MAC or PC) may permit other naming options, the interoperable nature of the Internet (everything has to work with everything else) means following this short list of rules:

✔ Use only letters, numbers, underscore (_), and hyphen (-) as characters in filenames.

✔ Leave no spaces between characters.

✔ Use mostly lowercase letters; uppercase letters may be used to distinguish words, for example, *STBirthdayParty.jpg*.

✔ When separating words, use the underscore mark (_), as in *green_earring.jpg*.

✔ Use a period (.) only to separate the extension from the rest of the filename, as in *dome.jpg*.

✔ Use a maximum of 16 characters when naming an image.

Internet service providers may supply you with an image upload area, but they may require you to use File Transfer Protocol (FTP) program. You may also be able to find a free or shareware (requiring a small fee) FTP program on sites such as the following:

✔ www.tucows.com

✔ www.download.com (formerly cNet)

✔ www.shareware.com

If you use the image editing program, Fast Photos (described in Chapter 16) you will get an FTP program as part of the software at no extra charge!

To upload a file to your ISP's server with a popular FTP program, Cute FTP (available at www.tucows.com), follow these steps:

1. **Choose File➪Connection Wizard from the Cute FTP main menu.**

   The Cute FTP Connection Wizard appears.

2. **Click the down arrow by the Choose Your ISP drop-down list, and select your ISP. Then click Next.**

3. **Type the user name and password that you use to log on to your Internet account. Then click Next.**

4. **Click the Browse button (shown in Figure 15-6) to locate the folder on your computer where you store your eBay images. Then click Next.**

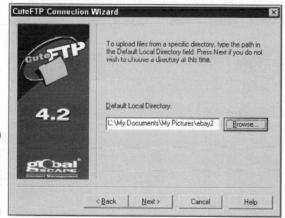

Figure 15-6:
Selecting
your default
folder.

5. **If you want to log on to your FTP space upon opening the Cute FTP program, click the Connect to This Site Automatically check box.**

   If not, don't change anything on this screen.

6. **Click Finish.**

From this point on, every time you open the program (provided you selected the automatic connection in Step 5), Cute FTP logs on to your Web space and displays the screen shown in Figure 15-7. Notice that the left side of the program is open to the folder you selected as the default for your eBay images. The right side of the screen shows what is currently on your ISP-provided home page.

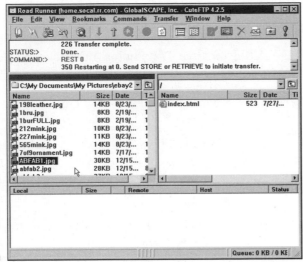

Figure 15-7: Signing on to your FTP space.

To upload an image, double-click it. Faster than we could take a screen shot (okay, we took it anyway, and it's Figure 15-8), the image is uploaded to our Web space!

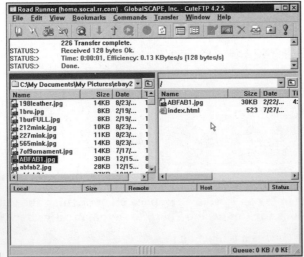

Figure 15-8: Instant image upload!

Uploading images to AOL

AOL handles image uploads a bit differently from other ISPs. (But those of you on AOL knew that already.) Many people love AOL because it provides an easy, step-by-step interface. As you probably imagine, uploading pictures is handled in that same AOL style.

To upload pictures to AOL, follow these steps:

1. **Sign on to your AOL account.**

2. **Display the FTP area of AOL:**

   For users of AOL 5.0: Select Keywords, type my ftp space in the text line, and click GO.

   For users of later versions of AOL: Search keywords for ftp-click go by typing it in the text line. On the next page, click members ftp space. Then double-click members.aol.com.

3. **Click See My FTP Space.**

   You're sent to your AOL storage area.

4. **Click Upload.**

   A screen appears so you can name the file you want to upload, which is called the *remote* file.

5. **In the Remote Filename box (see Figure 15-9), type a name for your picture.**

   Use all-lowercase letters — and no more than eight characters.

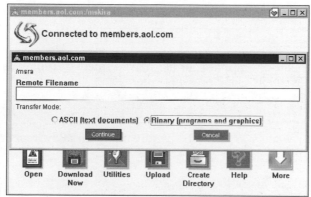

Figure 15-9: Giving your file a name for AOL.

6. Click Continue.

A window opens so you can locate the file on your computer, as shown in Figure 15-10.

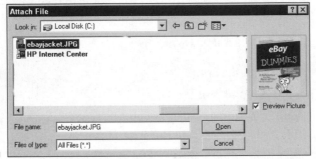

Figure 15-10:
Finding the
file on your
computer.

7. Locate the file, click its filename, and then click Open.

Your file will whiz through the wires to the server at AOL, as shown in Figure 15-11.

Figure 15-11:
The file is on
its way!

You can now double-check that your file arrived safely by typing its URL in your browser (as follows) and pressing Enter:

```
http://members.aol.com/yourscreenname/picturename.jpg
```

You use the URL when you insert the picture into your eBay item description, as follows

```
<img src= http://members.aol.com/yourscreenname/
          picturename.jpg>
```

Uploading your picture to eBay

eBay offers two versions of Picture Services. The basic version, which is shown in Figure 15-12, allows you to upload eBay-ready images as they appear on your computer. If you want to rotate or crop the picture, you need the more advanced picture service. We use the advanced version in the steps that follow.

Add pictures   👁 Live help
Use these tips to add a great photo to your listing.

| eBay Enhanced Picture Services | 📷 eBay Basic Picture Services | Your Web hosting |

Upgrade to eBay Enhanced Picture Services at no additional cost. It's faster, lets you upload pictures of any size, and enables you to preview, crop, and rotate your pictures.

Picture 1 (Free)
[   ] [Browse...]
To add pictures to your listing, click Browse.
Picture 2 ($0.15)
[   ] [Browse...]
Picture 3 ($0.15)
[   ] [Browse...]
Picture 4 ($0.15)
[   ] [Browse...]
Picture 5 ($0.15)
[   ] [Browse...]
Picture 6 ($0.15)
[   ] [Browse...]

Figure 15-12:
The basic
Picture
Services
photo-
hosting
page.

When you reach the part of the Sell Your Item form that allows you to add pictures, does the screen look like Figure 15-12? If so, scroll down and click the Upgrade to *eBay Enhanced Picture Services* link. This sends you to eBay's Enhanced Picture Services install screen, which is shown in Figure 15-13. If you've never used eBay's Enhanced Picture Services before, you'll be asked for permission to install a small program on your computer. This is safe (and the only way you can use eBay's Picture Service features), so click Yes.

Figure 15-13:
Here you
can install
Enhanced
Picture
Services.

| 📷 eBay Enhanced Picture Services | eBay Basic Picture Services | Your Web hosting |

Enhanced Picture Services Software Not Installed

The eBay Enhanced Picture Services software (ActiveX Control) is not installed or is damaged. Click the **Set Up Picture Services** button to re-install.

[Set Up Picture Services]

Having problems adding pictures? Try this troubleshooting help.

To complete the installation, here's the drill:

1. **Click the Set Up Picture Services bar.**

   On the resulting page, you're informed about accepting some security warnings and about the timeframe required to complete the installation process (which is just a few minutes).

2. **Click the Install Now bar when you're ready.**

3. **Okay the security warning, as shown in Figure 15-14.**

4. **When the installation is complete, click Finished.**

Figure 15-14:
It's okay to say OK to eBay!

Then, to upload your pictures, follow these steps:

1. **In the Enhanced Picture Services screen (refer to Figure 15-15), click the Add Picture button.**

   A window pops up, prompting you to open an image file on your computer.

2. **Navigate to the folder that holds your eBay images on your computer.**

3. **Click the image you want to upload in the browsing window.**

   The image name appears in the Filename box.

4. **Click the Open button.**

   The selected image appears in the picture frame.

   If you accidentally select the wrong picture to upload, click the X in the lower-left corner of the thumbnail version to make the picture disappear so you can select a different one.

5. **To rotate the image, click the circular arrow (at the upper right of the main image box).**

6. **To crop the image:**

    a. **Click the crop box in the right corner of the larger image.**

       Two squares appear at opposite corners of your main image.

    b. **Click the frame on the outside of your image, and move the bar until the offensive area is cropped out.**

       You can do this from the sides, top and bottom of the picture.

7. **To make further edits (such as adjusting brightness or contrast), click the Advanced Edit button (shown in Figure 15-15) and another window pops up.**

8. **When you're finished doing your edits, click Continue.**

   A pop-up window notifies you that your picture is being uploaded to eBay's picture server.

Figure 15-15:
eBay's
Enhanced
Picture
Services.

Using your hosted images

When you're filling out the Sell Your Item form on eBay, click the Your Web Hosting link and type in the URL, or address, for the image on your ISP or image-hosting server. We recommend that you use eBay's Picture Service for the first picture (because it's free), and you can insert more than one URL for the images in your description, also at no extra charge.

Using eBay's Picture Manager

If you really can't find a place to host your own pictures, you can store them with eBay's Picture Manager. Go to your My eBay page and click the Picture Manager link. The screen shown in Figure 15-16 appears.

Figure 15-16:
eBay's
Picture
Manager.

In the Picture Manager, you'll see any pictures you have uploaded, plus these four buttons:

- ✔ **Add Pictures:** Click this button to display the basic uploader. (Find more on the basic and full-featured uploaders at the end of this bullet list.)

- ✔ **Move:** Move a picture into another folder.

- ✔ **Rename:** If you don't like the name your camera gave the picture (and who would), you can rename the image here.

- ✔ **Copy Web Links:** When you put a check mark in the corner of one of your images and click this button, the Picture Manager gives you the HTML code to copy and paste into your auction description, as shown in Figure 15-17. From the Picture Dimensions drop-down list, you can choose HTML code for three picture sizes:

  Standard: 400 x 300 (bottom of the page size)

  Header: 200 x 150 (header image size)

  Thumbnail: 96 x 72 (gallery size)

- ✔ **Delete:** Clicking here will send your images out into hyperspace forever.

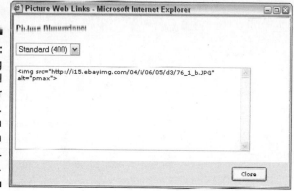

Figure 15-17:
Getting
universal
URL for your
images.
These can
be used on
any HTML
page.

Two upload screens are available in the Picture Manager: basic and full-featured. The basic uploader screen, which is shown in Figure 15-12, appears when you click the Add Pictures button on the Picture Manager screen. The basic screen uploads your pictures one at a time, as in the basic Picture Services.

Part IV
Advanced Applications for Your Newfound Skills

The 5th Wave   By Rich Tennant

"Try putting a person in the photo with the product you're trying to sell. We generated a lot of interest in our eBay listing once Leo started modeling my hats and scarves."

In this part . . .

Part IV is where we get into some advanced stuff, but in true Marsha & Patti fashion, we make it as simple as possible. You find out how to use the simplest of software tools to build your listings and clean up your pictures. (Although we feel you may have become such an expert at this point that you may not *need* software — just sheer charisma!) And we give you some extra tips on building your eBay store and applying everything you've learned to other online marketplaces.

Chapter 16

Making Perfect Pictures

*I*f there's one huge myth about taking photos for eBay, it's that you need to use a mammoth photo-editing software program. It's simply not true. In this chapter we're going to show you a few simple tips and tricks — but believe us, that's all you need. If you have to do any more editing, there's something major wrong with your image to start with. Get up from your cushy computer chair and take another picture. It's simple as that.

No eBay seller should spend hours playing with and perfecting images for eBay listings (although some very foolishly do). One pass through a simple image-editing software program gets any reasonable picture Internet-ready.

Then, after your pictures are, well, picture-perfect, look to Chapter 5 for some easy ways to upload your images to the Web.

Sizing for Dollars — and Quick Load Times

So many sellers ignore this — but it's one of the most crucial issues in eBay photography. Keep your file size small — that's right, in this case, size *does* matter, and small is beautiful. Limiting your image's file size means you don't bog down the prospective buyer's computer screen when somebody's trying to view your item page (especially if you're using multiple pictures in the item description). Why? It's simple mathematics: The larger your item's image files, the longer the viewer's browser takes to load the listing page. Most eBay users will click back out of a listing to avoid a long page load. We're looking for eyes on our items — we don't want to turn away the curious!

There are a few utilities on the Internet that you can use to measure how fast your page loads once you've completed your listing. Just search Google.com for *page load timer* and you should come up with a few services. One we tried out was at `www.numion.com/Stopwatch`. When you're viewing your listing, just copy its URL from the address line at the top of the browser into the timer page. Click *Start Stop Watch* and the program will load your requested page and tell you how long that loading takes. But realize that in this instance, the listing is loading at your computer's speed.

Pathetically, the United States (maybe because our country is so big?) lags behind the rest of the world in its percentage of broadband users. Without going into a political discussion of the high costs here in the U.S., let's just say that over 50 percent of users still dial up. Dialing up (if you broadband folks can remember back that far) means excruciatingly slow page loads.

To get a better idea of the size for the images you use online, remember that no matter which camera setting you choose, your image should be designed to be viewed on a monitor. Low resolution is just fine because the average computer monitor isn't an HDTV.

Don't confuse a printer's dots-per-inch with a monitor's pixels-per-inch. They are two different things. Check out Chapter 7 to get the full explanation.

Computer monitors measure resolution in pixels (tiny squares of on-screen light) per inch. The average monitor can only produce 72 pixels (some upper-end models can produce 96 pixels and better). This means that regardless of your vision, if an image exceeds 72-pixel resolution, *you won't be able to tell by looking at the monitor.* (The average printer can produce 600 dpi or better.) All you get for your effort is a huge file that takes forever to load.

To get a clearer picture (sorry) of why this matters, consider these average monitor-resolution settings (in pixels):

- 640×480 (VGA)
- 800×600 (Super VGA)
- 1024×768 (XVGA)

These settings determine the actual number of pixels that will be viewed on the screen. No matter how large your monitor is (whether 15, 17, or even 21 inches), it shows only as many pixels as *you determine* in its settings. On larger screens, the pixels just get larger — which makes your pictures fuzzy. That's why most people with larger screens set their monitors for a higher resolution.

Higher-resolution monitors make the screen images smaller — but a lower resolution, bigger image works better for most users. Also consider the aging baby boomers — they have become huge spenders these days (prime eBay customers), and they don't want to squint! Many of today's users keep their displays set to the 800×600 size for eye comfort, regardless of monitor size.

Of course, if you use eBay's Picture Services for your all eBay items, setting your image size is not a big issue. eBay Picture Services applies a compression algorithm that forces your pictures into eBay's prescribed size.

The more compression applied to computer images, the less sharp they appear. So you're ahead of the game if you select your image size *in your camera* or set your image-editing program to a monitor-friendly size.

Here's a checklist of tried-and-true techniques for preparing elegant, fat-free, fast-loading images to display on eBay:

- **Set your image resolution at 72 pixels per inch.** You can do this with the settings for your scanner. Although 72 ppi may seem a low resolution, it merely nibbles computer memory, shows up fast on a buyer's screen (even over a dial-up connection), and looks great on eBay.

- **When you're using a digital camera, set its resolution to no higher than the 800×600 format.** That's custom-made for a VGA monitor. You can always crop the picture if it's too large. You can even save the image at 640×480. It will display well on eBay but take up less space — so you can add more pictures!

- **Make the finished image no larger than 480 pixels wide.** When you size your picture in your image software, it's best to keep it no larger than 300×300 pixels or 4 inches square. These dimensions are big enough for people to see the image without squinting, and the details of your item show up nicely.

- **Crop any unnecessary areas of the photo.** Show only your item; everything else is a waste.

- **Use your software to darken or change the photo's contrast.** When the image looks good on your computer screen, the image also looks good on your eBay auction page.

- **Save your image as a .JPG file.** When you finish editing your picture, save it as a .JPG. (To do this, follow the instructions that come with your software.) .JPG is the best format for eBay; it compresses information into a small file that loads fast and reproduces nicely on the Internet.

- **Check the total file size of your image.** After you save the image, make sure it takes up no more disk space than about 40K (if it's too much bigger than that, see if you can crop judiciously — or compress your JPEG to reduce total size). That way eBay users will see the image appear on-screen in a reasonable amount of time.

✔ **If your image is larger than 50K, reduce it.** Small is fast, efficient, and beautiful. Big is slow, sluggish, and dangerous to your sales. Impatient eBay users will move on to the next listing if they have to wait to see your image.

Editing for Perfection (or Close Enough)

Pictures don't always come out of the camera in perfect form. However, you can make a few tweaks to bring them into near-perfection range:

✔ **Alter the size:** Reduce or increase the size or shape of the image.

✔ **Change the orientation:** Rotate the image left or right; flip it horizontally or vertically.

✔ **Crop the background:** Sometimes there's a little too much background and not enough product. Don't waste precious bandwidth on extraneous pixels. To *crop* your image means to cut away the unnecessary part of the picture.

✔ **Adjust the brightness and contrast:** These two functions usually work together in most photo programs. By giving your picture more brightness, you make the picture look brighter (duh) but too much brightness can obscure details. Raising contrast brings out detail; lowering it dulls the difference between light and dark.

No one brightness or contrast setting works equally well for all photo shoots. Experimentation is the name of the game here.

✔ **Sharpen:** If your camera was not perfectly in focus when you took the picture, applying a photo-editing program's sharpening feature can help. But easy does it. Sharpening too much can destroy the smoothness of the image.

If your image needs any more help other than these alterations, retake the picture. It's probably easier and faster.

Employing Image-Editing Software and Services

eBay sellers use a wide array of image-editing software. As a matter of fact, some listing software has built-in mini-editing capabilities. Choosing software for your images is like choosing an office chair: What's right for some people is dreadful for others.

When you buy a digital camera, it will no doubt arrive with a CD that includes some variation of image-editing software. Give it a try. If it works well for you, keep it. If not, check out the two options we mention further on in this chapter.

 Every image-editing software program has its own system requirements and capabilities. Study the software that comes with your camera or scanner. If you feel that the program is too complicated (or doesn't give you the editing tools you need), investigate some of the other popular programs. You can get some excellent shareware (software that you can try before you buy) at www.tucows.com and www.shareware.com.

 Just because a program is elaborate (and pricey) doesn't always mean it's *better* for your purposes. Marsha used to be happy using Adobe Photoshop, but it's a large, expensive program — and it's overkill for eBay images. Stay tuned for two simple, low-cost solutions: Fast Photos and eBay's own Enhanced Photo Services.

Quick touch-up and FTP in Fast Photos

If budget is a consideration (and it should be in any business), you might be happy giving Fast Photos by Pixby Software a try. It's a simple, all-in-one photo-editing program designed especially for e-commerce and eBay sellers. The developer of the software knew exactly what capabilities online sellers need for their images — and included just those — nothing else: cropping, JPEG compression, sharpening, resizing, enhancing, rotating, and adding watermark text and borders.

The software is a PC application that runs on Windows XP, 2000, ME, and 98 SE. For a 21-day *free* trial, visit their Web site at

www.pixby.com/marshacollier

 We call Fast Photos an *all-in-one* tool for eBay sellers because it not only allows you to touch up your images quickly, but also has a built-in FTP program so you can upload your images immediately after editing them.

Editing an image for eBay in Fast Photos is simple:

1. **Open the program.**

2. **Click Browse and find the directory containing your image.**

   This location can be a floppy disk (as it is for images from the Sony Mavica FD series), a Memory Stick, a CompactFlash card, or an area on your hard drive that you've set aside for storing your images.

3. **Once you've found the photo, click it, and then click the Add to Tray button (near the top of the screen).**

   Before you can settle on the correct image to edit, you have to get a good look at it, right? Figure 16-1 shows the selection process that puts it on-screen.

Figure 16-1:
Selecting a photo for editing in Fast Photos.

4. **Choose Edit.**

5. **Click to perform any of the following tasks (see the editing screen in Figure 16-2):**

   Rotate: If you've shot your picture sideways or upside down, you can rotate it here.

   Crop: In Crop mode, a gray rectangle appears with corner dots. Click a corner dot, hold, and drag the rectangle until it closes in on your item. If you want to adjust your cropping area, click and drag an edge or corner handle to adjust the rectangle's size. When you're satisfied with the cropping, double-click Apply. Poof! It crops itself and appears at your new size.

   Enhance: Brighten, darken, increase or decrease the contrast, and work with image *gamma* (how it appears on a monitor) and color. If you feel that the color of your image isn't vibrant enough or is too dark, adjust the brightness and contrast. Moving the sliders to the left or to the right will (respectively) increase and or decrease these values. The image in the main window will change as you perform your alterations, so you know what your image will look like before you save your changes. When you're happy with the image results, feel free to click Apply.

Don't worry, everything you do is visible on-screen — and it can be undone if you mess up.

Resize: You can resize your image to the standard eBay sizes or make the image a custom size.

Sharpen: Is your image a little fuzzy? Click here to bring out the details. You can apply 3 different strengths of sharpening to your pictures.

Add border: If you want a border or a drop shadow on your image, you can apply it here.

Add text: Type your user ID so you can *watermark* your images (add distinctive text in a see-through font that can help dissuade those who might try to use your images as their own).

JPEG compress: By moving a sliding bar, you can compress the image as much as you dare. The more you compress, the less detailed the image will be. Find a workable balance between clear detail and compact file size.

Create gallery thumbnail: You can create a perfect 192×192 thumbnail of your image on a white background for use in the eBay Gallery.

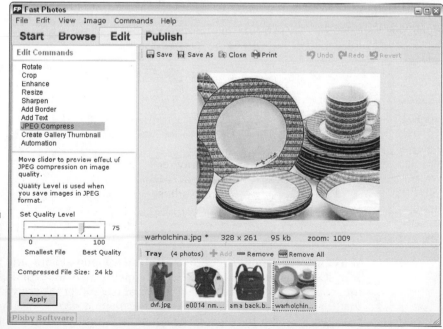

Figure 16-2:
Here we're compressing the size of the file after cropping.

6. **To save the changes you've made to your image, click Save As, give your file a name, and press Enter.**

Now you can upload your newly edited image to the Web. Those steps are just as fast:

1. **Choose Publish (on the toolbar).**

2. **Go to the Publish screen and click the Add button under the FTP accounts box.**

   This is the procedure for adding (setting up) an FTP account for uploading. The box shown in Figure 16-3 appears.

   Not to brag, but we can send 5MB worth of pictures to our ISP for free! Check to see what your ISP offers. You might want to check out mpire.com in Chapter 19 — they also have free image hosting.

3. **Input the data required for your FTP server and click OK.**

   Your image is ready to upload.

4. **Highlight the image(s) you want to upload and then click the Publish button.**

Figure 16-3:
Here's where to fill in the form with your FTP information.

Add Account

Account Name	Road Runner	Choose a name for account Example: My ISP Account

FTP Account Login Info

User Name	marshac	FTP account login
Password	*********	
Host Name	home.socal.rr.com	FTP server.host name or address Example: ftp.myisp.com
	☑ Connect in Passive Mode Test Connection...	

Remote Folder Setup

URL		URL (Web Address) of remote folder Example: http://users.myisp.com/user1
Server Folder		Name of hidden folder on server Example: www (Some ISP's require this)

Help   OK   Cancel

You can upload your images to the Web space individually or in a batch — with the same single mouse click. Once an image is uploaded, you'll see the word *done* appear in the status box at the top of the page. Notice that it showed up after we uploaded the image in Figure 16-4. You also see the URL suffix to call up the picture from your Web space.

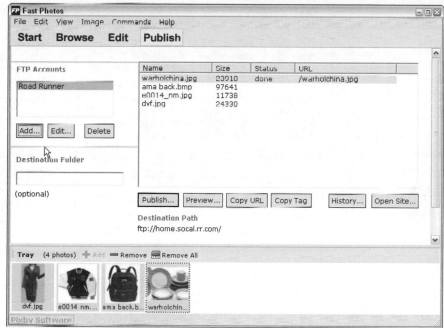

Figure 16-4:
Here we've
successfully
uploaded a
picture to
our ISP Web
space for
use in an
auction.

Using eBay's Enhanced Picture Services

Free tools — that actually work. How nice is that? eBay's Picture Services are now far more than a fancy FTP program. Now you can upload your images and perform minor editing right on your screen without and additional software.

The Enhanced Picture Services are great for quick one-off items and for beginners — but if you're selling many items on eBay, especially over the long term, you might want to invest in a more robust editing program like Fast Photos.

The Sell Your Item form is where you find the area that requests your images. Click the tab for Enhanced Picture Services. If you've never used this feature before, you may have to download a small program (see Chapter 15 for details).

To use this wonderful tool, follow these steps:

1. **Click the small Add Picture button.**

   Doing so opens a directory on your computer, as in Figure 16-5.

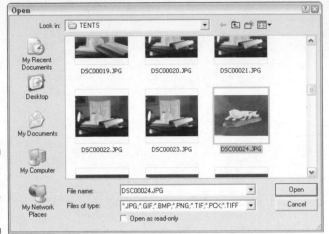

Figure 16-5:
Selecting a
picture for
uploading.

2. **Click an image to select it**.

The name of the file appears in the filename box.

3. **When you've selected the picture you want, click Open.**

Doing so adds the image to the main preview screen, as in Figure 16-6.

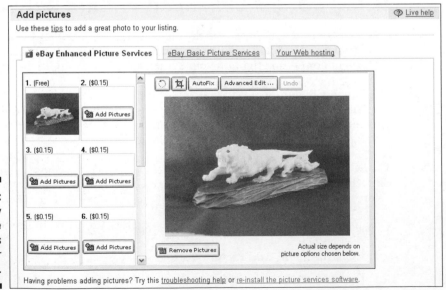

Figure 16-6:
Our lovely
lion figurine
picture is
ready for
editing.

4. Apply the appropriate controls to your picture, as follows:

- You can click the little circle if you want to rotate your image (as in Figure 16-7).

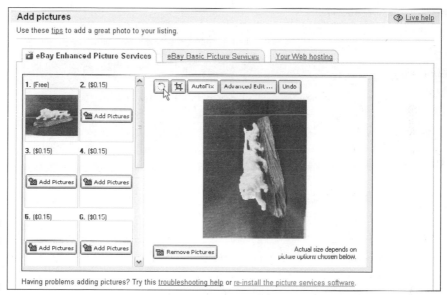

Figure 16-7:
Rotating the image.

- To crop your picture, click the crop marks. You can now drag the corners inward or outward to make your picture its best size for eBay (as in Figure 16-8).

- You can use AutoFix to let eBay's server decide what's best for your picture — but we don't recommend it. For more satisfying results, click the Advanced Edit button (as in Figure 16-9) so you have control over the changes made to your images.

- In Advanced Edit mode you can adjust contrast and brightness, along with the previously mentioned features. Thankfully, there is also the Undo button, to whisk away any overaggressive changes you may have made to your image.

5. When you've made all your changes, click Continue in the Sell Your Item form.

Your image is uploaded to eBay's server for use in your listing.

Figure 16-8:
Cropping an
image on
eBay.

Figure 16-9:
Clicking
Advanced
Edit opens
your image
in a new
smaller
screen.

The purpose of an eBay listing is to sell your stuff, and the purpose of this book is simply to demystify eBay listing. That's our mission here. We're not trying to sell you up to buy fancy software. Or to fill your head with pages upon pages of technobabble that will keep you awake all night. We're not here to make you feel bad if you can't remember what an f-stop is or remember the numeric coding for the color red (though of course you *can* worry about all that if you need another hobby). This is the simple deal. Explained this way, there's not much mystery, is there?

Chapter 17

Dolling Up Your eBay Store

*W*hen eBay Stores were first introduced, they were severely limited in their features. At the time, they provided a simple way for sellers to have all their listings displayed in one place, and that was about it . . .

They've come a long way since then! Features have burgeoned. These days eBay Store owners can choose quite an array of features to make their eBay Stores into online selling environments. Try these on for size:

- ✔ **Selling Manager:** This program keeps your sales ordered and tracked, adding professionalism even if you've never been to business school.

- ✔ **Phone support:** If you need help with your eBay Store and want to give eBay a phone call, this feature's got you covered.

- ✔ **Traffic reports:** Online visitors are the lifeblood of your eBay business; see how many folks have dropped by for a look at your wares, and how they got there.

- ✔ **E-mail newsletters:** Staying in touch with your customers — new, repeat, or regular — has never been easier.

- ✔ **Cross-merchandising:** If you have (say) a line of perfectly extreme guitar straps to go with those hot electric guitars you're selling, get those goods to help sell each other!

- ✔ **Custom non-inventory pages:** Here's where you can expand on your policies or terms and conditions, share your expertise — any non-inventory information you need to share.

- ✔ **Custom headers:** These give your store's Web pages a look that is consistent — but uniquely yours — that makes customers feel welcome.

- ✔ **Promotion boxes:** Catch that trend and ride it by calling attention to your latest hot item, or get that special sale up and running in no time.

Should you decide to open an eBay Store, you have three different levels you can choose: Basic, Featured, or Anchor. The Featured and Anchor levels have all of the same features of a Basic store, along with additional merchandising exposure and traffic reporting. To give you the big picture, this chapter covers the features that can help all eBay store owners enhance the look of their stores and their listings.

Deciding on Custom Pages

With each eBay Store, the seller can create a specific number of optional custom pages with additional information about the seller, the store, or the merchandise available for sale. A Basic store can have up to five custom pages. These pages provide a virtual blank slate for the seller to provide more information to their customers about their business and items for sale.

Follow these steps to create custom pages for your eBay Store:

1. **Go to your eBay Store.**
2. **Click the** <u>Seller, manage Store</u> **link at the bottom-right corner of the page.**
3. **Click the** <u>Custom Pages</u> **link on the left side of the page under Store Design.**
4. **Click the** <u>Create new page</u> **link to create a new custom page.**

For sellers who create an optional custom page, eBay offers a choice of layouts which include promotion boxes, item showcases, text sections, item lists, and picture placements.

How many custom pages you can create depends on the level of your eBay Store; the higher the level, the more custom pages you are allowed. When you've created the maximum number of custom pages, you have to delete an existing page before you can create a new one.

Setting Up a Theme

Chapter 4 makes the case that the best way to get return customers is for you to create a consistent look for your listings — a style or "brand" that sticks in your visitors' minds. The trick is to work up a standard color scheme, logo, and overall on-screen look that works for any and all of your merchandise. A perfect place to start is the look of your eBay Store.

eBay provides features you can use to define a theme for your eBay Store — using standard colors, fonts, and layouts, or customizing the colors and fonts you use — and you can choose from a virtual wonderland of possibilities — but here's a word to the wise . . .

If you have a logo, make sure its color scheme is made up of complementary shades. Garish, clashing colors are one way to drive your customers' eyes away from your listings. Who wants to buy what's hard to look at?

Follow these steps to customize the look of your eBay Store:

1. **Go to your eBay Store.**

2. **Click the** Seller, manage Store **link at the bottom right corner of the page.**

3. **Click the** Display Settings **link on the left side of the page under Store Design.**

4. **Click the** Edit current theme **link on the right side of the page in the Theme and Display section of the page.**

Customizing Your Store Header

The workhorse of the theme for your eBay Store is the *header* — a distinct, consistent, on-screen area that includes the seller's logo, store name, a brief description of the store, and a summary of the merchandise for sale. eBay recently provided the capability to expand the standard header with text, pictures, and links — which then appears on-screen below the standard header on every page of the eBay Store.

eBay offers several different ways to format the expanded header — and you can view current choices by going to the following page:

```
http://pages.ebay.com/storefronts/headerdesign.html
```

These options include

✔ One Main Featured Item and Two Sub-Featured Items

✔ Two Featured Items and Six Promotional Links

✔ Three Featured Items

✔ Four Featured Items

When you choose the link for the layout you prefer and fill in the options, eBay generates a paragraph of HTML commands, which you can then copy and paste when you create an expanded header. Speaking of which . . .

Follow these steps to create an expanded header:

1. **Go to your eBay Store.**

2. **Click the** <u>Seller, manage Store</u> **link at the bottom-right corner of the page.**

3. **Click the** <u>Display Settings</u> **link on the left side of the page under Store Design.**

4. **Near the bottom of the page in the Theme and Display section, click the** <u>Change</u> **link to the right of the *Store page header* designation.**

5. **Enter the text or HTML commands to be included in the new expanded header.**

Figure 17-1 shows an example of an expanded header that uses the Three Featured Items layout.

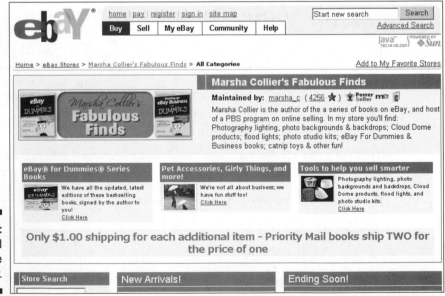

Figure 17-1: Expanded eBay Store header.

The expanded Store header appears on every page in an eBay Store, including any custom pages you've created.

Using eBay Store Promotion Boxes

One of the most flexible features that eBay offers its Store owners is the *promotion box* — which puts your hottest item right out front, calls attention to special sales, and adds some zip to your eBay Store. Promotion boxes come in various pre-designed formats that are seriously easy to use; they take you step-by-step through a guided setup process. The only limit on how to use a promotion box is the seller's imagination — imagine these uses, for example:

- Providing an alternative method for navigating through the store
- Highlighting specific listings
- Displaying a banner that calls attention to special information
- Promoting accessory items
- Announcing special sales

When you create a promotion box, you start by defining several parameters. Some of these work only with a specific type of promotion box (we get into the different types of promotion boxes later in this chapter). But several parameters are common to all promotion boxes.

- **Unique name:** You give a name to every promotion box you create. The name can be anything you want, but make sure it helps you identify the purpose of the promotion box. The box's name is never displayed in your eBay Store — your customers never see it.

- **Consistent colors:** The colors used for the promotion boxes are pre-set; they're the same ones you defined when you chose or created the theme for your eBay Store. If you want to get especially creative, you can redefine these colors (or not) for each promotion box you create.

- **Location:** You define where to put the promotion box on-screen as you create it. There are five different possible locations for promotion boxes (as detailed in the upcoming sections).

Follow these steps to create a new promotion box:

1. **Go to your eBay Store.**

2. **Click the** Seller, manage Store **link at the bottom-right corner of the page.**

3. Click the <u>Promotion Boxes</u> link on the left side of the page under Store Design.

4. Click the Create New Promotion Box button to create a new promotion box.

Promotion-box placement and size

Hey, even virtual real estate is valuable. So you get two standard, on-screen locations for the placement of promotion boxes on inventory pages — each of which has specific size limitations (summarized in Table 17-1).

If you want to use a promotion box on a custom (non-inventory) eBay Store page (as mentioned earlier in this chapter), all you have to do is choose one of the two promotion-box layouts while you're creating the custom page.

Each Store page gives you two places to put a promotion box:

✔ **The upper area of each Store page:** This area is just above the list of items for sale, and directly below the header. It's pretty handy — you can place *two* small promotion boxes there, side by side; these locations go by the names Top Left and Top Right (as shown in Figure 17-2). If you want to use this entire space for one double-wide promotion box, however, no problem.

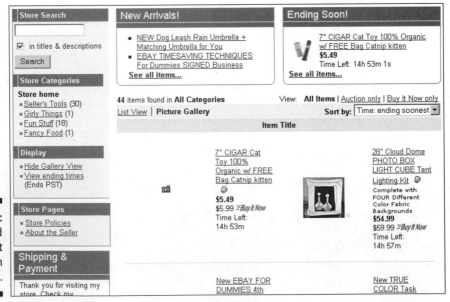

Figure 17-2:
Top Left and
Top Right
promotion
boxes.

✔ **Below the left Store Navigation bar:** Same deal here — you can put one or two promotion boxes in this area (depending on what does the job best for you), and they'll show up on every page in your eBay Store that shows a left navigation bar, as shown in Figure 17-3.

If you use eBay Store categories (if? but of course you do!), you can specify different Top promotion boxes for every separate store category page — and you can make them different from the Top Left and Top Right (or Single) promotion boxes you create for the All Categories page.

Table 17-1	Promotion Box Location Size Limits	
Promotion Box Location	*Size Limit (pixels)*	*Size Limit (characters)*
Top Left (with border)	275 wide×85 high	120 characters
Top Left (without border)	280 wide×115 high	140 characters
Top Right (with border)	275 wide×85 high	120 characters
Top Right (without border)	280 wide×115 high	140 characters
Single (with border)	575 wide×85 high	215 characters
Single (without border)	680 wide×115 high	300 characters
Upper (Left Navigation)	170 wide (unlimited height)	Unlimited
Lower (Left Navigation)	170 wide (unlimited height)	Unlimited

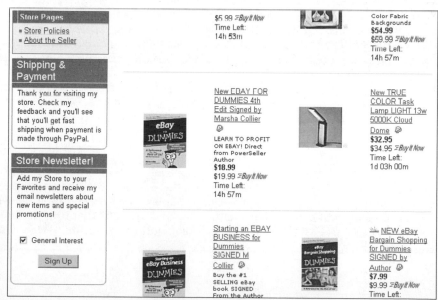

Figure 17-3: Upper and Lower promotion boxes.

Choosing a type of promotion box

eBay really started something when it introduced promotion boxes. They were so popular with eBay Store owners that many different formats were designed and made available. Customizing the look of an eBay store became as common as it was easy. The reason is simple: Most promotion-box formats are not only predefined, eBay guides you automatically through the setup process as you create them.

Custom Links

Using the Custom Links promotion box, you can display from four to ten customized links that take customers to specified pages within your eBay Store (or elsewhere on eBay). This promotion box has a border; the seller defines the border color and the words displayed in the title bar.

You can display no more than four links in either of the Upper promotion boxes. If you initially define a promotion box for one of the Left locations with more than four links, but later change the box's location to one of the Upper positions, only the first four links are displayed; the rest are hidden and not displayed.

Be sure that any links included in this promotion box are in compliance with the eBay Links policy — which (don't panic) you can find by going to

```
http://pages.ebay.com/help/policies/listing-links.html
```

Custom Text/HTML

Among promotion boxes, this one is the superhero of versatility. It allows the seller to enter virtually any text, HTML commands, or images (subject to the limitations outlined in Table 17-1). The border and title bar are optional; if you choose the border/title bar option when you create the box, you can enter the desired title — and change the color scheme if you want to.

A link to the eBay Stores HTML Builder is ready to hand just above the text-entry box for the Custom Text/HTML promotion box. See Chapter 19 for more information about HTML Builder — it's way too handy not to.

Ending Soon

The Ending Soon promotion box is predefined with a border and title bar; if you don't like the color scheme and the words in the title as supplied by eBay, you can change 'em. This box shows a picture and the title of an item whose auction is ending soon — followed by a link that the customer can use to see more listings that will be ending in the near future. (When you create

this promotion box, you can define the store category and/or the time period —
from one hour to one week — to determine which of those listings are displayed.) The Top Right box in Figure 17-2 is an example of the Ending Soon
promotion box.

If more than one listing will be ending in the time period defined for the
Ending Soon promotion box, it rotates the displayed listings randomly, and
shows them whenever the promotion box is included on a page viewed by a
customer.

Generic (Featured Listings)

The Generic promotion box features one or two individual listings. If a single
listing is featured, a link is displayed with the item's title and picture. If two
listings are featured, the box shows only the titles of the items — no pictures —
as links. Figure 17-2 shows what the box looks like for a single featured listing
(at Top Left) and for two separate featured listings (at Top Right).

When you create a Generic promotion box, you can choose the listings to be
featured — either manually or by defining specific criteria — say, listing
format, store category, keyword, price range. Either way, the featured listings
will be selected and updated automatically whenever a customer views any
page containing this promotion box.

Graphic

The Graphic promotion box displays an image, whether a custom picture
(supplied by the seller) or a predefined image supplied by eBay. You can
define this image as a link for the customer to click (gotta love that HTML!)
that displays a specific set of search results from listings in your eBay Store.
Using keywords and/or specific eBay Store categories, you can define exactly
which listings are displayed when a customer clicks this link.

If you define an image for use in the Graphic promotion box without making it
the exact size allowed for the location (as defined in Table 17-2), your image
is resized to fit that location — and the quality of the picture may suffer. For
example, if you supply a square image and the promotion box is rectangular,
the resulting graphic will show up distorted on-screen.

Table 17-2	Promotion-Box Sizes
Promotion-Box Location	*Image Size (in Pixels)*
Top Left	280 wide×115 high
Top Right	280 wide×115 high

(continued)

Table 17-2 *(continued)*	
Promotion-Box Location	*Image Size (in Pixels)*
Single (Top Area)	580 wide×115 high
Upper (Left Navigation)	170 wide (unlimited height)
Lower (Left Navigation)	170 wide (unlimited height)

Item Showcase

You can use the Item Showcase promotion box to highlight one to four specific listings at the top of category pages — and even display different listings on different category pages — either a horizontally or vertically. You can specify the listings you want displayed, or you can designate criteria that determine which items show up on-screen. And you can look ahead: If you defined your starting listings specifically, you can change them by setting criteria that pick out replacement listings when those listings end — all in the course of creating this promotion box.

The Item Showcase promotion box cannot be displayed in either the Upper or Lower locations below the left navigation bar. It won't fit.

If you've already defined the Top Left and or Top Right promotion boxes and you create an Item Showcase to put there, it'll go there but those previously defined promotion boxes change to Inactive status. You don't need to deactivate them yourself; eBay does that automatically for you when you place the Item Showcase.

Newly Listed

The Newly Listed promotion box is pre-defined with a border and title bar, although the seller may change the color scheme and the words in the title if they don't care for the title supplied by eBay. Links to two items recently listed by the seller are displayed in this promotion box, followed by a link to see more newly listed items. When creating this promotion box, you can set the store category and/or the time period — from twelve hours to one week — that determines which listings are displayed. The Top Left promotion box in Figure 17-2 is an example of the Newly Listed promotion box.

If you listed more than two items in the time period defined for the Newly Listed promotion box, it displays and randomly rotates those listings whenever it's included on a page being viewed by a customer.

Shipping & Payment Information

The Shipping & Payment Information promotion box highlights payment and shipping information for the customer. It's a predefined box with a border and title bar, although you can change the color scheme and the words in the title if eBay's defaults strike you as less than inspiring. The Upper promotion box on the left side of Figure 17-3 is an example of this promotion box.

Initially the text for this promotion box is the same as the settings defined on the Sell Your Item page (used when listing an item on eBay — see Chapter 2). Of course, you can change this information if you really want to, but keep in mind that if you change it for this promotion box, you don't change the settings for the Sell Your Item page for any subsequent new listings. (Chapter 2 also includes details on how to do that.)

Store Newsletter

The Store Newsletter promotion box displays a message about your eBay Store's e-mail-marketing mailing lists. This is a pre-defined box with a border and title bar; you can change the color scheme and the words in the title if you like. You type your promo information into a text-entry box, and if you want to work up a long-term, happy relationship with your customer (and what seller doesn't?), you can crate a Sign Up button. When the customer clicks that button, it adds your Store's owner (yep, that's you) to the customer's Favorite Sellers list on eBay, and to your mailing list. The Lower promotion box on the left side of Figure 17-3 is an example of this promotion box.

Creating and maintaining the eBay Store mailing lists is a whole other ball of wax. For the latest how-to for this powerful feature of your eBay Store, check out the following:

```
http://pages.ebay.com/help/specialtysites/
         email-marketing.html
```

Wow. All this from one basic notion: Put all the listings in one place. Looks like if you build it, they will come.

Chapter 18

Porting Your Listings to Other Sites

• •

In This Chapter

▶ Moving out into the browser battlefield

▶ Staying compatible with your customers' browsers

▶ Expanding your selling beyond eBay

▶ Setting up your own Web site and finding a host

• •

"**D**on't put all your eggs in one basket unless you want a sudden omelet." There's a reason those old sayings keep being repeated from one generation to another — they keep turning up true! There's more to eBay than just the auction site; you might lose a selling opportunity if you overlook the other available selling areas. And there's more to selling online than just selling on eBay (for openers, there's a whole Internet out there . . .). So here's where we discuss a few other sites to broaden your customer base, point out several other solutions provided by eBay the company — and maybe help you put a lot more eggs in a lot more baskets.

Selling on venues in the eBay community — or on your own Web site — is another reason to create a standard look (a.k.a. *brand*) for your listings (as discussed in Chapter 17). If a previous customer should recognize your listing layout on another Web site, it could be an incentive to purchase from you rather than from another seller.

Understanding Browser Compatibility

Before we talk about selling in different venues, we need to touch on making sure that your listings are compatible with multiple browsers. A browser, after all, is a program used to view Web sites on the Internet — not just eBay. If you're like most people, your first adventures with accessing the Internet probably got you used to the browser that was provided with your computer. Most probably, this browser was Microsoft Internet Explorer (call it a hunch).

More experienced users learn that other browsers are available, and wind up using several. They settle on one specific browser that they prefer for most uses, but keep one or two other browsers installed for use when those are required by specific sites.

In a galaxy far, far away . . .

In the early days of the Internet, there were only a few browser options. In the late 1990s, the first of the "browser wars" began between Netscape Navigator and Microsoft's Internet Explorer. Since Internet Explorer came already installed on any computer with a Windows-based platform, it became the *de-facto* standard browser, winning that war.

Recently, however, another browser war has begun — primarily due to the widespread use of Internet Explorer. Unfortunately, as the use of the Internet became more widespread, miscreants started spreading their own brand of trouble in this new landscape — creating viruses, computer worms, and malware targeted at Internet Explorer. Some even used Internet Explorer itself to spread malicious programs by taking advantage of its security flaws. Out of sheer self-defense, users have begun to explore other browsers.

Viewing a listing in various browsers

Virtually all Web pages look at least a bit different when viewed in different Web browsers. Sometimes the apparent difference is minor, such as a change in the spacing between sections of a page. But in other instances, the differences can be major — even to the point of a page that's perfectly legible in one browser being unreadable in another. This can occur because one browser might not be able to perform an HTML formatting command that the other browser handles easily.

Figure 18-1 shows the home page of Marsha's Web site (`www.coolebaytools.com`), viewed using Internet Explorer 6.0. Figure 18-2 is the same page viewed using Netscape Navigator 7.1.

And finally, Figure 18-3 is the very same page displayed in Firefox 1.5. The major difference in the three is that both Netscape Navigator and Firefox add a line break both above the header, and also between the header and the navigation bar. The border lines also appear bolder in Internet Explorer.

Although these differences in browser display appear to be minimal, there are occasions when a page viewed in a browser will look not at all like you expected, so it is very important to view all your listing pages in the browsers you expect your customers to be using.

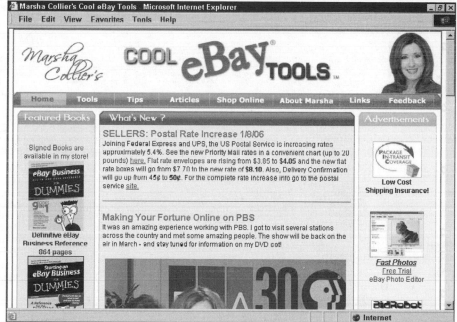

Figure 18-1: Internet Explorer's rendition of Cool eBay Tools.

Figure 18-2: Cool eBay Tools rendered in Netscape Navigator.

Figure 18-3:
Firefox view
of Cool eBay
Tools.

We recommend that you test out your listing in at least these three browsers commonly used by eBay customers:

- ✔ **Internet Explorer 6 Service Pack 1:** If you don't have it, you can download it at `microsoft.com/downloads`.

- ✔ **Netscape Browser 8.1:** Go find this browser at `http://browser.netscape.com`.

- ✔ **Mozilla Firefox 1.5:** You can get the latest version of this new, but increasingly popular browser at `www.GetFirefox.com`.

If you have access to an AOL account, viewing a listing now and then in their latest browser doesn't hurt either.

Checking Out Half.com, an eBay Company

Half.com, founded in July 1999, was the brainchild of Half.com's President Joshua Kopelman. He observed the insufficiencies of retailing in the area of used mass-market merchandise and went to work on developing a new outlet for second-hand merchandise. Kopelman's site was so successful that eBay bought out Half.com after its first year of business.

Selling at Half.com differs from selling in your eBay (or other online) personal store because you're selling in a fixed price marketplace. Your item is listed head-to-head against more of the exact same item that other sellers are selling. Half.com isn't a home for your store; you might say that each item has its own store, complete with competing sellers.

The what and how of selling on Half.com

You can sell a variety of goods at Half.com (see its home page in Figure 18-4). Half.com currently lists millions of items, including books, music CDs, DVDs and VHS video tapes, video games, and video game systems.

From a seller's point of view, the best features of Half.com are

- ✔ The item listing is free.
- ✔ The item stays on the site until the item is sold or until you remove it.

Half.com charges a commission after your item sells. Commissions for items sold in the Books, Music, Movies, and Games categories are a percentage of the selling price of the item only; the shipping cost is not added to the selling price when this commission is determined. For the most current commission rate, go to

```
http://pages.half.ebay.com/help/seller/getpaid.html
```

Figure 18-4:
The
Half.com
home page.

You'll find that some of the standard features you use at eBay — for example, feedback — also show up at Half.com. Although payments are processed via PayPal, this is transparent to both the buyer and the seller. Half.com collects the payment from the buyer, deducts the commission, and sellers get paid on a monthly basis — no worries about non-paying bidders here! And no need to determine shipping costs either; Half.com had a standard shipping reimbursement amount for each product type. For the latest on shipping costs, review the information at

```
http://pages.half.ebay.com/help/seller/fulfill.html
```

Listing your items at Half.com

To list an item for sale at Half.com, you first need to locate the item's Universal Product Code (UPC) or a book's International Standard Book Number (ISBN). In case you're wondering what an ISBN is, turn this book over and find the bar code on the back.

If you don't want to bring all your books, CDs, movies, or games to your computer, you can use an inexpensive hand-held scanner (one that holds memory) and take it over to your stacks of items. Scan all the ISBN or UPC numbers until the scanner memory fills up. Go back to your computer and download the data to input for sale.

When someone searches for an item, a book for example, at Half.com, a listing of all sellers who are selling that book appears. The listings are classified by the condition of the book — categorized as "Like New" or "Very Good" — depending on what the seller entered. The original list price of the book is included, as well as other descriptive information, and identical items listed on eBay. Other points to know about listing at Half.com include the following:

✔ When you enter the UPC or ISBN, Half.com comes up with a stock photo and description of your item, so you don't even have to take a picture for your sale. When an item is out-of-print, Half.com may not have an image to upload with the listing. In this case, a generic image appears in the area where the picture would appear.

✔ In addition to Half.com's stock description, you can also enter a short description of your item — plain text only — of up to 500 characters. It's where you tell buyers about the condition of your item. Up to 75 characters of this description display on the main product page, along with a link to display the full text.

✔ You can also add an optional expanded description of your item in either plain text or HTML. This expanded description appears on your item page underneath your comments.

The expanded description area, which allows you to enter HTML, is where you can provide an image of the item you have for sale. This feature is especially handy when Half.com doesn't have a stock photo available. (See Chapter 7 for the scoop on inserting a picture using HTML.)

As does eBay, Half.com has specific guidelines concerning what you can (and can't) include in your item description. Be sure you get up to speed on these guidelines by reviewing the Half.com policies, which you can find at

```
http://pages.half.ebay.com/help/seller/list.html
```

Trading Space on Amazon.com

Another online alternative is Amazon.com, where you'll find multiple options for selling your merchandise. We won't go into the specific details about how to list items on these alternative sites, but if you've listed items on eBay or Half.com, you'll find the listing pages on the other selling sites to be very similar. In fact, you can probably port your titles and descriptions to the other sites with very little modification.

As on eBay, Amazon.com gives you specific guidelines concerning what can be included in your item description. Check out Amazon's policies (so you can comply with them) by going to

```
http://www.amazon.com/exec/obidos/tg/browse/-/1161232/
        103-0118635-1456656
```

Similar to Half.com, Amazon.com has an area (called the Marketplace) where sellers can sell books, movies, music and associated items easily by simply entering the ISBN or UPC code. If the number is in the Amazon.com database, a stock photo and/or description is provided, and the seller needs to enter only a fixed price and the condition of the item they are selling. Amazon then provides a link to these fixed price items from their product information pages.

In addition, Amazon.com has a feature like eBay Stores, but only for fixed price listings. These listings (and any Marketplace listings the seller has) are included in the seller's zShop. And last but not least, Amazon.com has an area of its Web site where a seller can list items for auctions, just as at eBay.

To find out about selling on Amazon.com, just point your browser to the following Web page:

```
http://www.amazon.com/exec/obidos/subst/misc/
        sell-your-stuff.html
```

Selling Your Wares at Overstock.com

Overstock.com began its life as a Web site where consumers could buy (what else?) overstock items at a deep discount from the company itself. In 2005, Overstock.com opened an auction marketplace, which provides yet another outlet for selling your merchandise.

We won't cover the specific details about how to list items and sell at Overstock.com, but if you've listed items on eBay or Half.com, you'll no doubt find the selling process and format for listing items familiar, and you may be able to reuse many of the titles and descriptions you already have in place.

We advise you to look for and respect any specific guidelines that Overstock. com gives you concerning the information that's appropriate and necessary to include in your item descriptions. You can find out about its policies by following this link: `http://auctions.overstock.com/cgi-bin/ auctions.cgi?PAGE=FAQ`.

To get started selling on Overstock.com, just point your browser to the following Web page and let Overstock.com guide you from there: `http:// auctions.overstock.com/cgi-bin/auctions.cgi?PAGE=FAQ`.

Selling on Your Own Web site

Although your eBay Store can function as your sole online presence, you might at some point consider opening up your own Web site. There are literally hundreds of options available, with a wide, sometimes confusing array of options. The following bullet list highlights some of the things you need to consider when evaluating potential companies to host your Web site:

✔ Cost

- What is the basic cost per month?

- Is there an additional fee based on completed transactions?

- Is there a sign-up discount available?

✔ Disk Space

- Is there a limit for the amount of information transferred? (This limit is often based on thousands of megabytes per month)

- Will you be able to upload audio, video, and/or flash if necessary?

- Is there a limit to the number of pages, subdirectories, or sub-sites you can have?

✔ Password protection can be applied at several different levels; it's especially useful if more than one person will have access to the Web-site-building area.

✔ Site statistics or traffic reports should provide information about the number of visitors to your site and when they are visiting — the more detail the better.

✔ A Photo/File Manager will help with uploading, deleting, and relocating images, inventory, and text files.

✔ An HMTL Editor will make the task of maintaining the pages of your Web site a breeze.

✔ E-mail marketing tools can help you stay in contact with your customers — essential to garnering repeat business!

✔ Blogging Tools can put you on the cutting edge by helping you communicate with your customers via your very own blog — Weblogs are the latest thing!

✔ PayPal Payment Processing can ease the payment process for both buyer and seller.

✔ A Secure Payment Gateway is essential if you have your own merchant account for credit card payments.

✔ Is your own Domain name (`www.yourWeb site.com`) included, or will you need to get that yourself?

✔ E-mail addresses (How many do you need?)

✔ E-mail and/or phone support, tutorials, and setup wizards provided in a convenient and efficient form are essential in setting up and maintaining your Web site.

✔ Gift Certificate and Web Coupon Builders can help you create additional income sources quickly and easily.

✔ Automatic backup by the hosting company of your Web site — all of it — on a regular basis can assist in your peace of mind. (But you'll still need to make copies of essential information yourself!)

Choosing a Web-hosting company

Of course, not *all* these features are strictly necessary for the success of your Web site — and not all Web-site-hosting companies provide the same features. You have to determine which features are most important to you and your business, do your own comparison of several different hosting companies, and then decide which company offers the best place to set up your own online store.

One of the most important things to look for is sample Web sites that the company hosts — or you can ask the company for referrals to folks who use their service successfully (they won't mind referring you — call it a hunch). A current customer's evaluation can be very helpful when you're determining which Web-site-hosting service to use.

Checking out eBay's ProStores

eBay now provides a way for you to create your own Web site apart from your regular eBay Store: ProStores. Figure 18-5 shows the ProStores home page. If that looks intriguing, you can find more information about ProStores via a link at the bottom-left corner of the eBay home page (in the More eBay Sites block), or you can go directly to www.prostores.com.

As with most companies that provide Web-hosting services, ProStores has several levels of Web hosting available: ProStores Express, ProStores Business, ProStores Advanced, and ProStores Enterprise. Each level provides increasingly elaborate services — for an associated increase in cost.

As with any other Web-site-hosting company, be sure to evaluate all of the features available and estimate the expected total cost of a solution as you evaluate a potential host's services — before you sign up. Don't be afraid to shop around; the pros do.

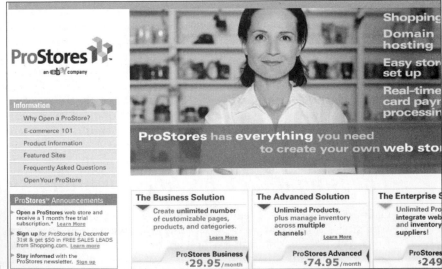

Figure 18-5: The ProStores home page.

Chapter 19

Automating with HTML Generators

*O*kay, by the time you've thoroughly used and dog-eared this book, you'll be champing at the bit to extend your eBay-listing mastery (call it a hunch) — so we'll just mention a few free HTML generators. Just remember that fancy auctions are nice to look at, but fancy doesn't make the item sell any better. Competitive pricing and low shipping rates — those are the practical nuts and bolts that work in your favor.

A clean, efficient listing with as many photos as necessary goes a long way to sell your product. The use of simple HTML doesn't slow the loading of your page, but if you dump in a lot of miscellaneous images (decorative backgrounds, animations, and other claptrap), viewing your auction becomes a chore for those who dial up. And forget the background music — that *really* slows things down (and it's so, well, '90s)!

Luckily, you don't have to know any highfalutin computer code to use these generators. So if you're stuck in a time constraint — or perhaps just like to automate your work, we found some excellent tools for you to use. These HTML generators can really help.

HTML Generator Symbols

When you use HTML generators, you will come across some universal symbols. Mostly they appear at the top of the text-input box — or in the design area. To save you confusion, here are the most common symbols and what they stand for:

B **Boldface** text

I *Italicize* text

U Underline text

Align text to the left

Center text

Align text to the right

Create a numbered list

Create a bulleted list

"Deindent" (Say what?) — that is, move indented text back to the left (Oh.)

Indent text to the right

Check the spelling in your description

You may also come to some other mysterious HTML symbols — well, okay, not so mysterious — as quests go, this one's pretty easy:

- ✔ **A double ring that looks like two chain links.** Clicking this enables you to set up a Web link.

- ✔ **The letters ABC with a check mark.** Clicking here will double-check the spelling in your text.

- ✔ **A bucket spilling paint.** (No, it isn't time to redo the living room.) Clicking the bucket brings out a color palette. Just click the color you want — and watch it will fill in the background.

Using eBay's Turbo Lister

Not much in this world is free, but (for now, anyway) eBay offers you a free, convenient tool you can use to list your items for sale: Turbo Lister. This powerful software helps you organize your items for sale, design your ads, and list them. It organizes your items for future relisting as well, saving your initial item input and allowing you to create folders for storage. Your items disappear from the program only if you delete them.

We like Turbo Lister because it's simple and easy to use, with a built-in WYSI-WYG (what-you-see-is-what-you-get) HTML editor that makes preparing your eBay listings offline a breeze. After you've input your items and are ready to list, you can just click a button and they're all listed at once. You can also stagger listings and schedule them for a later date (for a fee). Sound intriguing? Read on: This chapter gives you an inside look at how Turbo Lister works.

Although Turbo Lister is free, you're still responsible for any fees you incur by listing an item on the site.

Features and minimum requirements

eBay created a winner in Turbo Lister. It's robust software with the following seller-friendly features:

- **Self-updates:** Turbo Lister automatically updates itself regularly from the eBay site, and pops in any new eBay enhancements so your listings always take advantage of eBay's latest features. Whenever you invoke the program, it loads — and then immediately checks with the eBay server for updates. Well, okay, sometimes this can be a bit laborious (especially if the servers are busy or you have a slow Internet connection), so if you plan to list your items at a particular time, be sure to open Turbo Lister *earlier* so you can give it a few minutes to work its updating magic.

- **HTML templates:** Predesigned HTML templates are built into the program's Listing Designer. If you use one of eBay's multitude of colorful themes or layouts, you're charged an additional ten cents (horrors!) on top of your listing fees unless you're a subscriber to Selling Manager Pro — in which case, you can use the Designer for free — but what else can you get for a dime these days? You can use a template of your own design to jumpstart your ad design without incurring extra charge by pasting it into the HTML view. You can even use templates from other sources (such as those in Book V), as long as they are in HTML format.

- **WYSIWYG interface:** If you choose to design your own ads from scratch, you can do it with Turbo Lister's easy-to-use WYSIWYG (what you see is what you get) layout design.

- **Bulk listing tool:** Prepare your listings whenever you have the time. When you're ready to launch a group of them, just transfer them to the upload area and — go for it — upload them.

- **Item preview:** You can preview your listings to be sure they look just as you want them to.

- **All item listing capabilities are available offline:** By using Turbo Lister (and its constant auto-upgrading), you won't sacrifice any of the features available to you when you list on the site using the Sell Your Item form.

Although this software is hugely useful, you have to decide whether it's really for you. The first order of business is to check whether your computer meets Turbo Lister's minimum requirements.

- Your computer must be a PC, not a Mac (sorry, Mac users). You have to have the Windows 98, 98 SE, ME, NT 4+SP6, 2000, or XP operating system.

- The processor must be at least a Pentium II. The faster your processor, the better.

- You must have at least 64MB of RAM (and that's a bare minimum).

  The more RAM you have, the better things work.

- You should have at least 20MB of free space on your hard drive to run the installation.

- Minimum monitor setting of at least 800×600 resolution, 256 colors (8-bit). Keep in mind the software interface looks a lot better with 16-bit color and 1024×768 resolution. (All recent monitors these days have this capability, so you should be just fine there.)

- Microsoft Internet Explorer version 5.5 or later.

To check your version of Internet Explorer with the browser open, click the Help menu and then click About Internet Explorer command. On the top line, your Internet Explorer version number is listed.

Downloading Turbo Lister

Of course, to use Turbo Lister, you have to get hold of it first. Go to the download page at

```
pages.ebay.com/turbo_lister/download.html
```

After you install Turbo Lister on your computer, you can list auctions on the easy-to-use form. What could be simpler?

After you get to download page, follow these steps:

1. **Read the system Requirements.**

   The requirements for using Turbo Lister appear above the two links for downloading. Things change quickly in the eBay world and you need to be sure your computer is prepared for the installation.

2. **Click the Turbo Lister Web Setup link.**

   The Windows Security warning appears, cautioning that you're about to download something foreign to your computer.

3. **Click Yes.**

   Clicking Yes downloads Turbo Lister; clicking No doesn't. Just trust us (and eBay) and click Yes.

From this point on, installation is automatic. Voilà! Turbo Lister is on your computer!

Note that this procedure first downloads a small setup version of the program that checks your computer for preinstalled files. When that task is finished, Turbo Lister checks back with mothership eBay and automatically downloads any files it needs.

After you've installed the program, you'll see a new icon on your desktop — a little green man juggling magic pixie dust over his head. This is the icon for Turbo Lister. Double-click it and you'll see the Turbo Lister splash screen, which pops up every doggone time you open the program — which can get annoying. It doesn't do anything for you and wastes precious seconds of your time. If you want to avoid it, click the check box labeled *Do not show me this screen again,* and then click Start Here. The little green man will be forever banished.

When the program is open, the first thing you do is to set up a new Turbo Lister file, like this:

1. **Select the Start option from the opening screen, and click Next.**

2. **Fill in your eBay user ID and password, and then click Next.**

   Turbo Lister now wants to connect back to eBay to retrieve your eBay account information.

3. **Make sure your Internet connection is live, and then click the Connect Now button.**

   In a minute or so, a small window opens with your eBay registration information (your name, address, and e-mail address). Click Next.

4. **Click the button next to one of the three offered choices:**

   a. **Create a new item:** Click this one if you'd like to create a new listing item immediately.

   b. **Import Items from my eBay Selling Account:** This option allows you to prepopulate the program with your existing listings.

   c. **No Action:** The program does nothing until you give it a command. We like this option because — due to many disasters over the years — we've learned to "think first, *then* click."

5. **Click Finish.**

   The program awaits and you're ready to list.

Listing with Turbo Lister

Now that you have Turbo Lister at hand, you can prepare hundreds of eBay listings in advance and launch them with a single mouse click. Or, if you want to start your auctions at a particular date and time, you can select a scheduled item launching format.

Assuming you told the program to do nothing upon startup, we suggest that if you currently have items up for sale on eBay (and who doesn't?), you import your existing eBay listings into the program. If you have multiple stock items listed on eBay (that you've listed through the Sell Your Item page or with eBay's relist feature), you can import those listings into Turbo Lister for future use and relisting. Just choose File⇨Import Items⇨From eBay Listings, as we have in Figure 19-1.

Then you have choice to make about what to download:

✔ **Your active listings:** The items that you currently have up for sale on the site, whether they are in your store or on the auction site

✔ **Your ended listings:** Here you can download — by indicating 'em in the drop-down menu — your ended items from the past 24 hours, 7 days, 14 days, 31 days and All. Clicking *All* permitted us to download everything back to 90 days! The whole thing came to 321 items, so we backed off and only took 7 days' worth!

Click the Show Preview link (as in Figure 19-2) before you download your items. That's the way we found out that we didn't *need* all those 321 items eBay was ready to send to us!

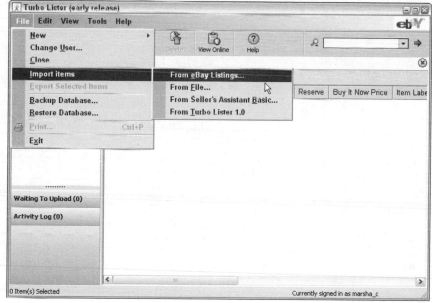

Figure 19-1:
Retrieving
our eBay
listings for
future
reuse.

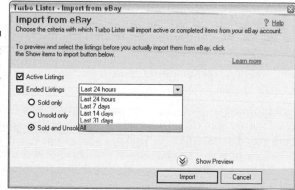

Figure 19-2:
Your have
many
choices
to make.
Be sure to
preview so
you're not
inundated!

If you sell individual items and have no repeat stock, don't bother taking the time to download your old listings. We *do* suggest that you indicate that you want all Unsold items for the past 90 days. That way you won't have to reinput them when it's time to resell.

Behold: In a moment or two, you're presented with a complete listing of everything you've asked for. (What a concept.) You can then save your listings as templates or for uploading at a later date. If you have duplicate of any items, you can highlight the ones you wish to remove; hit your Delete key and bid them begone. You can also highlight the items you want to remove and go to Edit➪Delete Items, as in Figure 19-3.

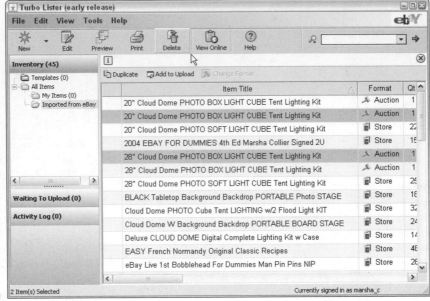

Figure 19-3:
Remove
unwanted
duplicates
from your
list before
you
download.

Here's the heart of the matter. Follow these steps to list an auction:

1. **Click the New button (the one with the starburst symbol) in the upper-left corner.**

   You see a menu where you can either *Create a New Item* or *Create Multiple Items with Pre-filled Item Information*.

   a. Creating Multiple items is handy if you are listing many items that are type of media, like CDs, DVDs or books. Selecting Multiple items gets you a screen like the one in Figure 19-4. You can also select whether you want to run these listings as Auctions, Fixed Prices, or as Store Listings.

   At this point, the items we asked for will show up in the Item Inventory box with our other items we've downloaded from eBay. (As Figure 19-5 shows, you can even edit those listings.)

   b. Selecting Create a New Item brings you to a screen where you decide the type of listing you want.

   From here on, let's assume we want an Auction format for our listing.

2. **Click the Auction option, and then click Next.**

   A page appears, waiting for you to enter all your listing information, including your title (and subtitle if you want).

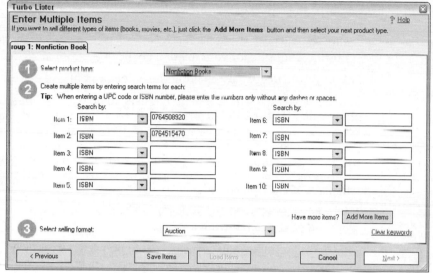

Figure 19-4:
We can list lots of books quickly by merely typing in their ISBN numbers.

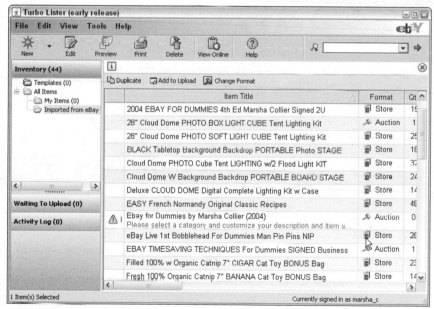

Figure 19-5:
You may now make edits on your pre-filled media listings.

You can save bunches of time if you write your titles and descriptions in Notepad or Word, at your leisure, before you go into Turbo Lister. You can use your own templates or use the program's Design view to doll up your text.

3. **In the Item Title box, enter the title.**

   If you want to use a subtitle, type that as well. Subtitles are handy for adding selling points that accompany your title in search results. (Entering a subtitle for your auction costs an additional fifty cents.)

4. **Select your category by clicking the Select box.**

   You are presented with a screen that lists all eBay categories in a hierarchal format. The main categories are listed with a plus sign next to them. When you find your main category, click the plus sign, and subcategories are displayed, as shown in Figure 19-6. To drop even lower into the world of nether-categories, keep clicking the plus signs next to subtopics. You know you've hit the bottom rung of the category ladder when you see only a minus sign.

5. **If you have an eBay Store, select a category for the item in your store from the next drop-down list.**

   This list is automatically populated from your eBay store with your custom categories when eBay updates your Turbo Lister installation. Select your desired Store category (if any) and click Next.

6. **Get Item Specifics.**

   Many products will have pre-filled data supplied by the manufacturer. In Figure 19-7, we searched and found the item we wanted to list by using the online Item Finder. You're now presented with some data to confirm, as well as a drop-down menu that offers three options: New, Refurbished, or Used. Note that this information may vary to match your item.

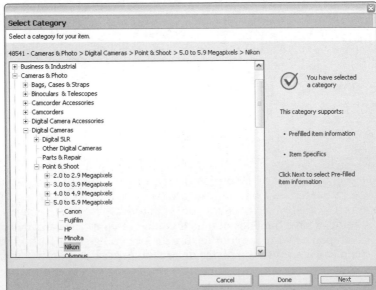

Figure 19-6:
Select
the final
category.

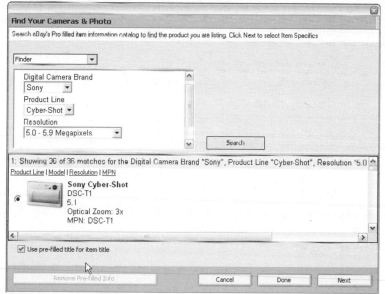

Figure 19-7:
Using the
online Item
Finder.

Once you've gone through the details given here, you'll be presented with listing software that closely mirrors the HTML capabilities of the Sell Your Item form (which we outline in Chapter 2).

Using Third-Party HTML Generators

It's (third-) party time! In addition to what you can get from eBay, there are plenty of software packages on the market that allow you to produce some amazing HTML designs. We actually found a couple of genuinely good HTML generators online. Have a look.

Mpire.com Launcher

We were blown away when we saw the quality of this tool — especially when we found out it was *free!* You can design and list your items right from the Mpire Web site. The point of Launcher is to familiarize you with Mpire.com's other services, but using Launcher is completely free. From here you get some pretty neat capabilities:

✔ You can host up to 10MB of images at no charge. *(That's FREE, gratis, no dinero!!)*

✔ You can schedule your listings for free. Mpire will launch them on eBay on a time schedule for you.

✔ You get to use a small, but nice, selection of templates. Over and over, in fact. You can put in your regular text just once — and use it again and again.

This is all pretty amazing! Take a look at Figure 19-8 to see Mpire Launcher's Sell Your item form.

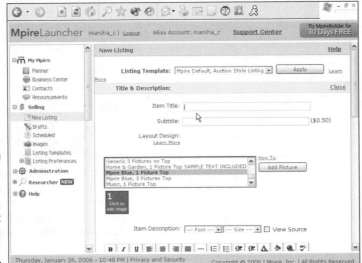

Figure 19-8:
Beginning
a listing
here is just
like using
Turbo Lister!

Once you've filled in your title and sub-title (if you wish) you can select one of Mpire's many colorful templates (check out the one in Figure 19-9) — or you can select a generic one that has no extra graphics and your own images can take center stage.

You can then input your text in an HTML generator and doll it up using the standard buttons. At the bottom of Mpire's form will be all your listing details — you can edit the items here in one swoop — then you've got a beautiful listing ready to upload to eBay.

Using ours: simple, quick, and free

Because there are times you're in too much of a hurry to fool with *anything* (and believe us, we've been there), we've put a free ad tool on the Web site:

www.coolebaytools.com

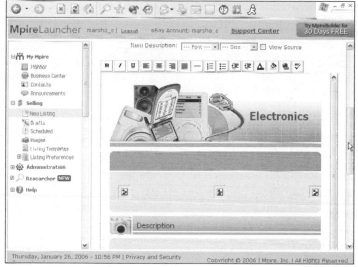

Figure 19-9:
An elegant graphic for an electronics listing.

When you land on the home page, click the link in the navigation bar labeled Tools. On the resulting page, click the Cool Free Ad Tool link and you jump to the instant template page, shown in Figure 19-10.

Figure 19-10:
The Cool Free Ad Tool page on Marsha's site.

To set up a quick eBay template using this tool, follow these steps:

1. **In the Title box, type the headline for your description.**

2. **In the Description box, enter a description.**

   You can copy and paste prewritten text from Notepad or a word-processing program, or just write your copy text as you go along.

3. **In the Photo URL box, enter the URL of your image.**

4. **In the Shipping terms box, type in pertinent information. If you don't want to include it, it's not necessary.**

5. **Enter the e-mail address that you use for eBay.**

   The address is used to put code in your description for an E-mail for Questions link. We do not keep your e-mail information (for oh, so many good reasons — and we figure you know 'em).

6. **Select the border and background colors from the drop-down menus.**

7. **Click View Ad.**

   You see how your new auction description looks. Ours is shown in Figure 19-11.

Take a minute to check your handiwork: With the description in place, scroll down until you see a box containing the auction description's HTML code, as shown in Figure 19-12.

You can copy and paste this code directly into the eBay description area of the Sell Your Item form (or any eBay listing tool). You can also add HTML codes and even another picture to your auction description.

Today eBay, tomorrow the planet.

Givenchy Winter in Paris Musical Snow Globe

Description

Elegant Givenchy "Winter in Paris" Musical Snow Globe would make an perfect gift; or a lovely addition to your Holiday Decor. This is a high quality snow globe with exquisite detail. The globe features a wintery scene of the Givenchy Building in Paris at Christmas time, with holiday wreaths hung on windows and doors. Both sides of this beautiful globe show a different view of the building. Plays: La Vie en Rose. Brass plaque on front reads Givenchy Globe measures approx 7" High x 4-1/2" Diameter True Glass globe with Wooden Base Wind-up musical globe and does not require batteries.

Shipping & Payment Terms

Winning bidder to pay calculated Priority Mail (2 to 3 day) shipping based on distance. Please use the eBay Shipping Calculator below. Type your zip code in the box below to determine your shipping rate. If time is not of the essence, please email and we will quote a lower FedEx Ground shipping rate. Please submit payment within a week of winning the auction. Credit cards graciously accepted through PayPal.

HAVE A QUESTION?

Figure 19-11: Your instant eBay ad.

Copy & Paste the following code into the auction's description box:

Figure 19-12: HTML coding for your auction.

```
<CENTER><table border="3" bordercolor="navy"
cellspacing="0" cellpadding="0" width="500"
bgcolor="#ffffff"><tr><td colspan="3"
bgcolor="#ffffff"><center><font face="arial black"
color="navy" size="+2">Givenchy Winter in Paris
Musical Snow Globe </font><br><br><table border="0"
width="500" bordercolor="#000000" cellspacing="0"
cellpadding="5"><tr><td width=500 align="center"><img
src="http://www.collierad.com/snowglobe.jpg"
hspace="0" vspace="0" border="0"></td></tr> <tr><td
align=center bgcolor="navy"><font color="white"
size="+1"
face="arial"><b>Description</b></font></td></tr><tr><td
align=center><font face="arial">Elegant
```

Part V
The Part of Tens

The 5th Wave   By Rich Tennant

"Maybe it would help our eBay sales if we perk up
the listings with images of our products in action."

In this part . . .

In traditional *For Dummies* style, we give you our Part of Tens. You get two chapters, each with ten nuggets of solid, no-baloney facts that will rush you ahead of the rest of the sellers.

Chapter 20

Debunking the Ten (or so) Online Photography Myths

In This Chapter

▶ How not to mess up your pictures with bad advice

▶ Don't waste your time on dressing up the picture

▶ Getting creative with manual camera settings

▶ Setting up your photo studio cheaply and reasonably

*W*e began this book with the reference to "all the misinformation we've seen about selling on eBay." This chapter carries on with that theme and plays mythbuster with some of the most common (and upsetting) selling myths passed around by the "experts." We'd like to take a shot at the "experts" right here: There are "experts," and there are **experts.** Just because you are an expert writer, an expert businessman, or even an expert photographer, it does not mean that you are also an expert eBay seller. Just ask anyone who sells products for a living on eBay.

Sellers pick up 1,001 selling nuances over time, and we like to include some of these as insights in our books. The "experts" who don't sell on eBay have to rely — not on experience — but on the truthfulness of people who inform them. And face it: No seller ever wants to give away his or her real trade secrets!

We put together this chapter's list of no-nos after reading several "expert" books about taking pictures for use on eBay (which were written by writers and photographers, *but not sellers!*). Please remember that *we do not recommend* the ideas put forth in any of these headings below. Don't e-mail us to complain that we told you to do any of this stuff. We didn't. We don't. Read on for the reasons why.

Putting together a makeshift photo studio from household items

Huh? Using a makeshift studio for photography makes about as much sense to us as using newspapers for baby diapers. If you shop with a keen eye for bargains (on eBay, of course), you can assemble a low-cost home version of a small *professional* photo studio.

People who decide that selling online isn't for them close out their businesses and sell perfectly good, gently-used photography tools. That's not to mention the individuals who understand eBay photography and make their business selling these items. (We like to do business with little guys like us — just be sure to check their feedback.) Be sure to shop smart and weigh the prices against the seller's feedback. A low-priced item plus a low-feedback seller could equal disaster.

Note some accessories suggested in other books and our offering of reasonably priced alternatives:

- ✔ **Metal Clamps.** Instead of using metal clamps to pull back fabric or to affix things to your lights, why not use clothespins? Marsha bought a bunch of them at the 99-cents store and has more than she can ever use for about a buck! By the way, when you use clothespins to affix diffusion material to a flood light, be sure to use *wooden* clothespins. Plastic clothespins may melt, and although there's a remote chance that wooden ones could catch fire, there's far less chance of self-immolation than you'd get from melted plastic when you're using a 100-watt bulb!

- ✔ **Clear plastic shower curtains.** In lieu of jury-rigging diffusion material from a snipped-out portion of a clear plastic shower curtain affixed to your flood light with metal clamps, why don't you just use what the pros use? Go online and buy a 10" x 10" or 12" x 12" diffusion gel (eBay sellers sell them). Although these items are considered disposable by professional cameramen and photographers, Marsha has used the same lowly piece of diffusion gel paper for months — and it shows no signs of self destructing.

  You can buy these diffusion-gel squares for around $2 apiece, and we think that's a way better deal than slicing up a shower curtain!

- ✔ **Poster board.** It's been suggested that you use poster board as a background for your pictures. And it is a good idea, but only if you're photographing a few items. Marsha used poster board when she first started photographing items for eBay, and it worked well. But before long, the board starts to curl or get dirty, which necessitates replacement. If you're shooting enough pictures you might have to replace the board every other day or so, and that's not very cost effective. Foamboard may be more durable, but it isn't bendable — and it's quite expensive!

Why not save a piece of poster board for reflecting emergency accent light — and purchase a portable backdrop stage for your background? Made of ABS plastic, backdrop stages are incredibly easy to clean and always stay their true color.

- **Beeswax.** Nope! None of their beeswax! Some sellers use beeswax to secure items in an irregular position for photography. For instance, when you want to hold a piece of jewelry or a gem at a specific angle, beeswax may be great. But we've found that it can often be very difficult to remove from the object we're photographing. Using museum putty (not the gel, the putty!) works much better; it holds even tighter, and is so very easy to remove from the item once we're finished taking its picture.

  You can buy a package of museum putty for about $6 on eBay, and it will last you virtually forever.

Dressing up your pictures for more appealing images

Yeah, well . . . no. Although dressing up items for a picture may *sound* like a great idea, it's not even a good one. In her early days working on retail holiday catalogs, Marsha thought that "dolling up the shot" with some decorative gewgaw was a great idea, too — until one day a photographer actually questioned what it was she was supposed to photograph. From that point, extraneous photo décor became limited to minimal greenery in the backgrounds.

Take a look at the picture shown in Figure 20-1. A prospective buyer might think that the background decorations are also part of the item for sale. Not dolling up your photo means this:

- **No filling the wine glasses you're selling because it looks cute:** When you do so, the buyer can't see whether there's any damage in the glass.

- **No putting flowers in the vase because they're pretty:** Again, you'd be obscuring important parts of the vase itself.

- **No clumsy accessories in the picture:** This is true no matter how homey you think they make your picture look.

These photos are quick pictures of merchandise for sale — not works of art.

Figure 20-1:
What
exactly are
we selling
here?

Saving time by taking a picture of one in a set

We found this one-in-a-set advice to be particularly offensive. The advice seemed to say that if you have a set of six items, why photograph all six? Instead, just shoot a picture of one and *tell* prospective buyers that there are six because "they all look the same."

So why is photographing just one item in a set not a good idea? Think about it: The buyer needs to know that all the items included in the package are for sale, and that they are all flawless and in perfect condition. You might get around not demonstrating the items' condition buy stating that the items are new and in a manufacturer's box — but why tempt fate? Shoot a picture of the whole shebang. Figure 20-2 shows the difference in the results.

Figure 20-2: Which picture portrays the set better?

Adding fancy camera attachments to make up for bad lighting

Hello? If you read Part III, you know that lighting your images is not the big deal you once thought it was. Why spend lots of money on extra camera attachments when you can use some of the great tools we use to prevent glare and color shifting?

At the very least, go for a full-spectrum light bulb that takes advantage of the camera's automatic white balance; it results in crisp, bright colors.

Using fancy backgrounds to make a "more interesting shot"

We swear — taking "interesting" shots is not the right idea. Looking at an item against a busy background can be like taking an eye test: Your prospective customer needs to see the item and understand immediately what they are looking at, without distractions. The photographic message must be simple and clear, not complicated like the scene depicted in Figure 20-3.

Figure 20-3:
We can't
say it
enough
times: Keep
the back-
ground
simple!

Saving your image without compression

Yes, we know that if we don't compress JPG photo files, they'll have more data and will also be very large. When you save your JPGs — as in the program Fast Photos (see Chapter 16) — be sure to compress the photo to the smallest size that still gives you an acceptable image.

If you do use image-editing programs, be sure to do any editing *before* compressing your image. Why? Because the more pixels you have to play with while editing, the better job you can do. Compressing a JPG should always be your last step.

Figure 20-4 shows you two images placed side by side for viewing online: One image was compressed mightily and the other not so much. We challenge you (without the obvious labels, of course) to tell which image is which. Pictures viewed on a computer screen — especially small photos like those you find on eBay — don't need tons of data and high resolution.

Figure 20-4:
The image on the right has been uber-compressed. Surprised?

Adjusting the f-stops and shutter speed

Using the manual settings of your camera to get a perfect shot may seem like a peachy idea, and it really may get you a better image. But hold on a minute: Tinkering with the manual settings is going to seriously eat into the time you have to devote to your eBay activities.

We advocate using your time differently — for example, use it to post your sales receipts and deposit your profits from your PayPal account. the idea is to make the best use of your eBay-selling time.

Using bright white bulbs for your lighting

All we need do with this "bright white" myth is point you to the images in the color section of this book. There you find one simple answer: Hands down, the winner for best lighting is a full-spectrum or true-color bulb with a temperature of 5000° or 5500° K and a brightness — or color-rendering index (CRI), as noted in Chapter 12 — in the 90s.

Chapter 21

Ten Tips for Your Auction Design

*T*hroughout this book, we give you many options for making your displays more effective — from designing your auctions (and other listings) to presenting the necessary information about your merchandise and offering customers a compelling first look at it. In this chapter, we give you our top ten tips for designing the perfect listing.

Writing a Detailed Description

One of the most important recommendations we can give you is to write the description for your listings as if there were no pictures. Describe your merchandise in detail, noting the size of the item, the color of the item, any flaws it may have — and don't forget to include its uses and benefits. If you write the description as if the pictures were not present, you probably won't leave out any important details — such as whether the box is included, or the actual dimensions of the item.

Additionally, there is a technical reason for writing a detailed description of your merchandise. Even the most reliable of services for hosting images — including eBay Picture Services — has short-term outages. (We've noted that such outages invariably happen in the last few hours of a listing's duration, thanks to Murphy's Law!) Words back up pictures.

Speaking of effective backups, let's hear it for the free picture eBay provides when you list an item for sale! Always use it — even if you host your images on another site and embed them in your listing description (as described in Chapter 7). If either hosted picture suddenly becomes temporarily inaccessible for technical reasons, your customer can still view at least one of the images. The odds are in your favor that either the hosted images or the free picture will still be available — and that could save a sale.

In the early days of eBay (which was then called Auction Web), few listings actually included digital pictures of the item for sale because widespread use of digital cameras among consumers was still years away. The most successful sellers were those who could write a description that painted a mental picture with such vivid clarity that the potential buyers had no question in their minds about what they were purchasing. Even though the tables have turned — now the majority of listings have at least one picture — the importance of writing a detailed description has not diminished. Doubt it? Ask any copywriter for an ad agency.

Taking Sufficient Pictures

A significant portion of this book discusses taking good pictures for your auction listings, sure — but just *once* more, we'd like to touch on the importance of taking *enough* pictures of your items. After all, shopping online isn't as tangible as shopping in a local department store — your customer can't pick up your merchandise to examine it closely. Therefore make sure that your images make a strong enough impression to make the customers forget they can't reach into the screen and pick up the item.

The task of taking multiple pictures from many different angles takes on more importance when your merchandise is an antique or collectible item. The condition of the item has a significant effect on the final selling price, and though your description plays an important part in conveying the condition of an item, multiple pictures can do the majority of the job for you.

In an earlier tip in this chapter, we suggest writing your description as if there were no pictures. Here's the flipside of the same idea: Take your pictures as if there were no description. Imagine that your pictures are the only information available for your customer to use when making their buying decision — *and* take enough pictures so they have no doubt about what they are purchasing, or its condition.

Using Color Only to Enhance

Color can provide a soothing break from the stark black and white of an unenhanced listing description. But avoid overuse of color. When new sellers first learn to change the color of their text with HTML commands, they often go wild and change colors every sentence. (Ow. Pass the aspirin.) Severely contrasting colors are the biggest problem, distraction, and (ultimately) turn-off — so make sure that your colors blend smoothly subtly enough that they're almost not noticeable.

Don't overuse color to the extent that the resulting description puts up a glare that hurts your customers' eyes when they view the page! There are far more effective ways to convey your enthusiasm (well-crafted descriptions, for example).

Keeping Your Customer Informed

One of the biggest mistakes new sellers make in their item descriptions is not including all the information a customer needs. In addition to every significant detail about the item you have for sale, each listing should include exact shipping costs. When viewing your item, the customer should know right up front what the final cost of the item will be, including shipping.

Although offering to provide a shipping quote is admirable, there is an inherent danger in doing so. Many buyers simply move on to another listing where all of the information is provided for them, rather than spend time haggling about shipping and waiting for a response from the seller. Even if some buyers do e-mail for a shipping quote, more often than not they continue to shop in the meantime — which increases the likelihood that they'll purchase from another seller who specifies the shipping costs.

Be sure to include other important information for your customers, including

- What payment methods you accept
- When they can expect their item to be shipped
- What guarantees you provide
- Your return policy

Establishing Your Brand Identity

After you determine a listing layout you like — one that works for virtually all your merchandise — use it consistently for all your listings. Doing so helps establish a *brand identity* for you and the items you sell. It's a proven technique; chain stores use the same look and layout for the items they sell. The idea is to make return customers comfortable so they know where to go to find exactly what they're looking for with minimum effort. Creating a standard layout for your online listings provides the same kind of comfort for your return customers.

Avoiding Unnecessary Complexity

A common mistake new sellers make is to include animated figures they've run across that they think are cute — or include a sound file that repeats their favorite song as long as a customer is viewing the listing. (Consider: Does a singing plastic trout in a store make you want to buy the things right next to it?) Remember the KISS — Keep It Simple, Stupid! — principle and don't plaster your listings with unneeded gewgaws. After all, if you include all of the other *practical* things we've told you are important, your listing will be complicated enough — but won't come across that way. Providing information about your merchandise is a better use of your customer's time (and yours).

Encouraging Multiple Purchases

If selling one item is a good thing, selling more than one to the same customer is even better. Here are some advantages for you when a customer makes multiple purchases:

- ✔ You can send a single, combined invoice.
- ✔ You have to prepare just one package for shipment
- ✔ You clear out more inventory with less effort.

There are several ways to encourage a customer to purchase more than one item. The first and most effective is to provide a discount on shipping for multiple purchases. Buyers love this option, and will often look at your other items for sale when they notice you offer a shipping discount, even if they were originally only interested in purchasing one item.

You can indicate any shipping discounts for multiple purchases when you list your item for sale on eBay. If you take advantage of this feature, eBay displays a special icon to call attention to your shipping discount, as shown in Figure 21-1.

Including links to your other listings is a good way of encouraging a customer to make a multiple item purchase. If you have an eBay Store, a built-in cross-promotion feature automatically displays other items available for purchase in your eBay Store. Which items are displayed is defined by the seller, and using this feature wisely will also encourage your customers to consider purchasing more than one item before leaving your store. Figure 21-2 shows how the cross-promotion box displays additional items.

Shipping, payment details and return policy

Shipping Cost	Services Available	Service Transit Time*	Available to
US $4.99	US Postal Service Priority Mail®	Estimated delivery 2-3 days	United States only

*Sellers are not responsible for service transit time. Transit times are provided by the carrier, exclude weekends and holidays, and vary with package origin and destination, particularly during peak periods.

Will ship to United States.

Pay only $1.00 shipping for each additional item from this seller's other listings!
Learn about shipping discounts

Shipping insurance
Not offered

Sales tax
Seller charges sales tax for items shipped to: CA (8.250%).

Seller's payment instructions
I will combine shipping if you purchase more than one item from me! Check my feedback and you'll see that you'll get fast shipping payment is made through PayPal. Autographed books are not returnable. Thanks for visiting!

Payment methods accepted

This seller, marsha_c, **prefers PayPal**.

PayPal

MasterCard · VISA · AMEX · DISCOVER · eCHECK

Figure 21-1:
Shipping-discount icon.

See More Great Items From This Seller

20" Cloud Dome PHOTO SOFT LIGHT CUBE Tent Lighting Kit	Cloud Dome W Background Backdrop PORTABLE ROAD STAGE	Cloud Dome PHOTO Cube Tent LIGHTING w/2 Flood Light KIT	PayPal For Dummies /V Rosenborg/ Marsha Collier:Editor
US $48.95	US $36.99	US $159.99	US $14.99
Buy It Now	Buy It Now	Buy It Now	Buy It Now

Visit seller's Store

Figure 21-2:
eBay Store cross-promotion display.

Be sure that any links you include in your listings adhere to eBay's Links policy, which can be found on the following Web page:

`http://pages.ebay.com/help/policies/listing-links.html`

If Chapter 17 hasn't yet convinced you to open an eBay Store, perhaps you'll reconsider opening one, if only for the additional merchandise exposure options that eBay automatically provides for eBay Store owners. The most effective of these is the *listing header* option. This option provides a header in each of your listings that, among other things, includes a search box that searches only the items in your eBay Store. What better way to encourage your customers to view other items you have available? Figure 21-3 shows an eBay Store header embedded in a listing. (See Chapter 17 for detailed instructions on how to add this feature to your listings after you open your eBay Store.)

Figure 21-3: An eBay Store listing header.

Using HTML to Your Advantage

Employing HTML commands to fluff up your listings makes them look nicer, perhaps even more colorful. But the most important reason for using HTML in your listings is to make them more readable for your customer.

Oddly enough, the most basic of HTML commands — the paragraph break (<P>) — can have the greatest effect on the look of your listings. Take a look at the listing shown in Figure 21-4, where no text breaks are provided. Difficult to read, isn't it?

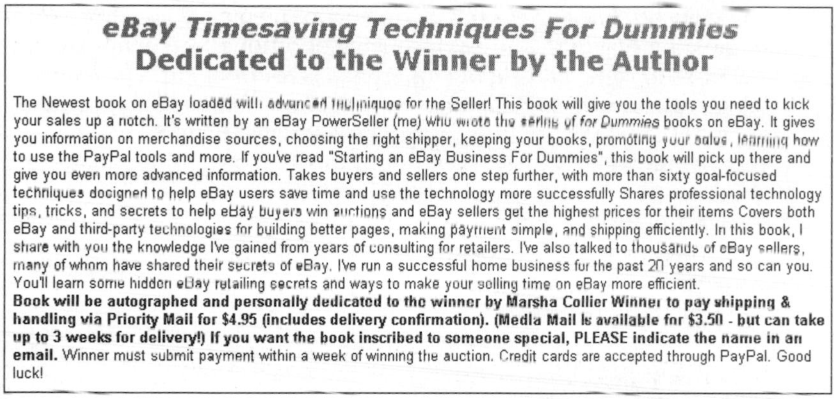

eBay Timesaving Techniques For Dummies
Dedicated to the Winner by the Author

The Newest book on eBay loaded with advanced techniques for the Seller! This book will give you the tools you need to kick your sales up a notch. It's written by an eBay PowerSeller (me) who wrote the series of for Dummies books on eBay. It gives you information on merchandise sources, choosing the right shipper, keeping your books, promoting your sales, learning how to use the PayPal tools and more. If you've read "Starting an eBay Business For Dummies", this book will pick up there and give you even more advanced information. Takes buyers and sellers one step further, with more than sixty goal-focused techniques designed to help eBay users save time and use the technology more successfully Shares professional technology tips, tricks, and secrets to help eBay buyers win auctions and eBay sellers get the highest prices for their items Covers both eBay and third-party technologies for building better pages, making payment simple, and shipping efficiently. In this book, I share with you the knowledge I've gained from years of consulting for retailers. I've also talked to thousands of eBay sellers, many of whom have shared their secrets of eBay. I've run a successful home business for the past 20 years and so can you. You'll learn some hidden eBay retailing secrets and ways to make your selling time on eBay more efficient. **Book will be autographed and personally dedicated to the winner by Marsha Collier Winner to pay shipping & handling via Priority Mail for $4.95 (includes delivery confirmation). (Media Mail is available for $3.50 - but can take up to 3 weeks for delivery!) If you want the book inscribed to someone special, PLEASE indicate the name in an email.** Winner must submit payment within a week of winning the auction. Credit cards are accepted through PayPal. Good luck!

Figure 21-4: A listing description that runs on and on and on.

Now look at the listing in Figure 21-5, where the information is separated by paragraph breaks. What an improvement in readability! Remember, the goal is twofold:

- ✔ To provide your customers with all the information they need to know about your merchandise and your policies.
- ✔ To provide that information in the most straightforward manner.

Making the text in your listing description easy to read is a good start. Just as important is proper placement of that information in your listing. The idea is to take full advantage of the space available.

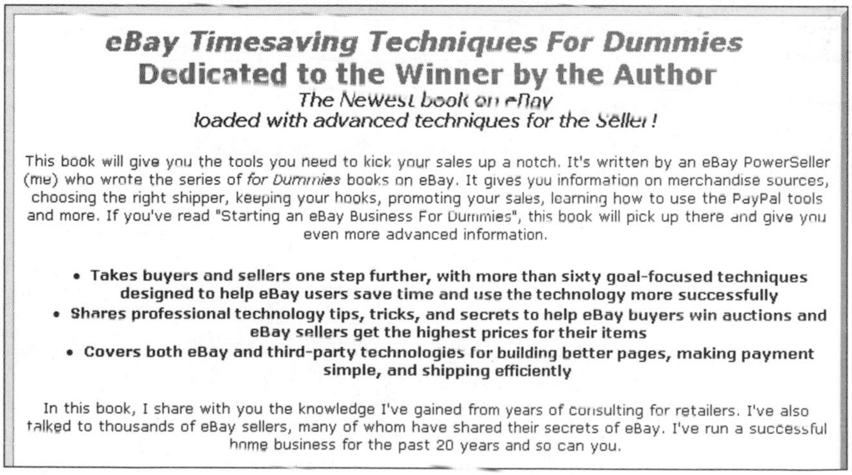

eBay Timesaving Techniques For Dummies
Dedicated to the Winner by the Author
The Newest book on eBay
loaded with advanced techniques for the Seller!

This book will give you the tools you need to kick your sales up a notch. It's written by an eBay PowerSeller (me) who wrote the series of *for Dummies* books on eBay. It gives you information on merchandise sources, choosing the right shipper, keeping your books, promoting your sales, learning how to use the PayPal tools and more. If you've read "Starting an eBay Business For Dummies", this book will pick up there and give you even more advanced information.

- **Takes buyers and sellers one step further, with more than sixty goal-focused techniques designed to help eBay users save time and use the technology more successfully**
- **Shares professional technology tips, tricks, and secrets to help eBay buyers win auctions and eBay sellers get the highest prices for their items**
- **Covers both eBay and third-party technologies for building better pages, making payment simple, and shipping efficiently**

In this book, I share with you the knowledge I've gained from years of consulting for retailers. I've also talked to thousands of eBay sellers, many of whom have shared their secrets of eBay. I've run a successful home business for the past 20 years and so can you.

Figure 21-5: A listing description with appropriate breaks in the text.

Though the commands you use to ensure proper placement are a little more complex, using tables to position images with the associated text aligned next to them can make a big difference. This technique is especially useful when you have multiple pictures — to show all sides of your merchandise (or several pieces of a multi-item lot). As shown in Figure 21-6, having the pictures and text interwoven (without tables) makes for a very long description that requires the customer to scroll up and down.

Figure 21-6:
A listing description that requires excessive scrolling.

Figure 21-7 shows that, with tables, the information can appear directly beside the picture it describes, which keeps the description compact and easy-to-read.

Figure 21-7:
Pictures and text properly placed using tables.

We can't emphasize this enough: Don't forget to check your listing in multiple browsers to be sure that the presentation in each one looks as you intend it to look. Some browsers are more forgiving of HTML errors than are others; what may look correct in one browser might not work at all in another.

Keeping an Eye on the Competition

Be sure to set time aside in your busy schedule to browse around the eBay site and view other sellers' listings. Call it research; you not only find out what your competition is doing, but you also get ideas about what works (and doesn't work) in their listing descriptions.

Don't copy another seller's listings, or any part of them, word for word. This sort of thing is against eBay's rules.

The first listings you should keep an eye on are those that offer items similar to yours (yep, your competition). In addition to making the obvious comparisons — such as purchase price and shipping costs — be sure to review what may seem less-significant details. Do they charge more for shipping, or offer only one method of shipment (and is it slower than yours)? If so, then emphasize your preferred shipping policy in your listings.

Review your competition's feedback; are there comments about poor packaging or slow shipment? If your packages can withstand a fall down a flight of stairs, make sure to state that in your description. What words do your competitors use in their titles? Are your listings showing up at the same time as their listings when customers search for items to purchase?

Don't forget to look at listings other than those of your direct competitors. Review other sellers' listings to see what works — and (more importantly) what doesn't!

You can learn as much from a bad listing as you can from a good listing. For example, watch for other sellers' listings that use animation, audio, or video. Take note on how long that listing page takes to load, and whether the whiz-bang stuff comes across as annoying. The longer a page takes to load, the greater the chance that the customer will go to another listing rather than wait. Just as you wouldn't put barricades around the entrance to a real-world store, don't put similar barricades in the way of customers who are viewing your listings — and take note of competitors who make this mistake.

Reviewing Your Listings

After you've designed dozens of listings, you might start to become complacent about the way they look. Don't fall prey to this!

At first, you find yourself reviewing every listing after it's submitted in order to be sure that it looks the way you designed it — and okay, you should. You should also view it in the top browsers your customers might use, to make sure that all your information looks correct (as described in Chapter 18). But don't stop there . . .

After a while, the temptation is to not review your listings after submitting them. After all, they've looked fine for weeks, and you've not made any significant changes to your listing format, so why waste the time checking the look of final listing? Well . . . mistakes will happen. Easy-to-miss goofs affect your listing layout. When editing your description, you might have accidentally deleted one part of a pair of HTML tags. Even worse, you might have removed a part of your shipping or payment policies. So every few weeks, take a close look at a few of your listings to make sure they still display all the information as you designed them to.

Last but far from least, every so often you should go to the eBay home page, pretend you're a buyer looking for one of the items that you're selling, and see what your imaginary shopping experience is like. Ask yourself what words you would use to search for your merchandise, and then do a search and make sure that your merchandise is displayed. Click one of your titles, and imagine you're viewing it for the first time. Is all the information available that you need before you can make a decision to purchase the item? Putting yourself in the shoes of a customer is an invaluable final step in making sure that your listings are visible and readable.

Appendix

Mechanizing Your Sales with Third-Party Management Tools

∙ ∙

In This Appendix
▶ Deciding among the available tools
▶ Checking out auction-management services
▶ Figuring out what tasks you can automate

∙ ∙

*W*hen you get to the point of running up to 20 auctions at a time, we highly recommend that you begin to also use a management tool. At this level of activity, using eBay's Selling Manager will suit you nicely, but when your eBay business begins to push 100 listings a week, we recommend that you get additional help in the form of *auction-management* services or software — capabilities designed to handle multiple auctions efficiently.

Whether you use an online service or have software residing on your own computer is a personal decision. Keep these overall ideas in mind as you make that decision:

- ✔ **With an online service:** You may find it easier to use an online system because you can log on to your selling information at any time from any computer. But if you have a slow Internet connection or pay usage fees by the hour, managing your eBay business online can become impractical.

- ✔ **With computer-based software:** You may find features that enable you to do your work on your computer and then upload (or download) your data when you go online. If having multiple locations to work from is not important, and you run your eBay business from a single computer in your office, you may feel more comfortable with a desktop-based software product.

In either case, if your business has reached a level that cries out for an auction-management tool — congratulations! In this appendix, we want to save you some time finding the service or software that's right for you. We outline some tasks that an auction-management product should provide, and we compare prices of several services.

Choosing Your Auction-Management Tools

If you searched the Internet for auction-management services and software, you'd come up with a bunch. For simplicity's sake, we've chosen to cover just a few of these services in this appendix. After speaking to many sellers, we found online services that offer two must-have features:

- ✔ **Uptime reliability:** Time, specifically uptime, is money; you don't want the server that holds your photos going down or mislaunching your auctions.

- ✔ **Update reliability:** Software that's continually updated to match the changes made to eBay keeps you current.

Using a site or software program to run your auctions takes practice, so we suggest that you try any that appeal to you and offer free preview trials. For each of these different applications, we provide a description and include a link so you can check them out further.

Some software and services work on the basis of a monthly fee; others use a one-time purchase fee. If a one-time-purchase software application is truly to benefit you, it *must* have the reputation for updating its software each time eBay makes a change in its system. The programs we discuss in this appendix have been upgraded continually to date.

Most services have a free trial period. Be sure that you don't spend a bunch of your precious time inputting your entire inventory, only to discover you don't like the way the service works. Instead, input a few items to give the service a whirl.

There's a huge difference between auction *listing* software and sites and auction *management* products. For many a seller, listing software like eBay's Turbo Lister may just do the trick. Combine that with eBay's Selling Manager (a *management* program) and your eBay business will be humming along just fine.

When your business activity increases and you turn to an auction-management solution for your eBay business, you should look for certain standard features (described next). Also consider what information-management features you currently have through your bookkeeping program. You have the data there, regardless of whether you use it in a management solution.

Many of the products listed have several pricing tiers, so Table A-1 shows the link to each product's pricing page. We've also listed minimum price for each company's *management* products. Some offer less expensive options for *listing* your auctions (complete with templates and all kinds of swell bells and whistles), but the price shown in the table is for the minimum *management* product.

Table A-1	Desktop Auction-Management Software			
Name	*URL*	*Prices Start At*	*Number of Closings*	*Image Hosting Included*
AAA Seller	`www.aaa seller.com`	$9.95/month	Unlimited	Yes
AuctionHawk	`http://www. auctionhawk.com/ html/pricing.html`	$12.99/month	110	Yes
AuctionTamer	`http://www. auctiontamer. com/auction/ purchase.asp`	$39.75/ 3 months	Unlimited	No
Auction Wizard 2000	`www.auction wizard2000.com`	$75 first year, $50 renewal	Unlimited	No
Auctiva	`www.auctiva.com`	Basic **FREE**	Unlimited	Yes
DEK Auction Manager	`www.dekauction manager.com`	$50 month	Unlimited	Yes
Shooting Star	`www.foodog software.com`	$60.00 flat fee/1 year	Unlimited	No
Spoonfeeder	`www.spoonfeeder. com/pricing.php`	$49.95 +/- $4.99/month	40	Yes
Zoovy	`www.zoovy.com`	$49.95 ($399.95 setup fee)	Up to 1000 listings	Yes

Never choose auction-management tools by price alone. Go to the various Web sites and take a look at everything you get for the price stated. You may find that a service charging a bit more may just be worth it because of all the extra tools it offers.

Looking for essential features

Here are some of the must-have features to look for when you evaluate the offerings of auction management services and products:

- ✓ **Image hosting:** Some Web sites dazzle you with high-megabyte storage numbers. But keep one thing in mind: If your average eBay image takes up around 40 KB, you could store 128 pictures in a 5MB storage space and about 2500 images in a 100MB storage space. Unless you're a mega-big-time seller, you really don't need that much space. Your eBay images should be archived on your computer (how about in a folder called eBay Images). Images for current listings should be on the hosted site only while the transaction is in progress. After the buyer has the item and all is well, you can remove the images from the remote server.

  You most likely already have free image hosting on your ISP's Web site.

- ✓ **Designing listings:** The basis of most of these products is a good listing function. You'll be able to select from supplied templates or design your own and store them for future use. An important feature now coming into use is a spell checker. There's nothing worse than a misspelling in a listing!

- ✓ **Uploading listings:** Most products have a feature that launches a group of listings to eBay all at once. They may also allow you to schedule auctions to get underway at a prescribed time.

  You can also expect to be able to put together your listings offline — at your leisure — and upload them to your service when they're ready. Most products archive your past listings so you can relist at any time. Many services also offer bulk relisting.

- ✓ **E-mail management:** You can expect to be provided with sample e-mail letters (templates) that you can customize with your own look and feel. The services should also offer auto-generated end-of-auction, payment received, and shipping e-mail services.

- ✓ **Feedback automation:** Post feedback in bulk to a number of your completed listings, or leave predesigned feedback one by one. Some products support automatic feedback when a buyer leaves you positive feedback.

- ✓ **Sales reports:** Some services (even the least expensive) offer you some sort of sales analysis. Be sure to take into account how much you really need this feature, based on data that you may already receive from QuickBooks, PayPal, eBay Stores, or SquareTrade.

Exploring advanced features

Depending upon the type of business you run, you may need some more advanced features offered by management products:

- ✔ **Inventory tools:** Management products may allow you create inventory records for your different products, permitting you to click a bunch to list automatically. When an item is sold, they will deduct the items from your inventory.

- ✔ **Sales-tax tracking and invoicing:** With full management, you can expect your sales tax to be calculated into your invoices and complete line-item invoices to be sent automatically. Multiple items, when purchased by the same buyer, will be combined.

- ✔ **Consignment tracking:** If you're a Trading Assistant, be sure to look for a product that enables you to separately track the products you sell for different clients. You should also be able to produce reports of consignment sales by customer.

- ✔ **Shipping:** Most of the services will give you the option of printing your packing lists and shipping labels directly from the product. Some of the larger services integrate with the major shippers, allowing you to go directly to the particular shipper's site and ship from their software.

Table A-2 gives you the dollars and cents of subscribing to the various online and offline services. To put together this table, we disregarded lower subscription levels, where companies offered only listing products. These are the lowest prices for products that are truly management tools.

Table A-2	Third-Party Auction Management Solutions			
Name	*URL*	*Prices Start At*	*Number of Closings*	*Image Hosting Included*
Auction Helper	`http://www. auctionhelper. com/ah/info/ fees.asp`	1.95% GMS and $0.02 (min $10.00/ month)	Unlimited	Yes
Channel Advisor	`pro.channel advisor.com/pro`	$29.95/month	500/month	Yes
InkFrog	`http://www.ink frog.com/index. php?file=plans`	$12.95/month	Unlimited	Yes

(continued)

Table A-2 *(continued)*				
Name	**URL**	**Prices Start At**	**Number of Closings**	**Image Hosting Included**
MarketWorks	`http://www.auctionworks.com/fees.asp`	2% GMS/month (min $29.95)	Unlimited	Yes
Meridian	`http://www.noblespirit.com/products-pricing.html`	$19.95/month	500/month	Yes
SpareDollar	`http://www.sparedollar.com/corp/pricing.asp`	$8.95/month	Unlimited	Yes
Vendio	`http://www.vendio.com/pricing.html`	$0.10/listing	Up to 50 listings	$0.10 each

Online or Offline Management?

You may want to run your business from any computer, anywhere in the world. If that's the case, you might do best with an online service. But if you want to run your business from a fixed location, you might feel more comfortable with downloadable software that will handle most of the chores on your own computer.

Online auction management sites

Auction management Web sites handle almost everything, from inventory management to label printing. Some sellers prefer online (or hosted) management sites because you can access your information from any computer. You might use every feature a site offers, or you might choose a bit from column A and a bit from column B and perform the more personalized tasks manually. Read on to determine what service might best suit your needs.

Although quite a few excellent online services for automating sales are available, we have room here to show you only a few. Many services are similar in format, so in the following sections we point out some of the highlights of a few representative systems. Remember that by using an online service, your information resides on a server out there in cyberspace; if you're a control freak, it may be a bit much to bear.

When selecting a service, look for a logo or text indicating that the service is an eBay Certified Developer, Preferred Solution Provider, or API licensee. These people have first access to eBay's system changes and can implement them immediately. Others may have a day or so lag time to update their software.

ChannelAdvisor

ChannelAdvisor's founder Scot Wingo got into the auction business around the turn of the century. His first foray into the eBay world was AuctionRover, a site that had tools to perform an extensive eBay search, list auctions, and check pricing trends. The company's cute Rover logo was fashioned after Wingo's Border Collie, Mack.

Fast forward to today. ChannelAdvisor is a highly popular management service for all levels of eBay sellers. They supply listing and management services to everyone from Fortune 1000 companies to the little old lady next door. How? They offer three levels of software: Enterprise for large businesses who want to outsource their online business, Merchant for midsized businesses and higher-level PowerSellers, and Pro for small businesses and individuals. These powerful software suites help eBay sellers successfully manage and automate the sale of their merchandise.

Starting at the entry level, you can get the Pro version of ChannelAdvisor for $29.95 a month. Here's what they offer the beginning level seller:

- **Listing design and launching:** Create your listings with their standard templates or use your own HTML to design auction descriptions. List your items immediately or schedule a listing. ChannelAdvisor will launch the auction when you tell them to.

- **Item and inventory management:** If you want to keep your inventory online, you can create it on their system. If you want to input your inventory offline, you can import it from their Excel template. You can also import open auctions or store listings to your ChannelAdvisor account for relisting or servicing.

- **Image hosting:** You get 250MB of space to host your images. You can upload images to the site four at a time, or use FTP to upload a large quantity.

- **Post-auction management:** This function merges your winning auction information and generates customized e-mail and invoices to your buyers. You can print mailing labels too.

To tour the various offerings of ChannelAdvisor and find out about their free trial period, visit

www.channeladvisor.com

MarketWorks

A group of collectors who saw the need for power tools for PowerSellers developed this highly graphical site (`www.MarketWorks.com`). We think they've succeeded. (They were known in the eBay community as AuctionWorks, but changed their name in June 2004.) A high percentage of eBay PowerSellers use the site. They launch approximately two million listings on eBay every month. MarketWorks offers help links at every turn, a first-rate online tutorial, free toll-free support (that's a free phone call and free support), and free interactive training classes for registered users. Here are just a few features:

- ✓ **Item and inventory management:** Features the ClickLaunch Single Step Launcher, which launches individual items to auction while adding them to inventory. (The site also has bulk item-launching capability.) LaunchBots provides automated launching of your listings. You can import existing auctions from eBay and import them with their bulk inventory upload form in Excel and MS Access.

- ✓ **Image hosting:** Enables you to bulk upload 15 images at a time to their servers. The basic account allows 100MB of storage. If your images average 30K each, you should be able to upload almost 3500 images into the 100MB image hosting space.

- ✓ **Auction reporting:** Generates accounts receivable, item history, and post-sales reports from the Reports area. MarketWorks has its own Traction System for sales and item tracking. Reports include customizable views of your sales data; item and auction data; accounts receivable, and sales tax by state!

- ✓ **Templates and listing:** MarketWorks uses their own trademarked Ballista template listing system. You can use their predefined color templates or use their macros with your own predefined HTML template, substituting the macros for stock areas in your template. By using their custom ad template option and well-thought-out macros, you can take your own HTML and make a MarketWorks template.

- ✓ **Post-auction management:** Sends out automated e-mail to your winners, linking them to your own branded checkout page. If customers want to pay with PayPal or your own merchant account, they have to link from there. MarketWorks combines multiple wins for shipping and invoicing. You have the option to set six different feedback comments, which you choose at the time of posting.

MarketWorks offers all their users a StoreFront with its own URL at no additional charge. If an item sells from your StoreFront, you pay the usual 2% commission. When you load items into inventory, you have the choice of immediately listing them in your StoreFront. All your items are seamlessly integrated. To get current information and sign up for a free trial, go to

`www.MarketWorks.com`

Dek AuctionManager

Dek was developed by eBay Titanium Power Seller David Hardin. Through his company's experience on eBay, he developed this service to fulfill all the needs of a high volume eBay seller, at a flat price of $50 a month.

- ✔ **Item and inventory management:** Includes calendar- and time-based (dates and times for launching) auction scheduling, automated auction launching and relisting, the ability to import past or current auctions, and the ability to import auction data from a spreadsheet or database.

- ✔ **Image hosting:** Offers space for storing pictures. You can upload bulk images to its Web site or FTP your images directly.

- ✔ **Auction reporting:** Generates current running auction statistics — the total number and dollars of current and past auctions — and an itemized report of each auction.

- ✔ **Post-auction management:** Allows you to send (manually or automatically) a variety of customized e-mails to winners and nonpaying bidders. Your invoices can link directly to PayPal.

The post-auction management features also include the capability to send automatic feedback — and to create mailing labels for each sale. If you want to make sure that feedback isn't posted until you're sure the transaction is successfully completed (wise move), you have the option of disabling the automatic feedback feature.

```
www.dekauctionmanager.com
```

Auction-management software

Many sellers prefer to run their auction businesses from their own computers. (Marsha happens to like the option of being able to reference old auctions on her backups.) Luckily, some valuable auction software programs are available to perform all the tasks you get from the online services. To those who would rather have the software at home, there are some solid choices other than the ones we examine in this section. You might also want to visit these other sites for their quality auction-management software.

You can accomplish almost all the same tasks on your own computer as you can with online services — except online auction checkout. (You can always use eBay's checkout as your final stop or include a link in your end-of-auction e-mail.) If you want, you can always set up a checkout page on your own Web site that gathers your auction information. If auction-management software sounds like the ticket to you, here's a quick tour of a few leading products.

Auction Wizard 2000

Way back in 1999, Standing Wave Software developed a product that would handle large inventories and meet the needs of the growing eBay population. Enter Auction Wizard. In 2000, the company introduced a more robust version, Auction Wizard 2000, to meet the challenges presented by changes happening on eBay itself.

This software is a tour-de-force of auction management, whose pieces are integrated into one program. Some of its special features enable you to

- **Handle consignment sales.** Handy way to keep track of consignment sales by consignees, including all fees.

- **Edit your images before uploading.** The software allows you to import your images, and crop, rotate, or resize those images for your auctions.

- **Upload your pictures with built-in FTP software while you're working on your auctions.** This feature eliminates the need for another piece of auction-business software.

The program interface is straightforward. If you follow Marsha's style (always plunging into new programs without reading the instructions), we think you'll be able to use the program successfully right off the bat. It's okay if you don't make it do acrobatics in the first five minutes; Auction Wizard 2000 has so many features that not many sellers have time to study them all.

To begin using the software, simply download your current eBay auctions directly into the program. When your auctions close, send customized e-mails (the program fills in the auction information) and manage all your end-of-auction business. Some sellers launch their auctions using Turbo Lister, and then retrieve them and handle the end-of-auction management with Auction Wizard 2000. For a 60-day free trial, go to their site at

```
www.auctionwizard2000.com
```

eBay's Turbo Lister

We like Turbo Lister because it's simple and easy to use. It has a built-in WYSIWYG (what-you-see-is-what-you-get) HTML editor and makes preparing listings offline easy. So, when you're ready, you can just click a button and they're all listed at once. You can also stagger listings and schedule them to launch at a later date for a fee.

Finding More to Automate

Now that eBay has become a world marketplace, a single-page auction or item listing is becoming an increasingly valuable piece of real estate. Millions of potential buyers view your sale — and the more auctions and fixed-price items you can list, the better your chance to make a good living. Time is money: You need to post your auctions quickly and accurately.

Auction posting, record keeping, inventory cataloging, photo managing, and statistic gathering are all tasks that you can automate. The more your business grows, the more confusing things can become. Automated tools can help you keep it all straight. But remember that the more paid tools you use, the more expense you may be adding to your business. Always keep your bottom line in mind when evaluating whether to use fee-based software and services.

You'll have to perform certain office tasks, no matter how few or how many auctions you're running. Depending on your personal business style, you may want to automate any or all of the following tasks. You may choose to use a single program, a manual method, or some features from one program and some from others. For folks who aren't ready for the automated plunge, we offer alternatives.

Setting up an auction photo gallery

Until you get your own eBay store, setting up a photo gallery is a great alternative. If your customers have a high-speed connection, they can browse your auctions through photographs. Some auction-management sites host your gallery. Some charge for this service; others do not. The best part is that you can produce your own gallery without any fancy programs or auction-management software — at no additional cost to you.

To make your own gallery on eBay without installing fancy scripts in your listings, you need to do two things: test your browser, and add a bit of HTML. So here goes: Test the following URL in your browser, substituting your own user ID where indicated in bold italics (Figure A-1 shows you a sample of what you will see).

```
http://search-desc.ebay.com/search/search.dll? MfcISAPI
      Command=GetResult&query=YoureBayUserID&ht=
      1&srchdesc=y&SortProperty=MetaEndSort&st=1
```

Now that you've seen a sample of your gallery, insert the following HTML into your auction to include a link to your gallery:

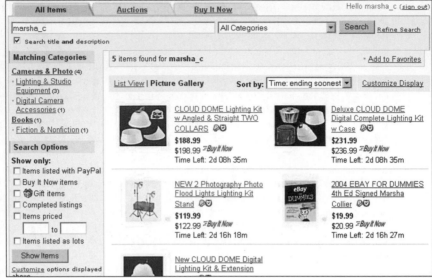

```
<a
href="http://search.ebay.com/_W0QQfcclZ1QQfclZ4QQfrppZ25QQ
        fsooZ2QQfsopZ2
QQsassZYoureBayUserID"> <B>Click <I>here</I> to view
        YoureBayUserID Gallery</B> <img src="http://
        pics.ebay.com/aw/pics/ebay_my_button.gif"
alt="My Gallery on eBay"></a>
```

As you can see in Figure A-2, this HTML snippet also inserts the custom eBay button.

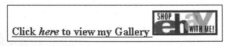

Sorting auction e-mail

A vital function of any auction software or system is the ability to customize and send e-mails to your winners. Many sellers use the default letters, which tend to be a bit — no, incredibly — impersonal and uncaring. You must decide whether you want the program to receive e-mail as well.

Most auction-management programs that are *computer-resident* (installed on your own computer instead of requiring that you go online to do your business) have their own built-in e-mail software. When you download your winner information from eBay, the program automatically generates invoices and congratulatory e-mails.

How you handle your auction-related e-mail is a personal choice. Although Marsha currently uses eBay's Selling Manager to send auction related e-mails, she receives auction e-mail through Outlook, using a separate folder titled *Auctions* that contains subfolders named *eBay Buy* and *eBay Sell*.

Automating end-of-auction e-mail

If you want to set up e-mails to be sent automatically after an auction ends, you must use a software application. The software should download your final auction results, generate the e-mail, and let you preview the e-mail before sending it out. Many of the online sites discussed previously in this appendix send out winner-confirmation e-mails automatically when an auction is over. That can work fine, but if you want to use this option, be sure you set your preferences to let you preview the e-mail before sending.

Keeping inventory

Many eBay PowerSellers depend on the old clipboard or notebook method — crossing off items as they sell them. If that works for you, great! Others prefer to use an Excel spreadsheet to keep track of inventory.

Most of the auction-management packages detailed in this appendix handle inventory for you. Some automatically deduct an item from inventory when you launch an auction. You have your choice of handling inventory directly on your computer or keeping your inventory online with a service that's accessible from any computer, wherever you are.

Marsha handles inventory on a desktop computer through QuickBooks. When she buys merchandise to sell and posts the bill to QuickBooks, it automatically puts the merchandise into inventory. Then, when she inputs a sale, QuickBooks deducts the items sold from standing inventory. This process lets her print a status report whenever she wants to see how much inventory she has left — or how much she needs to order.

One-click relisting or selling similar

Using auction software or an auction service speeds up the process of posting or relisting items. After you input your inventory into the software, posting or relisting your auctions is a mouse click away. All the auction management software packages detailed previously in this appendix include this feature.

If you buy your items in bulk, you might want to take advantage of eBay's free relisting tool. By clicking the Sell Similar link (see Figure A-3) on any successful listing, you can automatically relist your items. Sell Similar starts the listing as new, so if it doesn't sell, you can avail yourself of the Relist feature. This way, if the item sells the second time, your listing (insertion fees) for the first listing will be credited.

Although eBay says that Sell Similar is for relisting items, it works also when listing a duplicate of an item that has sold successfully. The only difference is that you aren't credited for the unsold item's auction-listing fee.

Click here to relist an unsold item

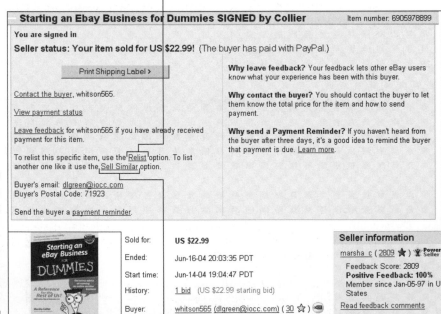

Figure A-3: The Relist and Sell Similar links on a completed auction page.

Click here to use the Sell Similar option

One savvy seller we know uses the eBay Sell Similar feature to post new auctions. She merely clicks the Sell Similar link, and then cuts and pastes her new information into the existing HTML format. That's why her auctions all have the same feel and flavor.

Scheduling listings for bulk upload

If you want to schedule the unattended launch of your auctions without incurring eBay's 10-cent fee, you must use an online management service (check out the "Online auction management sites" section). If you can be at your computer to send your auctions up to eBay singly or in bulk, you can use the Turbo Lister application, which eBay offers at no charge.

Hosting photos

If all you need is photo-hosting, and you've checked out your ISP and it won't give you any free Web space to use (are you sure??), you can always use eBay's picture services to host an additional picture in each auction at 15 cents an image.

Checking out

When someone wins or buys an item, eBay's checkout integrates directly with PayPal and also indicates your other preferred forms of payment. If you're closing more than a hundred auctions a day, that's all you need. eBay and PayPal will also send an e-mail to you and the buyer so you can arrange for payment.

Some online auction management services offer your own private checkout area that costs you a percentage of your sale, so you must decide whether your business warrants this option. A personalized winner's notification e-mail can easily contain a link to your PayPal payment area, making a checkout service unnecessary.

Printing shipping labels

Printing shipping labels without printing postage can be the beginning of a laborious two-step process. Two companies, Endicia.com and.Stamps.com, print your labels and postage all in one step.

Some sites, as well as eBay's Selling Manager, print your winner's address label without postage. That works well if you don't mind carrying your packages to the post office for postage. (Why would you do that? A burning need to stand in line?)

Tracking buyer information

Keeping track of your winners isn't rocket science. You can do it in an Excel spreadsheet or a Word document, both of which are exportable to almost any program for follow-up mailings promoting future sales. If you choose to have an online management service do this for you, be sure that you can download the information to your computer (in case you and the online service part ways someday).

Generating customized reports

Sales reports, ledgers, and tax information are all important reports that you should have in your business. Online services and software supply different flavors of these reports.

PayPal allows you to download your sales data into a format compatible with QuickBooks, a highly respected and popular bookkeeping program. You can also choose to download your data in Excel spreadsheet format (the downloads also work in Microsoft Works). PayPal reports are chock-full of intensely detailed information about your sales and deposits. Putting this information in a standard accounting software program — on a regular basis — makes your year-end calculations easier to bear.

Submitting feedback

If you're running a lot of auctions, leaving feedback can be a chore. One solution is to automate the submission of feedback through an online service or via software. But *timing* the automation of this task can be tricky.

We use eBay's Selling Manager Pro, which permits us to leave feedback automatically after a positive feedback has been left for us.

Don't leave feedback for an eBay transaction until *after* you've heard from the buyer that the purchase is satisfactory. Leaving positive feedback immediately after you've received payment from the buyer is too soon. After you receive an e-mail assuring you that the customer is satisfied, manually leaving feedback by going to the feedback forum (or the item page) can be just as easy as bulk-loading feedback — if not easier.

Index

• *M* •

BUSINESS, CAREERS & PERSONAL FINANCE

0-7645-5307-0

0-7645-5331-3 *†

Also available:

- Accounting For Dummies †
  0-7645-5314-3
- Business Plans Kit For Dummies †
  0-7645-5365-8
- Cover Letters For Dummies
  0-7645-5224-4
- Frugal Living For Dummies
  0-7645-5403-4
- Leadership For Dummies
  0-7645-5176-0
- Managing For Dummies
  0-7645-1771-6

- Marketing For Dummies
  0-7645-5600-2
- Personal Finance For Dummies *
  0-7645-2590-5
- Project Management For Dummies
  0-7645-5283-X
- Resumes For Dummies †
  0-7645-5471-9
- Selling For Dummies
  0-7645-5363-1
- Small Business Kit For Dummies *†
  0-7645-5093-4

HOME & BUSINESS COMPUTER BASICS

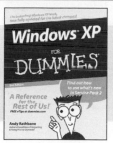

0-7645-4074-2

0-7645-3758-X

Also available:

- ACT! 6 For Dummies
  0-7645-2645-6
- iLife '04 All-in-One Desk Reference
  For Dummies
  0-7645-7347-0
- iPAQ For Dummies
  0-7645-6769-1
- Mac OS X Panther Timesaving
  Techniques For Dummies
  0-7645-5812-9
- Macs For Dummies
  0-7645-5656-8

- Microsoft Money 2004 For Dummies
  0-7645-4195-1
- Office 2003 All-in-One Desk Reference
  For Dummies
  0-7645-3883-7
- Outlook 2003 For Dummies
  0-7645-3759-8
- PCs For Dummies
  0-7645-4074-2
- TiVo For Dummies
  0-7645-6923-6
- Upgrading and Fixing PCs For Dummies
  0-7645-1665-5
- Windows XP Timesaving Techniques
  For Dummies
  0-7645-3748-2

FOOD, HOME, GARDEN, HOBBIES, MUSIC & PETS

0-7645-5295-3

0-7645-5232-5

Also available:

- Bass Guitar For Dummies
  0-7645-2487-9
- Diabetes Cookbook For Dummies
  0-7645-5230-9
- Gardening For Dummies *
  0-7645-5130-2
- Guitar For Dummies
  0-7645-5106-X
- Holiday Decorating For Dummies
  0-7645-2570-0
- Home Improvement All in One
  For Dummies
  0-7645-5680-0

- Knitting For Dummies
  0-7645-5395-X
- Piano For Dummies
  0-7645-5105-1
- Puppies For Dummies
  0-7645-5255-4
- Scrapbooking For Dummies
  0-7645-7208-3
- Senior Dogs For Dummies
  0-7645-5818-8
- Singing For Dummies
  0-7645-2475-5
- 30-Minute Meals For Dummies
  0-7645-2589-1

INTERNET & DIGITAL MEDIA

0-7645-1664-7

0-7645-6924-4

Also available:

- 2005 Online Shopping Directory
  For Dummies
  0-7645-7495-7
- CD & DVD Recording For Dummies
  0-7645-5956-7
- eBay For Dummies
  0-7645-5654-1
- Fighting Spam For Dummies
  0-7645-5965-6
- Genealogy Online For Dummies
  0-7645-5964-8
- Google For Dummies
  0-7645-4420-9

- Home Recording For Musicians
  For Dummies
  0-7645-1634-5
- The Internet For Dummies
  0-7645-4173-0
- iPod & iTunes For Dummies
  0-7645-7772-7
- Preventing Identity Theft For Dummies
  0-7645-7336-5
- Pro Tools All-in-One Desk Reference
  For Dummies
  0-7645-5714-9
- Roxio Easy Media Creator For Dummies
  0-7645-7131-1

* Separate Canadian edition also available
† Separate U.K. edition also available

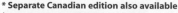

WILEY

SPORTS, FITNESS, PARENTING, RELIGION & SPIRITUALITY

0-7645-5146-9

0-7645-5418-2

Also available:

- Adoption For Dummies
  0-7645-5488-3
- Basketball For Dummies
  0-7645-5248-1
- The Bible For Dummies
  0-7645-5296-1
- Buddhism For Dummies
  0-7645-5359-3
- Catholicism For Dummies
  0-7645-5391-7
- Hockey For Dummies
  0-7645-5228-7

- Judaism For Dummies
  0-7645-5299-6
- Martial Arts For Dummies
  0-7645-5358-5
- Pilates For Dummies
  0-7645-5397-6
- Religion For Dummies
  0-7645-5264-3
- Teaching Kids to Read For Dummies
  0-7645-4043-2
- Weight Training For Dummies
  0-7645-5168-X
- Yoga For Dummies
  0-7645-5117-5

TRAVEL

0-7645-5438-7

0-7645-5453-0

Also available:

- Alaska For Dummies
  0-7645-1761-9
- Arizona For Dummies
  0-7645-6938-4
- Cancún and the Yucatán For Dummies
  0-7645-2437-2
- Cruise Vacations For Dummies
  0-7645-6941-4
- Europe For Dummies
  0-7645-5456-5
- Ireland For Dummies
  0-7645-5455-7

- Las Vegas For Dummies
  0-7645-5448-4
- London For Dummies
  0-7645-4277-X
- New York City For Dummies
  0-7645-6945-7
- Paris For Dummies
  0-7645-5494-8
- RV Vacations For Dummies
  0-7645-5443-3
- Walt Disney World & Orlando For Dummies
  0-7645-6943-0

GRAPHICS, DESIGN & WEB DEVELOPMENT

0-7645-4345-8

0-7645-5589-8

Also available:

- Adobe Acrobat 6 PDF For Dummies
  0-7645-3760-1
- Building a Web Site For Dummies
  0-7645-7144-3
- Dreamweaver MX 2004 For Dummies
  0-7645-4342-3
- FrontPage 2003 For Dummies
  0-7645-3882-9
- HTML 4 For Dummies
  0-7645-1995-6
- Illustrator CS For Dummies
  0-7645-4084-X

- Macromedia Flash MX 2004 For Dummies
  0-7645-4358-X
- Photoshop 7 All-in-One Desk Reference For Dummies
  0-7645-1667-1
- Photoshop CS Timesaving Techniques For Dummies
  0-7645-6782-9
- PHP 5 For Dummies
  0-7645-4166-8
- PowerPoint 2003 For Dummies
  0-7645-3908-6
- QuarkXPress 6 For Dummies
  0-7645-2593-X

NETWORKING, SECURITY, PROGRAMMING & DATABASES

0-7645-6852-3

0-7645-5784-X

Also available:

- A+ Certification For Dummies
  0-7645-4187-0
- Access 2003 All-in-One Desk Reference For Dummies
  0-7645-3988-4
- Beginning Programming For Dummies
  0-7645-4997-9
- C For Dummies
  0-7645-7068-4
- Firewalls For Dummies
  0-7645-4048-3
- Home Networking For Dummies
  0-7645-42796

- Network Security For Dummies
  0-7645-1679-5
- Networking For Dummies
  0-7645-1677-9
- TCP/IP For Dummies
  0-7645-1760-0
- VBA For Dummies
  0-7645-3989-2
- Wireless All In-One Desk Reference For Dummies
  0-7645-7496-5
- Wireless Home Networking For Dummies
  0-7645-3910-8